FOOTBALL NOW

**MIKE
LEONETTI
and
JOHN IABONI**

FIREFLY BOOKS

A Firefly Book

Published by Firefly Books Ltd. 2006

First printing

Publisher Cataloging-in-Publication Data (U.S.)
Leonetti, Mike, 1958-
     Football now! / Mike Leonetti ; and John Iaboni.
[176] p. : col. photos. ; cm.
Summary: Profiles of over ninety National Football League players.
ISBN-13: 978-1-55407-149-4 (pbk.)
ISBN-10: 1-55407-149-6 (pbk.)
1. National Football League — Biography. 2. Football players — United States — Biography.
I. Iaboni, John. II. Title.
796.332/ 64/ 0973 dc22   GV955.5.N35L45 2006

Library and Archives Canada Cataloguing in Publication
Leonetti, Mike, 1958-
     Football now! / Mike Leonetti and John Iaboni.
ISBN-13: 978-1-55407-149-4
ISBN-10: 1-55407-149-6
1. Football players — Biography. 2. National Football League — Biography. 3. Football players —
Pictorial works. 4. National Football League — Pictorial works. I. Iaboni, John II. Title.
GV939.A1L455 2006 796.332'640922 C2006-901668-2

Published in the United States by
Firefly Books (U.S.) Inc.
P.O. Box 1338, Ellicott Station
Buffalo, New York 14205

Published in Canada by
Firefly Books Ltd.
66 Leek Crescent
Richmond Hill, Ontario L4B 1H1

Printed in Canada

The publisher gratefully acknowledges the financial support for our publishing program by the Government of Canada through the Book Publishing Industry Development Program.

The authors would like to dedicate this book to the men and women stationed at home and abroad, protecting our rights and freedoms while cheering on the teams and stars that comprise *Football Now!*

TABLE OF CONTENTS

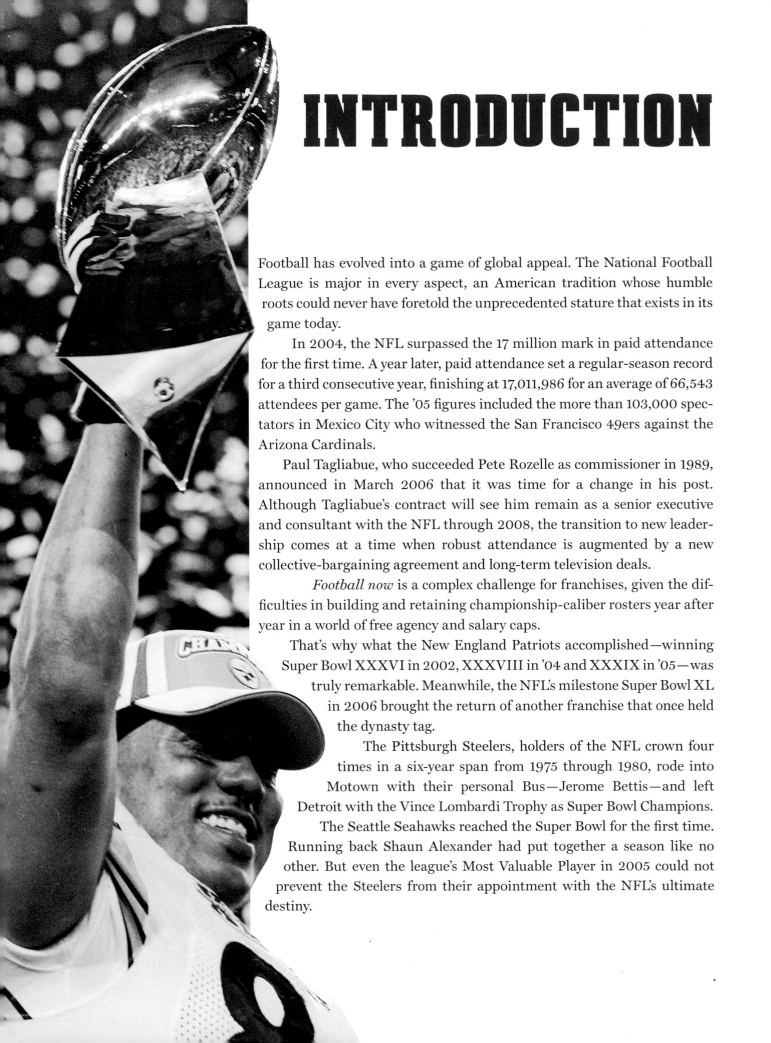

INTRODUCTION

Football has evolved into a game of global appeal. The National Football League is major in every aspect, an American tradition whose humble roots could never have foretold the unprecedented stature that exists in its game today.

In 2004, the NFL surpassed the 17 million mark in paid attendance for the first time. A year later, paid attendance set a regular-season record for a third consecutive year, finishing at 17,011,986 for an average of 66,543 attendees per game. The '05 figures included the more than 103,000 spectators in Mexico City who witnessed the San Francisco 49ers against the Arizona Cardinals.

Paul Tagliabue, who succeeded Pete Rozelle as commissioner in 1989, announced in March 2006 that it was time for a change in his post. Although Tagliabue's contract will see him remain as a senior executive and consultant with the NFL through 2008, the transition to new leadership comes at a time when robust attendance is augmented by a new collective-bargaining agreement and long-term television deals.

Football now is a complex challenge for franchises, given the difficulties in building and retaining championship-caliber rosters year after year in a world of free agency and salary caps.

That's why what the New England Patriots accomplished—winning Super Bowl XXXVI in 2002, XXXVIII in '04 and XXXIX in '05—was truly remarkable. Meanwhile, the NFL's milestone Super Bowl XL in 2006 brought the return of another franchise that once held the dynasty tag.

The Pittsburgh Steelers, holders of the NFL crown four times in a six-year span from 1975 through 1980, rode into Motown with their personal Bus—Jerome Bettis—and left Detroit with the Vince Lombardi Trophy as Super Bowl Champions.

The Seattle Seahawks reached the Super Bowl for the first time. Running back Shaun Alexander had put together a season like no other. But even the league's Most Valuable Player in 2005 could not prevent the Steelers from their appointment with the NFL's ultimate destiny.

The Indianapolis Colts flirted with perfection in 2005, running their record to 13–0 before losing 26–17 at home to the San Diego Chargers on December 18.

The New Orleans Saints will be remembered for 2005 as well, not so much for their record (3–13), as for the fact that they actually completed the full season after the devastation of Hurricane Katrina. The Saints fled to training quarters in San Antonio, Texas, and played all 16 games on the road, forever reminding football fans everywhere of the spirit of New Orleans.

Wide receiver/kick returner Steve Smith overcame a serious leg injury sustained in the season-opening game of 2004 and almost led the Carolina Panthers to the Super Bowl in 2005.

Tedy Bruschi, the emotional inside linebacker for the Patriots, was riding high after New England's Super Bowl win in 2005. But three days removed from his first Pro Bowl appearance he suffered a mild stroke. He even endured an operation to repair a hole in his heart. Yet on October 30, 2005, Bruschi and the Patriots beat the Buffalo Bills, a stirring return to be sure.

But Edgerrin James won't be back with the Colts, signing instead with the Arizona Cardinals during the bevy of free-agent signings across the NFL.

After five years of helping the San Diego Chargers head in the right direction, Drew Brees liked what New Orleans offered and inked a deal with them in the off-season. That development raises hopes that with Brees at QB, and explosive, exciting and tough running back Reggie Bush from USC in the fold, the Saints will be blessed with a solid foundation.

The Houston Texans passed on Bush and Texas Longhorns quarterback Vince Young to select 6´7˝, 294-pound North Carolina State defensive end Mario Williams with the number 1 overall selection in the 2006 NFL draft. Bush went number 2, followed by Young, who went to the Tennessee Titans.

What follows is an overview of many of the NFL's biggest names and prime-time performers. It's a look at the current era and an introduction to some potential future stars—personalities representing the fascinating, thrilling world of *Football Now*.

QUARTER

THE FIELD GENERALS OF THE NFL

BACKS!

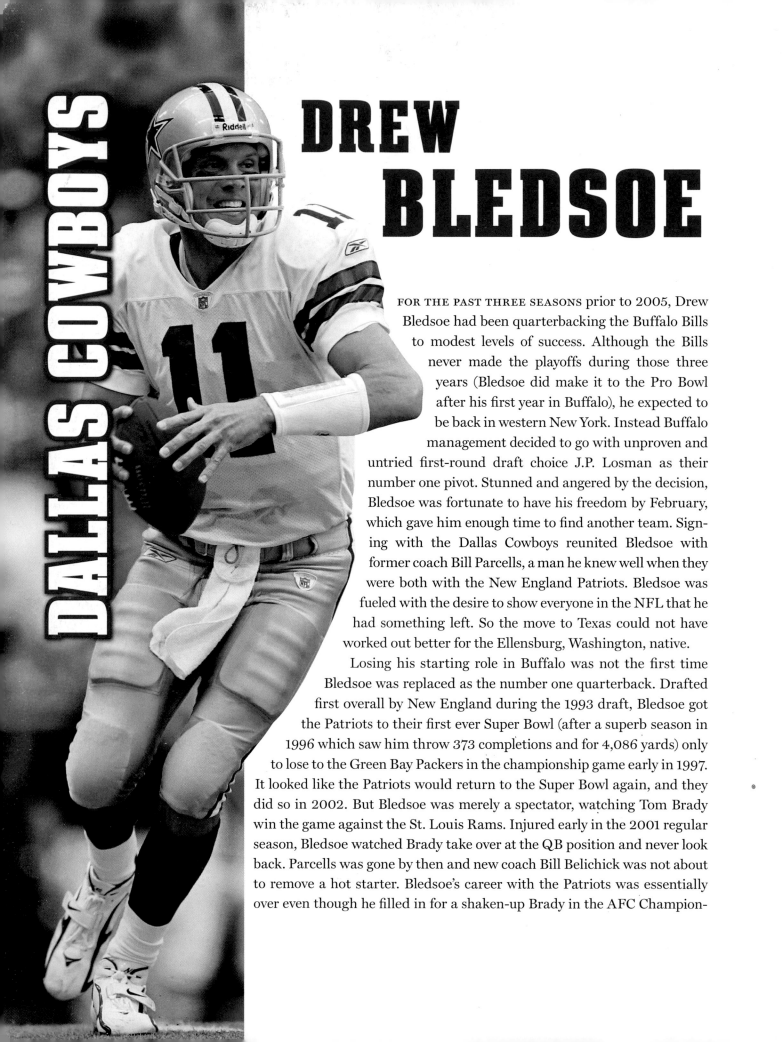

DALLAS COWBOYS

DREW BLEDSOE

FOR THE PAST THREE SEASONS prior to 2005, Drew Bledsoe had been quarterbacking the Buffalo Bills to modest levels of success. Although the Bills never made the playoffs during those three years (Bledsoe did make it to the Pro Bowl after his first year in Buffalo), he expected to be back in western New York. Instead Buffalo management decided to go with unproven and untried first-round draft choice J.P. Losman as their number one pivot. Stunned and angered by the decision, Bledsoe was fortunate to have his freedom by February, which gave him enough time to find another team. Signing with the Dallas Cowboys reunited Bledsoe with former coach Bill Parcells, a man he knew well when they were both with the New England Patriots. Bledsoe was fueled with the desire to show everyone in the NFL that he had something left. So the move to Texas could not have worked out better for the Ellensburg, Washington, native.

Losing his starting role in Buffalo was not the first time Bledsoe was replaced as the number one quarterback. Drafted first overall by New England during the 1993 draft, Bledsoe got the Patriots to their first ever Super Bowl (after a superb season in 1996 which saw him throw 373 completions and for 4,086 yards) only to lose to the Green Bay Packers in the championship game early in 1997. It looked like the Patriots would return to the Super Bowl again, and they did so in 2002. But Bledsoe was merely a spectator, watching Tom Brady win the game against the St. Louis Rams. Injured early in the 2001 regular season, Bledsoe watched Brady take over at the QB position and never look back. Parcells was gone by then and new coach Bill Belichick was not about to remove a hot starter. Bledsoe's career with the Patriots was essentially over even though he filled in for a shaken-up Brady in the AFC Champion-

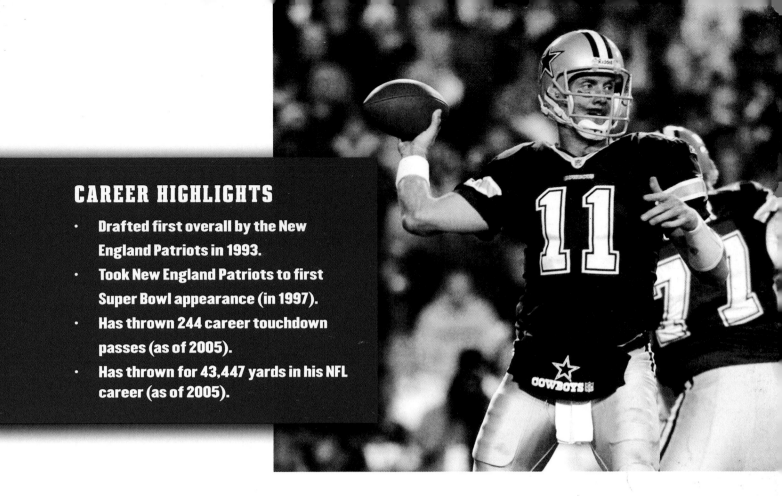

CAREER HIGHLIGHTS

- Drafted first overall by the New England Patriots in 1993.
- Took New England Patriots to first Super Bowl appearance (in 1997).
- Has thrown 244 career touchdown passes (as of 2005).
- Has thrown for 43,447 yards in his NFL career (as of 2005).

ship Game and pulled out a win over Pittsburgh. He left as the Patriots all-time leading passer with 29,657 yards.

The Bills wanted to bring an established QB onto the team and grudgingly gave up a number one draft choice (in 2002) to the Patriots for the rights to Bledsoe. At first Buffalo was excited about their new acquisition, and Bledsoe turned in a fine year with 24 touchdown tosses while throwing for 4,359 yards. But the next two years were not as good statistically, and a last-game-of-the-season loss to Pittsburgh (who were using many of their backups in the contest) sealed Bledsoe's fate as a Bill. In Dallas the coaching staff just wanted Bledsoe to avoid getting sacked too often (a severe criticism of a 6′5″, 238-pound QB) and not to throw as much. The Cowboys were confident they could mount a good running game and that a revamped offensive line could give Bledsoe the much-needed protection that was missing in Buffalo.

The Dallas passing game picked up considerably in 2005 and Bledsoe had the time to throw down the field to quality receivers like Keyshawn Johnson and Terry Glenn. Bledsoe looked much more confident, especially after a come-from-behind victory to open the season against the San Diego Chargers on the road. A 26 out of 37 performance by Bledsoe versus the New York Giants

IN THE HUDDLE

Drew Bledsoe holds the NFL record for most pass attempts in one season — 691 (in 1994).

gave the Cowboys a big win at home and a 4–2 record. The Cowboys stayed in playoff contention all year long, but losses to Washington and the New York Giants saw Dallas finish with a 9–7 record. Bledsoe's performance in '05 (passing for 3,639 yards and 24 touchdowns) showed that he is still capable of taking a team to the playoffs.

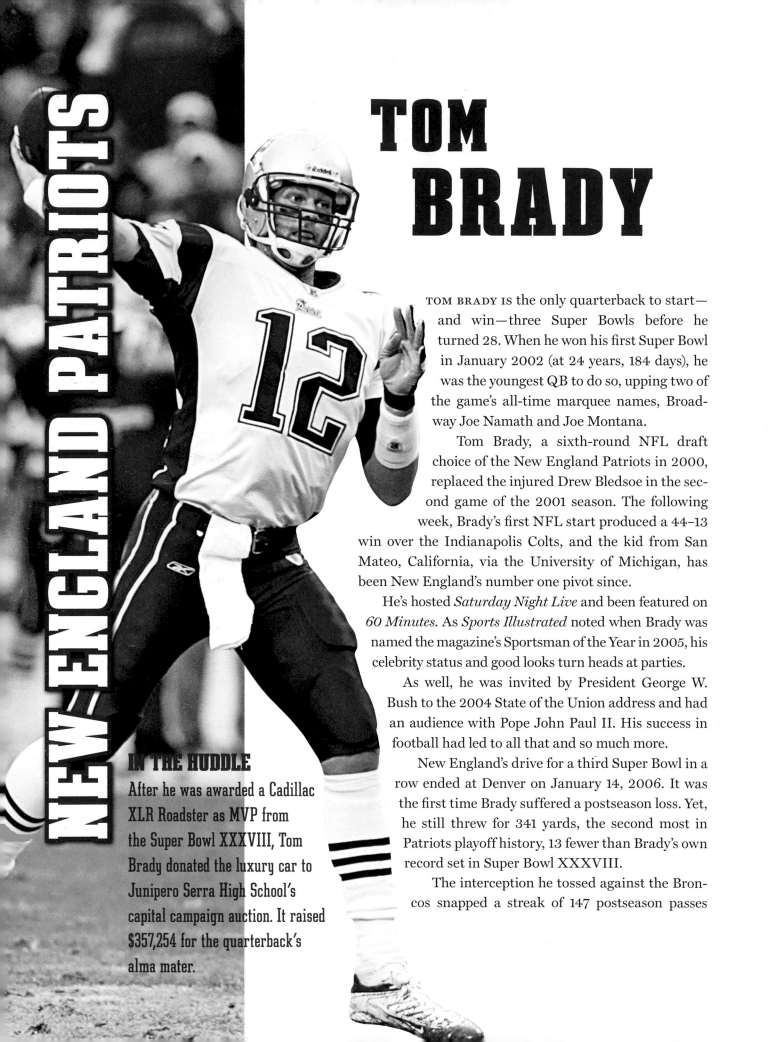

NEW ENGLAND PATRIOTS

TOM BRADY

TOM BRADY IS the only quarterback to start—and win—three Super Bowls before he turned 28. When he won his first Super Bowl in January 2002 (at 24 years, 184 days), he was the youngest QB to do so, upping two of the game's all-time marquee names, Broadway Joe Namath and Joe Montana.

Tom Brady, a sixth-round NFL draft choice of the New England Patriots in 2000, replaced the injured Drew Bledsoe in the second game of the 2001 season. The following week, Brady's first NFL start produced a 44–13 win over the Indianapolis Colts, and the kid from San Mateo, California, via the University of Michigan, has been New England's number one pivot since.

He's hosted *Saturday Night Live* and been featured on *60 Minutes*. As *Sports Illustrated* noted when Brady was named the magazine's Sportsman of the Year in 2005, his celebrity status and good looks turn heads at parties.

As well, he was invited by President George W. Bush to the 2004 State of the Union address and had an audience with Pope John Paul II. His success in football had led to all that and so much more.

New England's drive for a third Super Bowl in a row ended at Denver on January 14, 2006. It was the first time Brady suffered a postseason loss. Yet, he still threw for 341 yards, the second most in Patriots playoff history, 13 fewer than Brady's own record set in Super Bowl XXXVIII.

The interception he tossed against the Broncos snapped a streak of 147 postseason passes

IN THE HUDDLE

After he was awarded a Cadillac XLR Roadster as MVP from the Super Bowl XXXVIII, Tom Brady donated the luxury car to Junipero Serra High School's capital campaign auction. It raised $357,254 for the quarterback's alma mater.

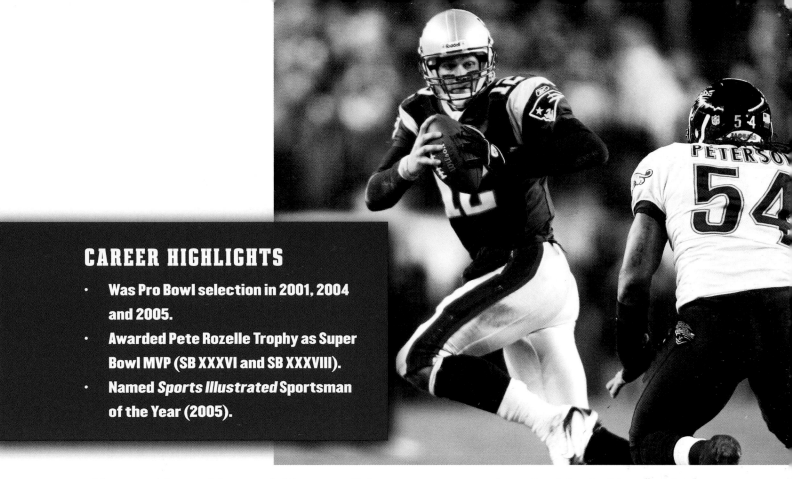

without a pick. Brady's remarkable accomplishments should come as no surprise. After all, he began his NFL career by setting a league record for the most consecutive passes without an interception to start a career (162).

On his way to getting where he is today, Brady graced the halls of Junipero Serra High School. In addition to Tom, the school's Hall of Famers include his older sister, Maureen, and Barry Bonds, Lynn Swann, Jim Fregosi and Gregg Jeffries.

Brady's multisport prowess became evident when he was selected by the Montreal Expos (now the Washington Nationals) in the 18th round of the 1995 Major League Baseball draft. The standout catcher, however, preferred football, and his pursuit of that game carried him east to Michigan.

He was the backup to Brian Griese when the Wolverines won the national title in 1997. While he wasn't always a starter over the next couple of seasons, he quietly went about his business as a constant team player. Brady's win–loss record as a starter was impressive (20–5), as were some of his passing performances.

Looking back on it now, though, the fact that he lasted into the sixth round and was taken 199th overall seems mind-boggling. Fate, indeed, shone brightly on the Patriots, who finally called his name.

Brady is known for using all his receiving options, but he and wide receiver Deion Branch have formed a spectacular duo, especially in key games. Although he set career highs for completions (373) and attempts (601) in 2002, Brady's best passing yardage total (4,110) occurred in 2005 when he led the NFL. He's never been picked off more than 14 times in one season, and after tossing 18 TD passes in 2001, he's hit for 23 or more TDs in each season since. Through 2005, Brady had connected for 123 TD passes and been intercepted 66 times.

With all he's done already, he's a lock for the Pro Football Hall of Fame.

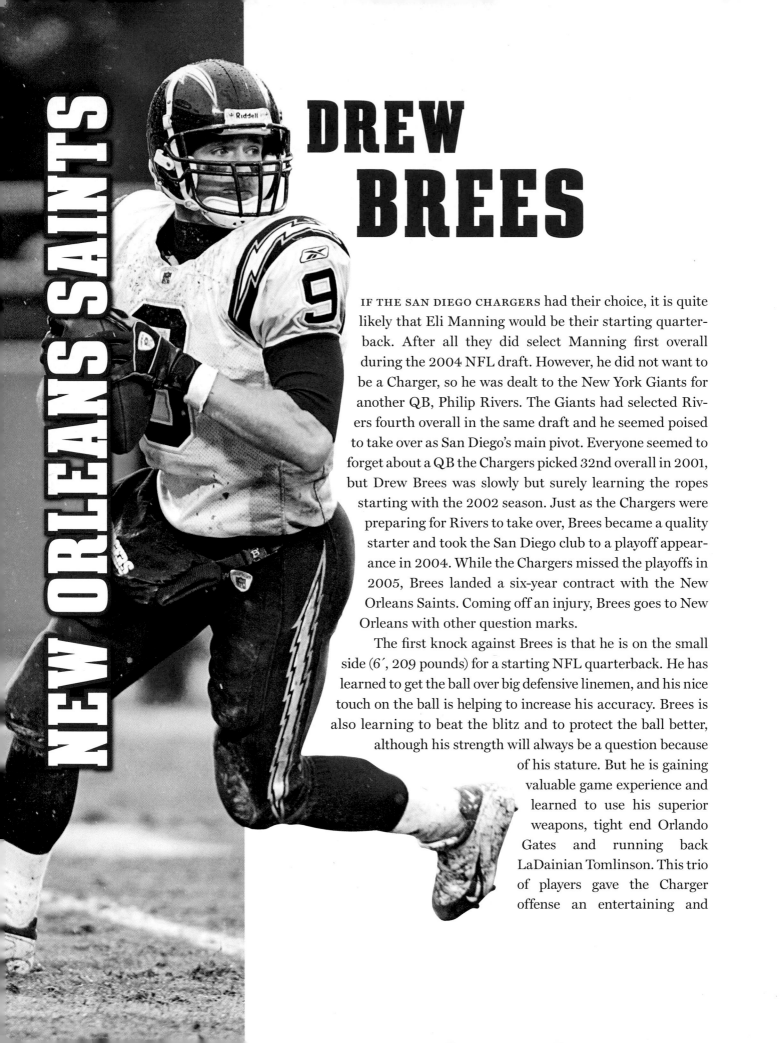

NEW ORLEANS SAINTS

DREW BREES

IF THE SAN DIEGO CHARGERS had their choice, it is quite likely that Eli Manning would be their starting quarterback. After all they did select Manning first overall during the 2004 NFL draft. However, he did not want to be a Charger, so he was dealt to the New York Giants for another QB, Philip Rivers. The Giants had selected Rivers fourth overall in the same draft and he seemed poised to take over as San Diego's main pivot. Everyone seemed to forget about a QB the Chargers picked 32nd overall in 2001, but Drew Brees was slowly but surely learning the ropes starting with the 2002 season. Just as the Chargers were preparing for Rivers to take over, Brees became a quality starter and took the San Diego club to a playoff appearance in 2004. While the Chargers missed the playoffs in 2005, Brees landed a six-year contract with the New Orleans Saints. Coming off an injury, Brees goes to New Orleans with other question marks.

The first knock against Brees is that he is on the small side (6´, 209 pounds) for a starting NFL quarterback. He has learned to get the ball over big defensive linemen, and his nice touch on the ball is helping to increase his accuracy. Brees is also learning to beat the blitz and to protect the ball better, although his strength will always be a question because of his stature. But he is gaining valuable game experience and learned to use his superior weapons, tight end Orlando Gates and running back LaDainian Tomlinson. This trio of players gave the Charger offense an entertaining and

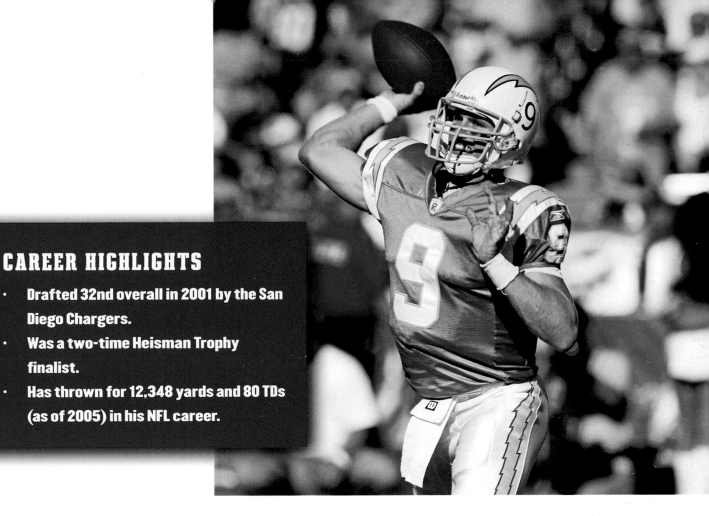

very productive attack. In the 2004 season the Charger attack led the team to a first-place finish in the West Division of the AFC and a spot in the playoffs with an unexpected 12–4 record. Only an overtime loss to the New York Jets stopped the San Diego season. Brees threw for 3,159 yards and 27 touchdowns (with only seven interceptions), proving that he belonged.

Brees began the 2005 season with the franchise player tag slapped on him by the Chargers, who then had to reward him with a one-year $8-million-dollar contract. Brees approached the season with the attitude that he had to improve (a sentiment that endeared him to head coach Marty Schottenheimer) and that he needed to have a big season (especially with Rivers under contract in an expensive multiyear deal).

The 2005 schedule for the Chargers proved a very difficult one as a result of their success in '04. They opened with two losses but rebounded to beat the Giants and then the defending champion New England Patriots right in Foxborough. The Chargers finished with a 9–7 record (a loss

IN THE HUDDLE

Drew Brees caught his first NFL touchdown pass from running back LaDainian Tomlinson against the Oakland Raiders on September 28, 2003.

late in the year to Kansas City ended their playoff hopes), and Brees demonstrated that he could lead the team back from a poor start and keep his club in contention (throwing for 3,576 yards and 24 touchdowns in '05) for a postseason spot. A severe shoulder injury (requiring surgery) that Brees suffered in the last game of the season set him back, but he's looking forward to taking the helm with the Saints and working with top draft pick Reggie Bush.

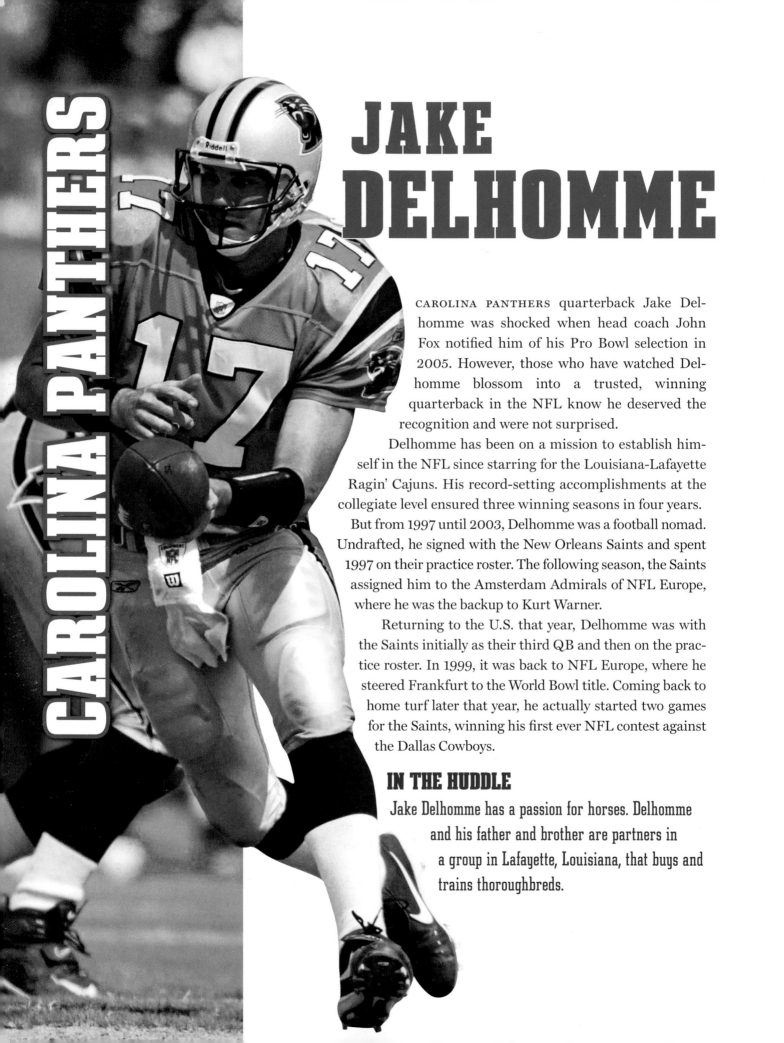

CAROLINA PANTHERS

JAKE DELHOMME

CAROLINA PANTHERS quarterback Jake Delhomme was shocked when head coach John Fox notified him of his Pro Bowl selection in 2005. However, those who have watched Delhomme blossom into a trusted, winning quarterback in the NFL know he deserved the recognition and were not surprised.

Delhomme has been on a mission to establish himself in the NFL since starring for the Louisiana-Lafayette Ragin' Cajuns. His record-setting accomplishments at the collegiate level ensured three winning seasons in four years. But from 1997 until 2003, Delhomme was a football nomad. Undrafted, he signed with the New Orleans Saints and spent 1997 on their practice roster. The following season, the Saints assigned him to the Amsterdam Admirals of NFL Europe, where he was the backup to Kurt Warner.

Returning to the U.S. that year, Delhomme was with the Saints initially as their third QB and then on the practice roster. In 1999, it was back to NFL Europe, where he steered Frankfurt to the World Bowl title. Coming back to home turf later that year, he actually started two games for the Saints, winning his first ever NFL contest against the Dallas Cowboys.

IN THE HUDDLE

Jake Delhomme has a passion for horses. Delhomme and his father and brother are partners in a group in Lafayette, Louisiana, that buys and trains thoroughbreds.

CAREER HIGHLIGHTS

- Undrafted. Signed by Carolina as an unrestricted free agent on March 7, 2003.
- Was Pro Bowl selection in 2005.
- Guided Carolina to Super Bowl XXXVIII in his first full season as an NFL starter.
- Celebrated the World Bowl Championship in 1999 with the Frankfurt Galaxy of NFL Europe.

From 2000 through 2002, he was still around the Saints, seeing limited action in four games in 2002. Granted his free agency, Delhomme's best options in 2003 were the Cowboys and the Panthers.

When he chose the Panthers, it would be the most momentous and rewarding decision of his pro football career. The Panthers posted a record of 1–15 in 2001 and 7–9 in 2002. With Delhomme at the helm starting 15 of 16 games in 2003, the Panthers, at 11–5, came within a win of equaling the franchise record.

He completed almost 60 percent of his passes during the regular season, then compiled a 3–1 record in the postseason. The Panthers won their first ever NFC Championship and came just short of winning Super Bowl XXXVIII, a 32–29 heartbreaker against the New England Patriots.

Delhomme completed 16 of 33 passes in that game for 323 yards—31 fewer yards than New England's Tom Brady. Delhomme matched Brady with three TD passes, but, by virtue of the win, Brady captured the Super Bowl MVP honor.

Nonetheless, Delhomme's NFL career was solidified with that campaign. He'd become the second unrestricted free-agent QB (Baltimore's Trent Dilfer in 2000 was the first) to lead his team to the Super Bowl in his first season with the club.

Delhomme's postseason record and 106.1 passer efficiency in that run were impressive totals. His passer efficiency of 113.6 in Super Bowl XXXVIII was the highest by a first-year QB since San Francisco's Steve Young (134.8 in Super Bowl XXIX).

His postseason magic brought the Panthers to the NFC Championship again in 2006. This time, the banged-up Panthers were smothered by the Seattle Seahawks, who contained Delhomme and wide receiver Steve Smith. Delhomme was picked off three times and had an uncharacteristically low 34.9 passer rating. That was a far cry from the 100.6 rating in the 23–0 Wild Card victory over the New York Giants and the 120.6 rating in the Divisional Playoff triumph over the Chicago Bears.

The Panthers receiving corps, led by Smith, has worked efficiently with Delhomme, who has surpassed 3,000 yards passing in each of his first three seasons (3,219, 3,886 and 3,421). He's thrown 72 TD passes over those three seasons and been picked off 47 times.

Delhomme, with little fanfare and better late than never, has provided stability and brought winning confidence to the NFL home he sought so long ago.

TRENT GREEN

KANSAS CITY CHIEFS

ON NEW YEAR'S DAY 2006, quarterback Trent Green guided the Kansas City Chiefs to a 37–3 season-ending victory over the Cincinnati Bengals. By compiling 344 passing yards on a 23-for-29 day, Green finished with 4,014 passing yards—the third consecutive season he'd toppled the significant 4,000 barrier.

That same day, Larry Johnson had rushed for 201 yards and three TDs. But other issues dominated the news. The first was the fact that, despite a 10–6 season in 2005, the Chiefs missed the playoffs. And the second was the impending retirement of Chiefs head coach Dick Vermeil. Green heaped praise on Vermeil, not only for his guidance in Kansas City but also during an earlier connection with the St. Louis Rams.

As the discussion turned to Green's own intentions, the 35-year-old quelled any rumors that he was thinking of winding down his career. He signed a seven-year contract with the Chiefs on February 27, 2003, and he intends to honor that commitment.

Acknowledged as one of the "good guys" in pro sports and as a constant giver to the community, Green isn't about to step aside, especially when he's playing at the top of his game and the exciting Chiefs are on the edge of challenging for a title.

His passing efficiency in 2005 (90.1) made him the only NFL quarterback with a current streak of four seasons at a 90.0 rating. He's 12–0 in games at Arrowhead Stadium after December 1, and he's the second QB in Chiefs history to surpass 20,000 passing yards (with 20,117 through 2005).

Recognition has come late in his career, but his staying power and his determination to find a permanent home and overcome injuries are now being rewarded.

He was an eighth-round selection of the San Diego Chargers in 1993 after starring with the Indiana Hoosiers. When the Chargers released him in August 2004, he headed to Canada, where he

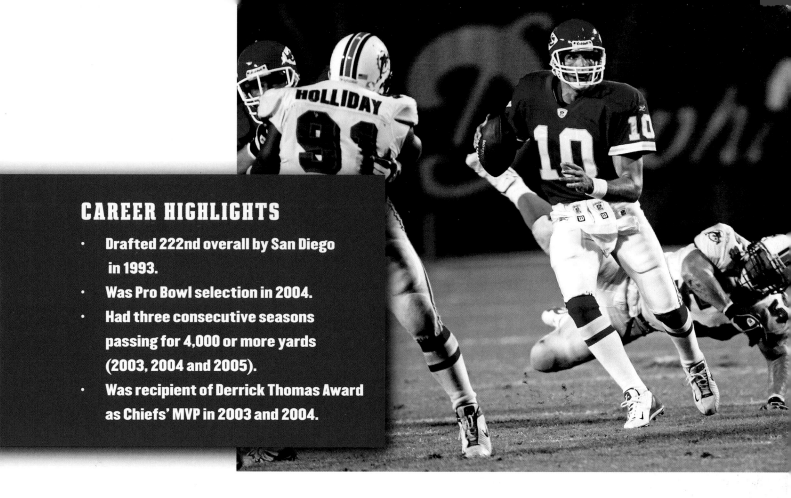

CAREER HIGHLIGHTS

- Drafted 222nd overall by San Diego in 1993.
- Was Pro Bowl selection in 2004.
- Had three consecutive seasons passing for 4,000 or more yards (2003, 2004 and 2005).
- Was recipient of Derrick Thomas Award as Chiefs' MVP in 2003 and 2004.

signed with the British Columbia Lions. He even dressed for a couple of games with the power-house Lions, but saw no action. The Lions released him in November 2004, and next it was off to the Washington Redskins, who inked him on April 5, 1995.

He spent two seasons as the third QB for the Redskins, finally making his NFL debut on December 21, 1997, with an incompletion against the Philadelphia Eagles.

An injury sustained by Gus Frerotte on September 6, 1998, proved an opportunity for Green as he played 15 games, starting 14, and completed 54.6 percent of his passes with 23 TDs and 11 interceptions.

Green was elated to sign as a free agent with the Rams on February 16, 1999, because it brought him and his family back to his St. Louis home. But just as it appeared his star was rising, he suffered a serious injury to his left knee during the Rams' third preseason game. He missed

the entire 1999 season, and that opened the door for Kurt Warner to take over the helm and charge his way to NFL MVP honors in 1999 and 2001.

The Chiefs welcomed Vermeil in 2001 and they reunited him with Green when they completed a trade with the Rams on April 20, 2001. Green and a fifth-round draft selection headed to K.C. for the Chiefs' first-round position (12th overall).

IN THE HUDDLE

The Trent Green Family Foundation (established in 1999 to help numerous children's causes) gained a $30,000 windfall in 2003 when Green demonstrated a keen ability to solve puzzles on *Wheel of Fortune* during NFL Week.

Green started every game in his first five seasons with the Chiefs, providing stability, expertise, leadership and plenty of wins along the way.

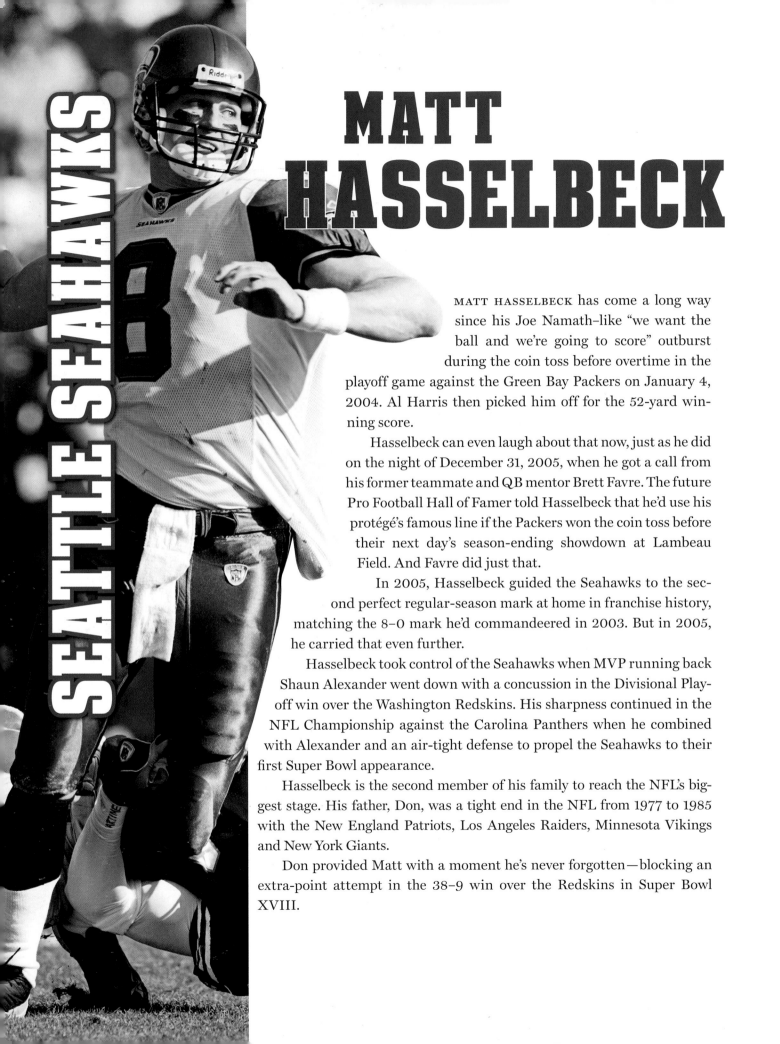

MATT HASSELBECK

MATT HASSELBECK has come a long way since his Joe Namath–like "we want the ball and we're going to score" outburst during the coin toss before overtime in the playoff game against the Green Bay Packers on January 4, 2004. Al Harris then picked him off for the 52-yard winning score.

Hasselbeck can even laugh about that now, just as he did on the night of December 31, 2005, when he got a call from his former teammate and QB mentor Brett Favre. The future Pro Football Hall of Famer told Hasselbeck that he'd use his protégé's famous line if the Packers won the coin toss before their next day's season-ending showdown at Lambeau Field. And Favre did just that.

In 2005, Hasselbeck guided the Seahawks to the second perfect regular-season mark at home in franchise history, matching the 8–0 mark he'd commandeered in 2003. But in 2005, he carried that even further.

Hasselbeck took control of the Seahawks when MVP running back Shaun Alexander went down with a concussion in the Divisional Play-off win over the Washington Redskins. His sharpness continued in the NFL Championship against the Carolina Panthers when he combined with Alexander and an air-tight defense to propel the Seahawks to their first Super Bowl appearance.

Hasselbeck is the second member of his family to reach the NFL's biggest stage. His father, Don, was a tight end in the NFL from 1977 to 1985 with the New England Patriots, Los Angeles Raiders, Minnesota Vikings and New York Giants.

Don provided Matt with a moment he's never forgotten—blocking an extra-point attempt in the 38–9 win over the Redskins in Super Bowl XVIII.

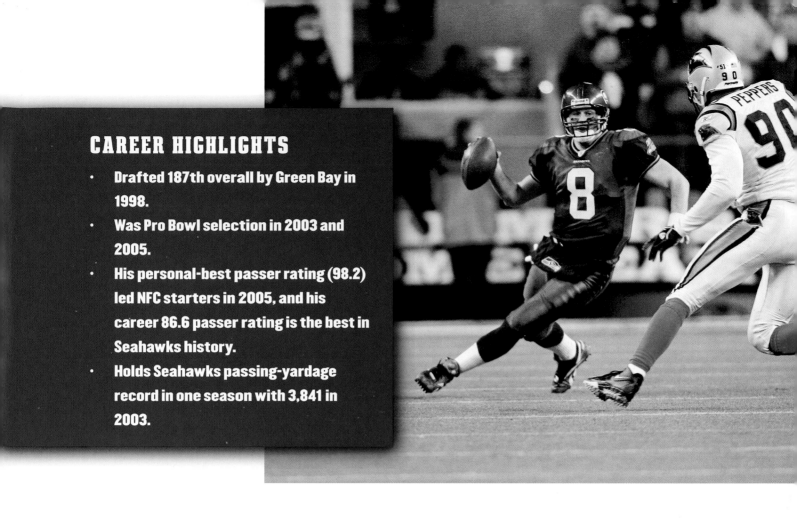

CAREER HIGHLIGHTS

- Drafted 187th overall by Green Bay in 1998.
- Was Pro Bowl selection in 2003 and 2005.
- His personal-best passer rating (98.2) led NFC starters in 2005, and his career 86.6 passer rating is the best in Seahawks history.
- Holds Seahawks passing-yardage record in one season with 3,841 in 2003.

From Xaverian Brothers High School in Westwood, Massachusetts, to Boston College, Matt Hasselbeck refined his game. The Packers, with Mike Holmgren as head coach, used a compensatory selection in the sixth round to select Hasselbeck in the 1998 NFL draft. After spending 1998 on the Packers' practice squad, Hasselbeck earned the understudy role to Favre.

On March 2, 2001, Holmgren, who'd left the Packers for the Seahawks in 1999, made one of the most significant trades in franchise history—obtaining Hasselbeck and Green Bay's first-round selection in the 2001 NFL draft (17th overall) for Seattle's first-round (10th overall) and third-round spots. Holmgren then used Green Bay's 17th spot to draft eventual perennial Pro Bowl guard Steve Hutchinson.

After Hasselbeck struggled as a starter in 2001 and launched 2002 as the backup to Trent Dilfer, injuries to Dilfer eventually placed him as

IN THE HUDDLE

Matt Hasselbeck isn't Don's only son with football experience. Matt's younger brother, Tim, was also once a starting QB at Boston College, and he spent 2002 with the Philadelphia Eagles, 2003 and 2004 with the Washington Redskins, and 2005 with the New York Giants. Another brother, Nathanael, was a wide receiver at Boston College and at the University of Massachusetts.

the Seahawks' starter in 2002. Hasselbeck has passed for more than 3,000 yards in every season since 2002, and he's thrown 20 or more TD passes for the past three seasons. Calm, cool and very much Favre-like, Hasselbeck has established himself as a dependable leader. Even though the Seahawks lost Super Bowl XL to Pittsburgh, it appears Hasselbeck's time has finally arrived.

NEW YORK GIANTS

ELI MANNING

THE GLARE, GLORY and scorn centers on quarterbacks more than on any other position in football. That's magnified even more if, as in the case of Eli Manning, the stage is the Big Apple and the bloodlines happen to be giants like his father, Archie, and his brother, Peyton.

In many respects, Eli has already shown the gutsy resolve he'll require to withstand the heat of life with the New York Giants. He took more than his share of lumps when he took over as the number one quarterback in 2004. He lost his first six starts before savoring a win in the season finale against Dallas. His first-year stats weren't impressive: 95 of 197 passing (48.2 percent) for 1,043 yards, six TD passes and nine interceptions.

Manning had set 47 game, season and career records at Ole Miss because of a fierce competitiveness, a cannon arm and talent. He began to display all those components in 2005 when he passed for 3,762 yards—fifth in the NFL—and completed 294 of 557 passes. He threw 24 TD passes and was intercepted 17 times. In conjunction with that output, the

IN THE HUDDLE

The Manning brothers, Eli (2004) and Peyton (1998), were both number one overall selections in the NFL draft. Their father, Archie (1971), was the number two selection in the NFL draft, going to New Orleans after the Boston Patriots picked Jim Plunkett.

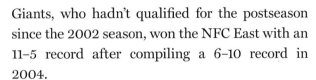
Giants, who hadn't qualified for the postseason since the 2002 season, won the NFC East with an 11–5 record after compiling a 6–10 record in 2004.

With Manning in firm control, receivers Plaxico Burress, Amani Toomer and Jeremy Shockey hauling in his passes, and the backfield getting plenty of mileage from All Pro Tiki Barber and Brandon Jacobs, the Giants' offense averaged 361.7 yards per game. That was the highest average for the Giants since 1972 and it ranked fifth in the NFL.

The Giants scored 422 points, up 119 from 2004. Their production in 2005 placed second in club history, bettered only by the 448 in 1963. And for the fifth time in NFL history, a team boasted five players with seven or more TDs: Barber with 11 and Burress, Toomer, Shockey and Jacobs all at seven. Four of that group had 50 or more receptions: Burress (74), Shockey (65), Toomer (60) and Barber (54).

Even after he resisted overtures from and declared no interest in playing for San Diego, the Chargers went ahead and drafted Manning with the number one spot in 2004. The Giants acquired him by shipping QB Philip Rivers (selected at the number four position by the Giants), a third-round pick in 2004, plus the first- and fifth-round selections in 2005.

The "but" in the Eli Manning feel-good story of 2005 came in the postseason, a disastrous 23–0 Wild Card loss at home to the Carolina Panthers. Manning was 10 of 18 for 113 yards and three interceptions. His QB rating for the game was 35.0, with only one QB—Washington's Mark Brunell at 25.7—worse that weekend. But Brunell, at least, was part of a winning team.

A headline in the *New York Post* read: "Giants Simply Mann-Handled." Another in the *New York Daily News* proclaimed: "Eli Fails 1st Playoff Test." Meanwhile, Fox analyst Jimmy Johnson chimed in, stating that Eli Manning would be fine—in time. After all, Johnson added, Peyton Manning lost his first three postseason games.

Eli Manning intends to learn from that bitter experience just as he did from his much-heralded arrival and early struggles in the NFL.

PEYTON MANNING

INDIANAPOLIS COLTS

EVEN THOUGH PEYTON MANNING was the son of a great NFL quarterback, his father, Archie, would not allow him to play organized football until he was in the seventh grade. Waiting to formally play a game made young Peyton even more hungry when he finally got his chance, and he has never lost his intensity. He did play baseball as a child and never liked it when he lost a game, and did not like it at all when a coach tried to explain away losses as "ties." Manning knows the difference between winning and losing, and his passion to win has led him to great heights as an NFL starting quarterback. His statistical achievements are too numerous to mention, but Manning knows that he is now playing for one reason—to win a Super Bowl. Simply put, there is nothing else left for him to achieve.

Drafted first overall by the Indianapolis Colts in 1998 after a college career at the University of Tennessee, the 6′5″, 230-pound Manning is perfectly suited to play the most vital position in football. What makes Manning so good is that he is prepared for everything he might encounter on the field. He practices extremely hard and his study of film is becoming almost legendary. The Colts pivot does not mind putting in the time to study the opposition—he knows that for three hours once a week his work will all be on the line. No detail is too small as far as Manning is concerned, and he hopes that he can recognize a situation at just the right moment (he does not hesitate to change a play call at the line) to capitalize on a big play at some point in the game. Manning can make any type of throw with equal dexterity, and he can pick apart any defense, given the time needed.

He is a firm believer that any football game usually comes

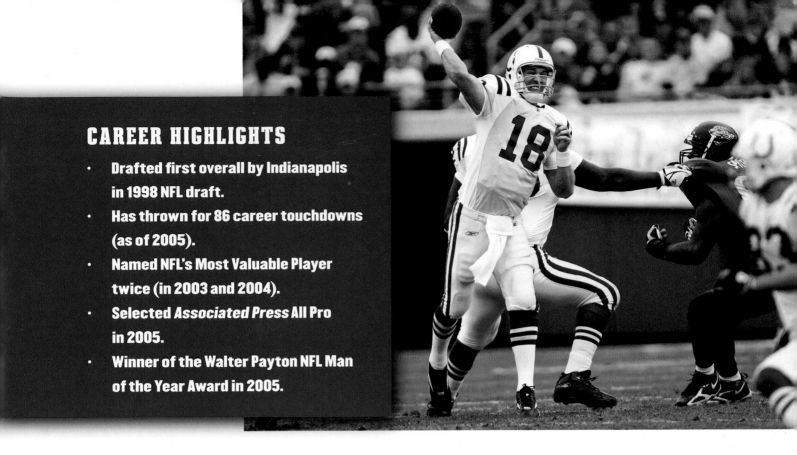

CAREER HIGHLIGHTS

- Drafted first overall by Indianapolis in 1998 NFL draft.
- Has thrown for 86 career touchdowns (as of 2005).
- Named NFL's Most Valuable Player twice (in 2003 and 2004).
- Selected *Associated Press* All Pro in 2005.
- Winner of the Walter Payton NFL Man of the Year Award in 2005.

down to four or five plays, and they might happen in any quarter of the contest. This approach keeps Manning sharp and alert throughout the entire game, and his results prove that being prepared is the key to his success.

A starter since he joined the Colts in 1998, Manning had his great NFL season in 2004 when he threw for a record 49 touchdowns (with only 10 interceptions) and passed for 4,557 yards. The 12–4 Colts made it to the AFC Championship Game only to lose to the eventual champion New England Patriots. It was expected that Indy would have a big year in '05, and they certainly did not disappoint, winning their first 13 games. Talk of a perfect season was everywhere the Colts went. However, a couple of losses scuttled that hope, and they ended the year with the best record in the league at 14–2. Manning was his usual self with 305 completions in 453 attempts for 3,747 yards and 28 TDs, lower numbers than the previous year, but the team was poised for a run at the Super Bowl.

But a funny thing happened on the way to what seemed like a sure championship—the Pittsburgh Steelers rolled into town and walked away with a 21–18 win that ended the Colts' dream once again. Manning was not as his best during the game against Pittsburgh and made things even worse after the game by saying his offensive line did not have a good day. He may have to mend some fences before the next season begins. Still, Manning is a player who demands and gets respect.

IN THE HUDDLE

As of the end of the 2005 season, Peyton Manning's record as a starter in the regular season is 80-48 and 3-6 as a starter in the playoffs.

The Colts became contenders virtually from the moment Manning arrived on the scene (the team has won 10 or more games six times since '98). He will keep his team in the hunt because of his enormous talent and his intense drive to succeed. It remains to be seen if he has what it takes to get to a Super Bowl and win it. Manning knows that is the standard by which he will be measured for the rest of his career.

PHILADELPHIA EAGLES

DONOVAN McNABB

DONOVAN McNABB is a pretty tough guy—both mentally and physically. He has to be in order to survive in Philadelphia, where they judge their sports heroes with a very critical eye. It all started the day the Eagles decided to take the 6′2″, 240-pound quarterback with the second overall pick during the 1999 NFL draft. Eagles fans wanted the club to select running back Ricky Williams with the choice and were quite upset when the team took McNabb instead.

It just goes to show that those in management need to be true to their own beliefs, and Eagles fans are happy now that they have seen how uneven Williams' career has been over the years. It would have been even worse if the Eagles had had a chance to select QB Tim Couch, who was taken first overall by Cleveland. He's not even in the league anymore! Any controversy over his selection did not seem to bother McNabb in the least. He praises his parents for teaching him that the best way to answer the critics is to keep your head up and show them what you can do. Since becoming the Eagles' full-time starter in 2000, McNabb has taken his team to the NFC Championship Game for four consecutive years (2002 to 2005) and to one appearance in the Super Bowl (a loss to the New England Patriots in '05). NcNabb has had to fight off the rantings of an uninformed national critic (Rush Limbaugh) and the verbal jabs of a loose-cannon former teammate (Terrell Owens); through it all he has always kept his dignity and composure. He looks forward to every game as a chance to lead his team to victory and wants to silence the dissenters with another trip to the Super Bowl.

McNabb has a strong throwing arm and uses his size and strength very well. He does not hesitate to put the ball in the air, and throwing 30 to 40 passes does not bother him in the least. As much as Owens was a pain for McNabb to deal with, having an outstanding wide receiver was good for his career. In 2004, for example, he threw for 31 touchdowns and had only eight interceptions (he was the first NFL QB to accomplish this feat—more than 30 TDs and fewer than 10 INTs in one season). Philadelphia's running game is good but not spectacular, so McNabb is often in a position where he has to throw the ball while facing a strong blitz from the opposition.

He also never hesitates to run if he has to. As a result he has endured some injury problems, but he is undaunted about playing the game. During the 2005 season he took a vicious hit in the opening game against the Atlanta Falcons. He came back to play with a bruised sternum, and later it was revealed that he had a sports hernia that required surgery. McNabb could have taken an out and undergone the surgery, but he knew that might cost his team a shot at the playoffs. During the second game of the year against the San Francisco 49ers, he threw for 342 yards and five touchdowns!

IN THE HUDDLE

Along with his mother, Wilma, Donovan McNabb has done television commercials in which they extol the virtues of eating soup.

The determined QB remained in the lineup by taking anti-inflammatories and doing his stretching exercises, preferring to stay away from painkillers. However, during a loss to the Cowboys, McNabb aggravated his injury, which forced him to end his season after playing in just nine games. The Eagles slumped to a 6–10 record while McNabb recovered from surgery. The end of Owens' stay with the Eagles should help McNabb as he comes back in 2006 to reclaim his place among the elite quarterbacks in the NFL.

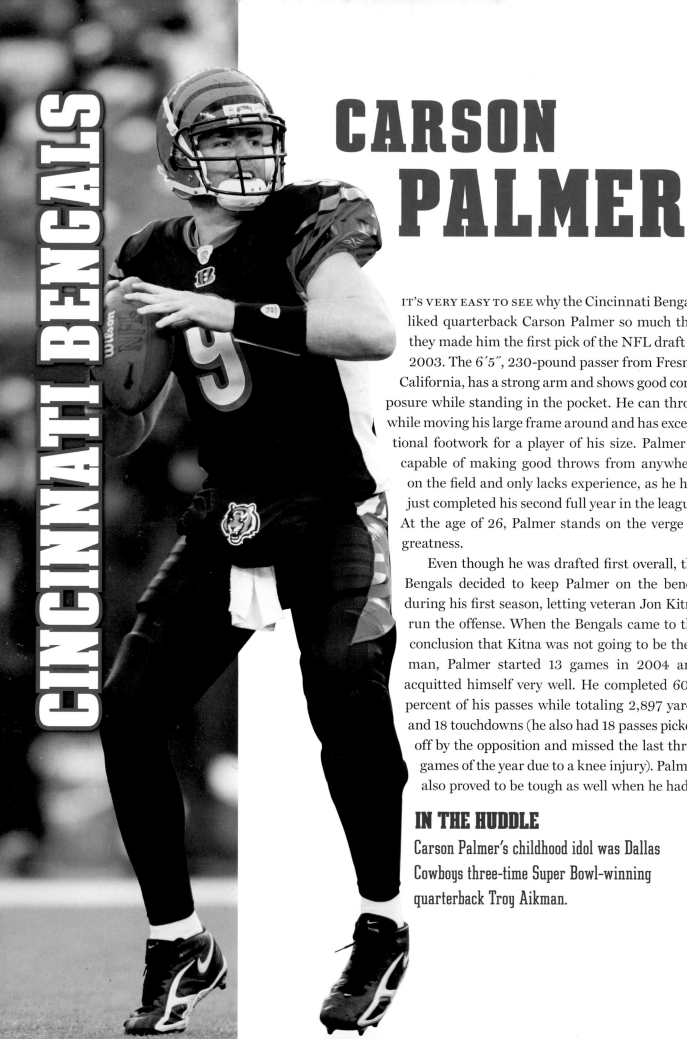

CINCINNATI BENGALS

CARSON PALMER

IT'S VERY EASY TO SEE why the Cincinnati Bengals liked quarterback Carson Palmer so much that they made him the first pick of the NFL draft in 2003. The 6′5″, 230-pound passer from Fresno, California, has a strong arm and shows good composure while standing in the pocket. He can throw while moving his large frame around and has exceptional footwork for a player of his size. Palmer is capable of making good throws from anywhere on the field and only lacks experience, as he has just completed his second full year in the league. At the age of 26, Palmer stands on the verge of greatness.

Even though he was drafted first overall, the Bengals decided to keep Palmer on the bench during his first season, letting veteran Jon Kitna run the offense. When the Bengals came to the conclusion that Kitna was not going to be their man, Palmer started 13 games in 2004 and acquitted himself very well. He completed 60.9 percent of his passes while totaling 2,897 yards and 18 touchdowns (he also had 18 passes picked off by the opposition and missed the last three games of the year due to a knee injury). Palmer also proved to be tough as well when he had a

IN THE HUDDLE

Carson Palmer's childhood idol was Dallas Cowboys three-time Super Bowl-winning quarterback Troy Aikman.

four-touchdown performance against the Cleveland Browns after missing most the practice week because of a back injury. Although his record as the starter was only 6–7, the Bengals finally had some hope at the key position—a hope they have not had since the days of Boomer Esiason!

Palmer was smart enough to realize that he could not be too satisfied with his performance in '04. He asked Kitna for help when he was the backup and then studied how Colts QB Peyton Manning spread the ball around to all his receivers in an effort to improve his own play. Palmer is generally a cool customer and worries more about winning the game than looking spectacular. It's been a little slow in terms of development, but Palmer is making steady progress, as evidenced by his play during the 2005 season.

Under coach Marvin Lewis the Bengals have put together a formidable group of young players. Along with Palmer, Cincinnati had added receivers Chad Johnson and T.J. Houshmandzadeh to go along with running back Rudi Johnson, giving the Bengals good talent at the key ball-handling

positions. Good linemen in center Rich Braham, young guard Eric Steinbach and Pro Bowl guard Willie Anderson help give Palmer the protection he needs to get the ball down the field. The Bengals started the '05 season with four straight wins but failed during the first big test, when division rival Pittsburgh beat them at home in a close contest. However, the maturing Cincinnati squad bounced back to beat the Steelers 38–31 late in the season with Palmer going 22 of 38 for 227 yards and throwing for three touchdowns. That victory helped the Bengals win their division with an 11–5 record and a playoff appearance for the first time in 14 years!

A playoff loss to Pittsburgh coupled with a major knee injury to Palmer certainly put a damper on the end of the year. The team is confident that Palmer (who was signed to a new deal that keeps him a Bengal until 2014) will make a full recovery, and the Bengals believe they are poised to do great things. This franchise now seems to have the necessary ingredients to make itself a contender for years to come.

DENVER BRONCOS

JAKE PLUMMER

QUARTERBACK JAKE PLUMMER's third season with the Denver Broncos was his best yet, despite ending on a sour note in the AFC Championship against the Pittsburgh Steelers.

For starters, the Broncos completed 2005 with a record of 13–3. Then they toppled the dynasty of the New England Patriots to set up their AFC Championship showdown against the Pittsburgh Steelers. Unfortunately for the Broncos, it wasn't a memorable day for Plummer as he lost two fumbles and tossed two interceptions against the tough Steelers defense in the 34–17 Broncos loss.

That detracted from how well he had played up until that point. Plummer had completed 277 of 456 passes for 3,366 yards during the 2005 regular season, tossing 18 TD passes and yielding but seven interceptions. He set a Broncos record when he went for a period of 229 consecutive passes over eight games without throwing an interception.

In 2004, Plummer had erased John Elway's club single-season mark for yards passing with 4,089 (Elway had 4,030 in 1993). Plummer established the Broncos' record for most passing yards in one game with 499 against Atlanta on October 31, 2004. Through 2005, he'd compiled a regular-season record of 32–11 as a starter with the Broncos—a sparkling winning percentage of .744, another franchise record.

So why, after all this, does it seem Plummer is still in a show-me situation? Well, until he could guide the Broncos to Super Bowl glory—as Elway had done—fans weren't about to be as forgiving of him.

Plummer's statistics with Denver have turned his career around. Adding his work in six seasons with the Arizona Cardinals to the mix left him with

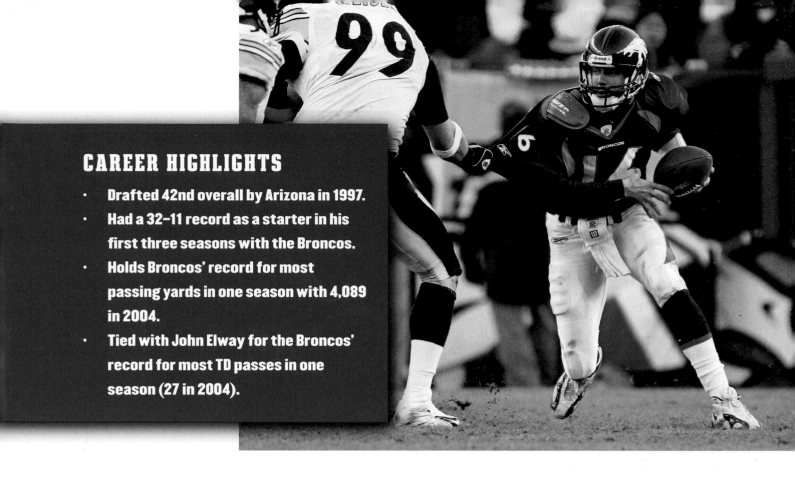

only two more career TD passes (150) than interceptions (148). His career passing efficiency (75.1) has been climbing since he has been a Bronco—he's posted ratings of 91.2, 84.5 and 90.2.

He didn't throw more TD passes than interceptions in any NFL season until his fifth season with the Cardinals and compiled a 9:24 TD pass-to-interception ratio in 1999. This was the same guy who had starred at Arizona State, and Bill Walsh, the once great mastermind of the San Francisco 49ers, even mentioned him in the same breath as Joe Montana.

For Plummer, life with the Cardinals wasn't what it had been with the Sun Devils. Year after year of futility, however, ended on March 7, 2003, when the unrestricted free agent inked a deal with the Broncos.

His teammates note that he keeps things loose in the locker room, but he is a man who argues for his principles. He was at odds with the NFL in 2004 when he declined to remove a helmet decal in honor of his good friend Pat Tillman,

a former Cardinals teammate who had been killed by friendly fire while on military duty in Afghanistan. The issue of a league fine was avoided when Plummer finally removed the decal. He did so after making a video in honor of veterans, which was shown in NFL stadiums.

But he was fined by the NFL in 2004 for making an obscene gesture. He also had a run-in with a gossip columnist in 2005 over a reference

IN THE HUDDLE

In 2005, Jake Plummer helped the Broncos become the third team in NFL history to field a 3,000-yard passer (Plummer), a 1,000-yard receiver (Rod Smith with 1,105) and two 900-yard rushers (Mike Anderson with 1,014 and Tatum Bell with 921) in the same season.

to his girlfriend. Then, during the 2005 playoffs, attention turned to his Grizzly Adams looks. Throughout all these potentially distracting incidents, Plummer found a way to keep on winning.

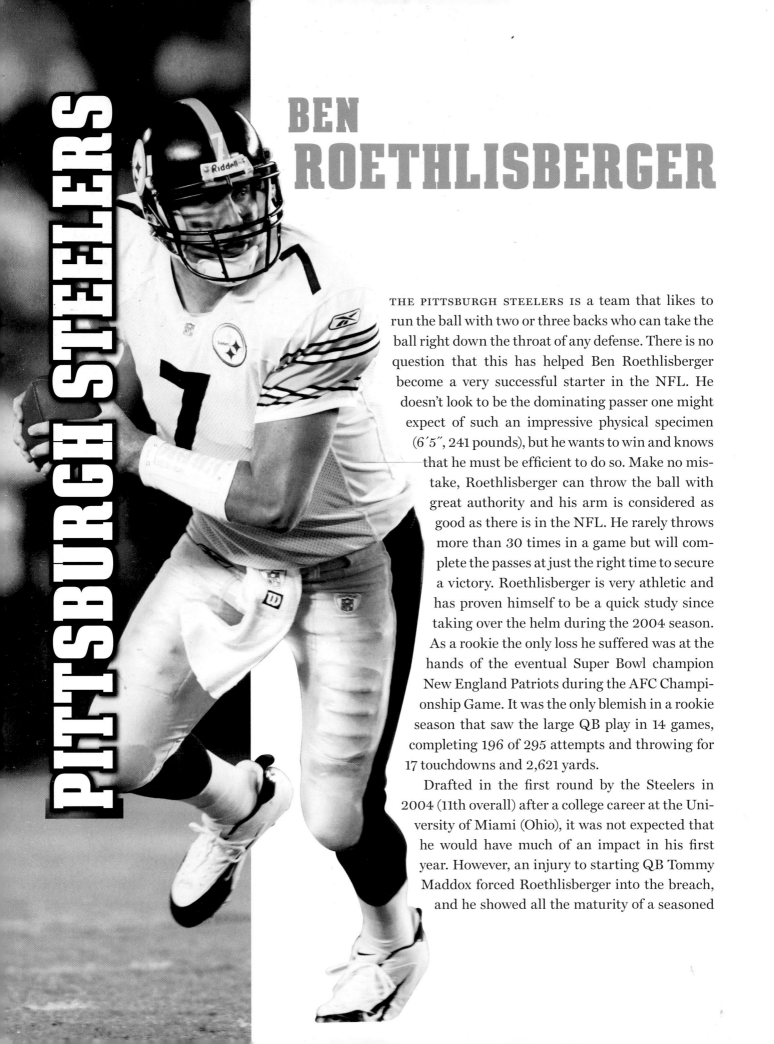

PITTSBURGH STEELERS

BEN ROETHLISBERGER

THE PITTSBURGH STEELERS IS a team that likes to run the ball with two or three backs who can take the ball right down the throat of any defense. There is no question that this has helped Ben Roethlisberger become a very successful starter in the NFL. He doesn't look to be the dominating passer one might expect of such an impressive physical specimen (6′5″, 241 pounds), but he wants to win and knows that he must be efficient to do so. Make no mistake, Roethlisberger can throw the ball with great authority and his arm is considered as good as there is in the NFL. He rarely throws more than 30 times in a game but will complete the passes at just the right time to secure a victory. Roethlisberger is very athletic and has proven himself to be a quick study since taking over the helm during the 2004 season. As a rookie the only loss he suffered was at the hands of the eventual Super Bowl champion New England Patriots during the AFC Championship Game. It was the only blemish in a rookie season that saw the large QB play in 14 games, completing 196 of 295 attempts and throwing for 17 touchdowns and 2,621 yards.

Drafted in the first round by the Steelers in 2004 (11th overall) after a college career at the University of Miami (Ohio), it was not expected that he would have much of an impact in his first year. However, an injury to starting QB Tommy Maddox forced Roethlisberger into the breach, and he showed all the maturity of a seasoned

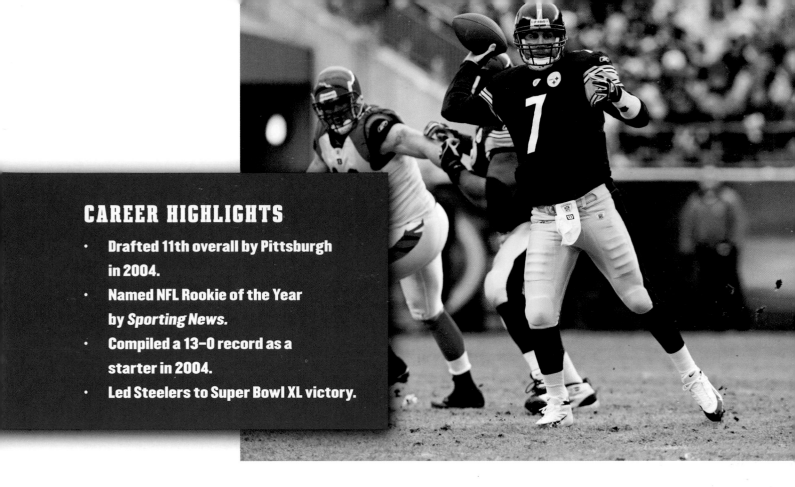

CAREER HIGHLIGHTS

- Drafted 11th overall by Pittsburgh in 2004.
- Named NFL Rookie of the Year by *Sporting News*.
- Compiled a 13–0 record as a starter in 2004.
- Led Steelers to Super Bowl XL victory.

veteran. He quickly became a fan favorite, and Steelers fans began reminiscing about another first-round pick of many years ago named Terry Bradshaw. Roethlisberger was certainly aware of the Hall of Fame quarterback who took Pittsburgh to four Super Bowls, and he liked the fact that Bradshaw did whatever it took to win. He saw himself in the same way, and if any QB could take the Steelers back to the glory days of the '70s, it had to be Roethlisberger.

The Steelers QB started 12 games during the 2005 season (he missed three due to injury) and led his team to an 11–5 record and a spot in the playoffs as a Wild Card entry. Ranked as the sixth seed in the AFC, the Steelers proceeded to defeat Cincinnati, Indianapolis and Denver to earn a berth in the Super Bowl. During the AFC Championship Game against the Broncos, Roethlisberger went 21 for 29, for 275 yards and two touchdowns. Perhaps his greatest contribution came as a tackler when he knocked down

Colts defensive back Roland Harper after a fumble recovery that was about to turn into a sure Indianapolis touchdown. It was a great play by Roethlisberger, who saved teammate Jerome Bettis from a terrible embarrassment.

IN THE HUDDLE

A Pittsburgh-area restaurant has honored Ben Roethlisberger with the "Roethlis burger." It sells for $7, to match his sweater number.

Roethlisberger did not have a spectacular game in Super Bowl XL (though he did throw a key block on a TD pass tossed by Antwaan Randle El). But the Steelers won the contest to raise his overall win–loss record as a starter to an unbelievable 27–4.

In June 2006, Ben Roethlisberger was seriously injured in a motorcycle accident. His ability to recover will determine his future in football.

SPEED, POWER, AGILITY: A THREAT TO
RUNNING

BREAK LOOSE FOR A TD AT ANY MOMENT

BACKS!

SEATTLE SEAHAWKS

SHAUN ALEXANDER

QWEST FIELD IN SEATTLE was aglow with a passionate love-in involving the Seahawks and *all* their 12th men in the stands when running back Shaun Alexander capped the NFC Championship triumph over the Carolina Panthers by taking the George Halas Trophy for a jog.

Alexander had the designation of the franchise player for the Seahawks in 2005. With free agency looming, the running back who had set the NFL record for most touchdowns in one season with 28 (27 rushing and one through the air) had delivered once more for the Seahawks; fans hoped his parading the Halas Trophy wouldn't be the last run he'd make at Qwest Field in a Seattle uniform.

One more gigantic challenge remained—Super Bowl XL at Detroit.

In addition to establishing the NFL's single-season TD mark in 2005, Alexander became the first player in the league's history with 15 or more touchdowns in five consecutive seasons. He is the fourth player in NFL history with back-to-back 20-or-more-touchdown seasons.

Alexander led the NFL in 2005 with a Seahawks-record 1,880 yards rushing, eclipsing by 184 yards the standard he had set the previous year. His 2005 production featured 11 games of 100 or more yards rushing, including a 173-yard game against Arizona on November 6. He is the franchise record-holder, with 7,817 yards rushing in his six seasons with the Seahawks.

He scored a first for the Seahawks when he won the *Associated Press* NFL Most Valuable Player award in 2005.

Alexander left the Alabama Crimson Tide as that school's all-time leader in rushing yards, with 3,565, and clutching 15 records for 'Bama. Before going to Alabama, he'd starred at Boone County High School in Kentucky, initially as a defensive back and kick returner. He developed his style and approach by

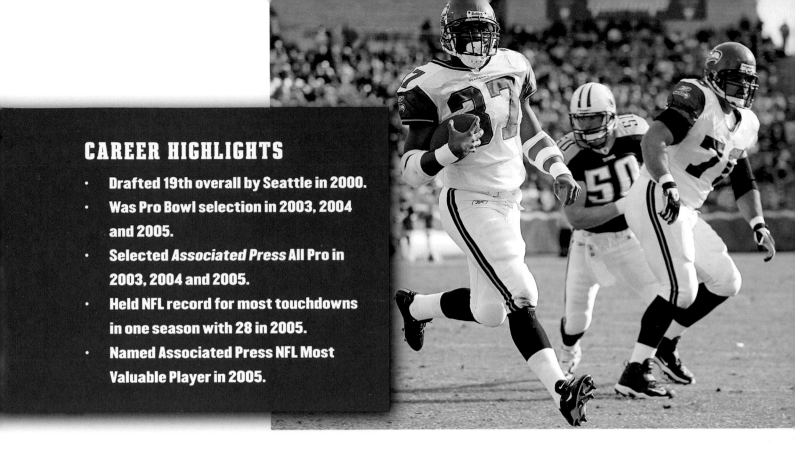

studying great running backs like Marcus Allen, Barry Sanders and Emmitt Smith.

Alexander started one of the 16 games he played in 2000 and saw most of his duty on short-yardage situations. Getting 12 starts in 2001, largely because Ricky Watters was sidelined by shoulder and ankle injuries, Alexander became the fourth player in Seahawks history to surpass 1,000 yards rushing in a season, with a record of 1,318 yards.

Alexander had a then franchise record of 16 rushing TDs and 18 overall TDs in 2002, rushing for 1,175 yards and catching a career-high 59 passes for 460 yards. His first Pro Bowl appearance came after a 2003 season that featured 1,435 yards rushing.

But when he finished with 1,696 yards rushing in 2004—one fewer than NFL leader Curtis Martin of the New York Jets—Alexander said he felt like head coach Mike Holmgren had "stabbed him in the back" by not calling his number on a one-yard scoring play against Atlanta in the season finale. Alexander played that down the next day.

After a concussion sidelined him during the Divisional Playoff against Washington in 2006, Alexander was back a week later to set the Seahawks' playoff record with 132 yards rushing (and two TDs) against Carolina in the NFC Championship. He also contributed 95 yards along the ground during Super Bowl XL, but the Seahawks lost 21–10 to the Pittsburgh Steelers.

IN THE HUDDLE

By rushing for four touchdowns against Arizona on September 25, 2005, and against Houston on October 16, 2005, Shaun Alexander became the fourth NFL player with two games of four rushing TDs in the same season.

In March 2006, Alexander signed an eight-year, $62 million deal to stay with Seattle. He is a man driven by strong religious beliefs, which the names his daughters, Heaven and Trinity, reflect. He also has faith in his game, where he's gone from anonymity to celebrity as the Seahawks gained Super Bowl status.

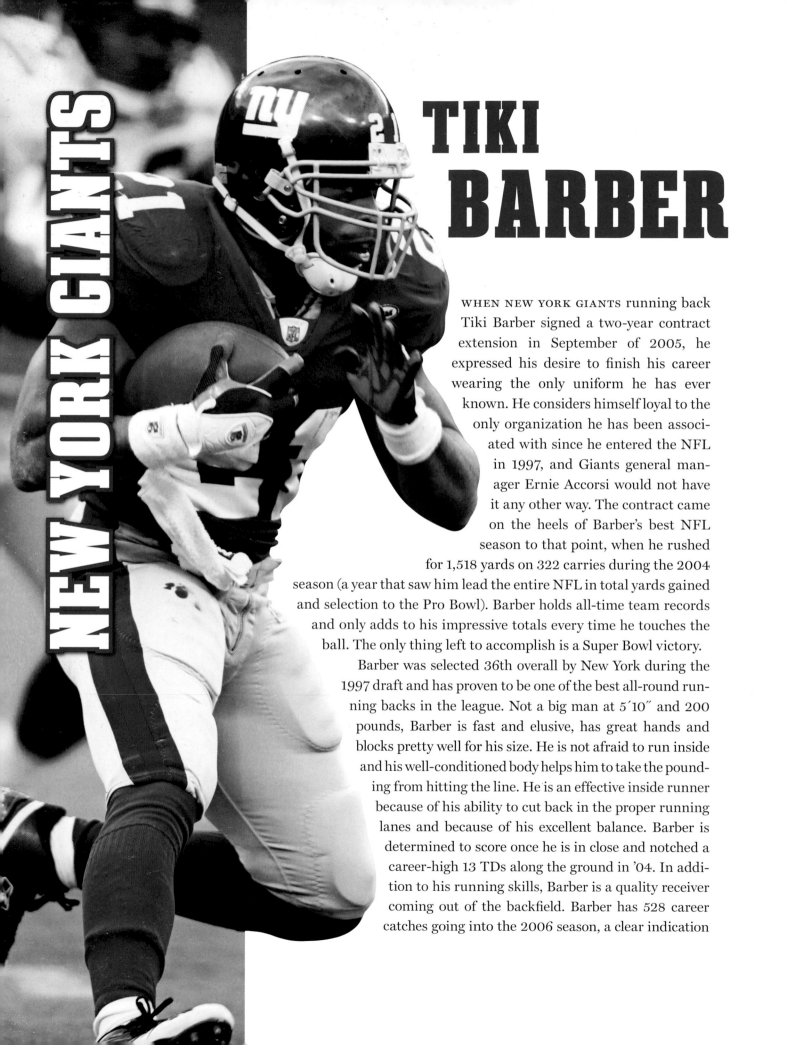

NEW YORK GIANTS

TIKI BARBER

WHEN NEW YORK GIANTS running back Tiki Barber signed a two-year contract extension in September of 2005, he expressed his desire to finish his career wearing the only uniform he has ever known. He considers himself loyal to the only organization he has been associated with since he entered the NFL in 1997, and Giants general manager Ernie Accorsi would not have it any other way. The contract came on the heels of Barber's best NFL season to that point, when he rushed for 1,518 yards on 322 carries during the 2004 season (a year that saw him lead the entire NFL in total yards gained and selection to the Pro Bowl). Barber holds all-time team records and only adds to his impressive totals every time he touches the ball. The only thing left to accomplish is a Super Bowl victory.

Barber was selected 36th overall by New York during the 1997 draft and has proven to be one of the best all-round running backs in the league. Not a big man at 5´10˝ and 200 pounds, Barber is fast and elusive, has great hands and blocks pretty well for his size. He is not afraid to run inside and his well-conditioned body helps him to take the pounding from hitting the line. He is an effective inside runner because of his ability to cut back in the proper running lanes and because of his excellent balance. Barber is determined to score once he is in close and notched a career-high 13 TDs along the ground in '04. In addition to his running skills, Barber is a quality receiver coming out of the backfield. Barber has 528 career catches going into the 2006 season, a clear indication

that he has soft hands and makes good catches. He thrives on hard work and always remembers that his mom tells him to "play proud."

Although Barber faces the knock that he has a tendency to fumble and he has to battle nagging hamstring injuries, the ninth-year pro got off to a great start in '05. He had a total of 62 yards rushing in the season opener and scored one touchdown by bouncing inside and then going right up the middle for 21 yards in a 42–19 win over Arizona. During the second week of the season, Barber racked up two more touchdowns (one on a pass, the other on a run) against New Orleans in a 27–10 victory. His running TD versus the Saints featured Barber bowling over one of his own teammates at the goal line to score!

Another top effort came in a game against division rival Washington Redskins when he ran for 206 yards along the ground as the New York club won 36–0. As if Barber needed any more motivation, the contest against Washington came after the death of Giants owner Wellington Mara,

a man who had a great influence on the star running back's career. Mara would have loved nothing more than to see one of his all-time favorite Giants chew up the opposition.

IN THE HUDDLE

Tiki Barber set a Giants team record for longest run from scrimmage when he ran 95 yards for a touchdown agaitns the Oakland Raiders on December 31, 2005, during a 30-21 victory.

The surprising Giants finished the season with an 11–5 record, good for first place in the tough East Division of the NFC. Barber ended the year strongly with three games of more than 200 yards rushing, including a team record 220 yards against the Kansas City Chiefs. In all Barber carried the ball 357 times for a career-best 1,860 yards and a 5.2 yards-per-carry average. He also made 54 catches, earning 530 yards and a place on the All Pro team.

ATLANTA FALCONS

WARRICK DUNN

THE ATLANTA FALCONS were backed up to their own five-yard line against the pesky New York Jets in the second quarter. The hometown Falcons were not supposed to have much difficulty with the injury-riddled Jets, but the New York club had them in a bad spot, hoping to hold Atlanta and gain a good field position. But then the ball was given to the spunky Warrick Dunn, and the Falcons running back cut off tackle and then burst straight ahead. Before he was brought down, Dunn had ripped off a 65-yard run (he would have scored a touchdown but ran out of room and gas) and got Atlanta out of a tough spot. Dunn's run (he totaled 155 yards in the contest) set up a field goal, and the Falcons won the game 27–14 to up their record to 5–2 just before the halfway point of the 2005 season.

His run against the Jets was the typical sort of play the scatback runner pulls off time and again for the Falcons. Dunn is not a big back at 5´9´´ and 180 pounds. However, there are few tougher players in the entire NFL. The underappreciated back can not only run effectively, but he is also a valuable asset coming out of the backfield. His speed in the open field makes him very dangerous, and with defenses having to worry about multitalented quarterback Michael Vick, the Falcons' offense can sting an opponent in many ways. Dunn has tremendous balance and excellent body control to go along with a catlike quickness (he has been clocked at 4.44 seconds over 40 yards). His elusiveness means he rarely takes hard hits squarely, and in 2004 he was able to play in every game for the Falcons and

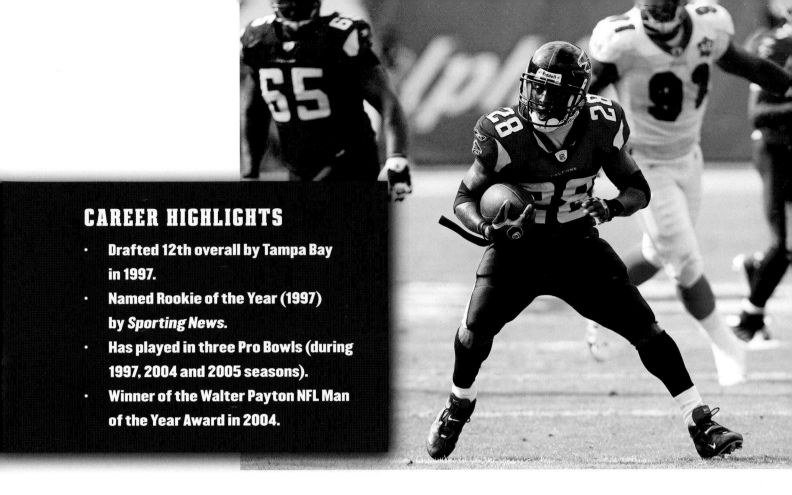

had 1,106 yards (his second-best career total for one season) rushing based on 265 carries, with nine TDs along the ground (a career high).

Dunn played three positions in high school but played running back at Florida State, where he recorded more than 3,000 combined yards in each of his last two seasons as a Seminole. His performance caught the attention of the Tampa Bay Buccaneers, who made him the 12th overall pick at the 1997 NFL draft (a year in which other fine running backs were available, including Tiki Barber, Priest Holmes, Corey Dillon, Duce Staley and Antowain Smith).

His rookie year was very impressive for the Baton Rouge, Louisiana, native as he piled up 1,440 yards of total offense, earning a trip to the Pro Bowl. His second season saw Dunn rush for 1,026 yards but his total dipped to 616 the following year. He bounced back in 2000 to rush for 1,133 yards but slipped back to 447 the following season. Tampa Bay allowed him to become an unrestricted free agent, and he signed a $4.6 million-per-year deal with the Falcons in 2002.

IN THE HUDDLE

Warrik Dunn developed a community project in Atlanta called "Homes for the Holidays." The program helps single-mother families buy homes by assisting with the down payment.

The Falcons made it to the NFC Championship Game in '04 but lost to the Eagles. They were one of the favorites in the NFC for the '05 campaign, and Dunn had another superb year with a career-best 1,416 yards along the ground (earned on a career-high 280 carries).

Falcons coach Jim Mora has to get his club to win the games they should if they have aspirations to make it to the Super Bowl. Another 8–8 year will not do it. However, another great season from Warrick Dunn is certainly expected, and the Pro Bowl player is quite likely to deliver it.

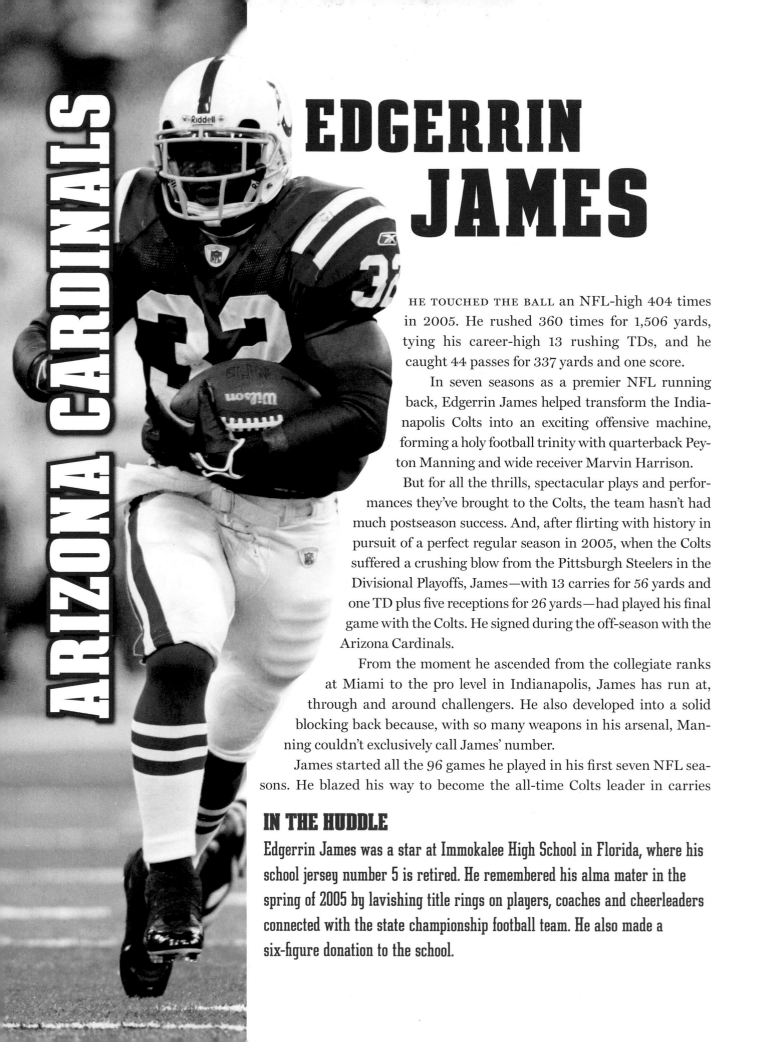

ARIZONA CARDINALS

EDGERRIN JAMES

HE TOUCHED THE BALL an NFL-high 404 times in 2005. He rushed 360 times for 1,506 yards, tying his career-high 13 rushing TDs, and he caught 44 passes for 337 yards and one score.

In seven seasons as a premier NFL running back, Edgerrin James helped transform the Indianapolis Colts into an exciting offensive machine, forming a holy football trinity with quarterback Peyton Manning and wide receiver Marvin Harrison.

But for all the thrills, spectacular plays and performances they've brought to the Colts, the team hasn't had much postseason success. And, after flirting with history in pursuit of a perfect regular season in 2005, when the Colts suffered a crushing blow from the Pittsburgh Steelers in the Divisional Playoffs, James—with 13 carries for 56 yards and one TD plus five receptions for 26 yards—had played his final game with the Colts. He signed during the off-season with the Arizona Cardinals.

From the moment he ascended from the collegiate ranks at Miami to the pro level in Indianapolis, James has run at, through and around challengers. He also developed into a solid blocking back because, with so many weapons in his arsenal, Manning couldn't exclusively call James' number.

James started all the 96 games he played in his first seven NFL seasons. He blazed his way to become the all-time Colts leader in carries

IN THE HUDDLE

Edgerrin James was a star at Immokalee High School in Florida, where his school jersey number 5 is retired. He remembered his alma mater in the spring of 2005 by lavishing title rings on players, coaches and cheerleaders connected with the state championship football team. He also made a six-figure donation to the school.

(2,188), rushing yards (9,226) and rushing touchdowns (64).

On December 18, 2005, in the game where the San Diego Chargers ended the 13–0 start by the Colts, James ran past Lenny Moore for the club's rushing-TD mark.

A two-year starter with the Hurricanes, in the 17 games he played he totaled 2,960 yards rushing, to rank second on Miami's all-time list. He is the only Hurricane with back-to-back 1,000-yard rushing seasons.

Quarterbacks were plucked in positions one through three in the 1999 NFL draft as the Cleveland Browns grabbed Tim Couch from Kentucky, the Philadelphia Eagles chose Donovan McNabb from Syracuse and the Cincinnati Bengals selected Akili Smith from Oregon.

The Colts followed by taking James with Texas running back Ricky Williams, then going fifth to the New Orleans Saints. James became the 13th rookie—joining the likes of Jim Brown, Eric Dickerson and Earl Campbell—to win the NFL rushing title, piling up 1,553 yards and scoring 13 TDs.

The following season, James established the Colts record with 1,709 yards—50 more than Dickerson had achieved in 1988. James suddenly found himself the fifth player to win consecutive rushing titles in his first two seasons, matching Bill Paschal, Brown, Campbell and Dickerson.

After piling up 855 yards from scrimmage in the first six games of 2001, injury did what no other opponent could do: it stopped James. On October 25 he went down with a wounded knee after rushing for 102 yards against the Kansas City Chiefs and missed the balance of the season.

As if coming back from reconstructive knee surgery wasn't enough, he sustained ankle, rib and hamstring injuries in 2002, when he rushed for 989 yards. But despite battling a back injury in 2003, he did exceed the 1,000-yard rushing total again with 1,259. His rushing production once again returned to the upper echelon in 2004 (1,548) and '05 as James kept adding to his Colts legacy.

KANSAS CITY CHIEFS

LARRY JOHNSON

WHEN INJURIES FORCED running back Priest Holmes to the sidelines in 2004 and 2005, Larry Johnson answered the prayers of the Kansas City Chiefs. Johnson's accomplishments in 2005 earned him the Derrick Thomas Award as Most Valuable Player for the Chiefs and his first NFL Pro Bowl and *Associated Press* All Pro selections.

Those honors in 2005 were amazing considering that Johnson had only taken over the starting duties on November 6. He reeled off a club-record nine consecutive games of at least 100 yards rushing, including a Chiefs-record 211 yards at Houston on November 20 and 201 yards versus Cincinnati on January 1.

From November 1, 2005, through January 1, 2006, Johnson generated 1,351 rushing yards and 1,627 yards from scrimmage, setting NFL high-water marks. The 1,351 rushing yards represented the best total in NFL history from November 1 through the end of a

IN THE HUDDLE

Larry Johnson and his father share a connection to Penn State. This connection extends to other family members: Larry's brother, Tony, was a wide receiver with the Nittany Lions from 2000 to 2003, while his sister, Teresa, played third base with Penn State's softball squad in 2001-02.

regular season. He became the first Chief to win the NFL AFC Offensive Player of the Month Award twice in the same season (November and December/January).

He finished his phenomenal season with a Chiefs-record 1,750 rushing yards to lead the AFC and rank third in the NFL. His 20 rushing touchdowns in 2005 ranked second to the 27 scored by Seattle's Shaun Alexander and his 21 total TDs were also runner-up to Alexander's tally of 28.

Johnson vindicated Chiefs president and general manager Carl Peterson, who had stuck his neck out by drafting the standout running back from Penn State with Kansas City's first selection in the 2003 NFL draft. Peterson had ignored pleas from head coach Dick Vermeil, Chiefs fans and football analysts, who insisted that defensive help should be at the top of Kansas City's shopping list.

The Chiefs traded down with the Pittsburgh Steelers, who badly needed a safety and got him in Troy Polamalu from USC. Peterson obtained his man in Johnson while also acquiring Pittsburgh's selections in the third and sixth rounds.

Johnson is strong-willed and plays with anger; he is often referred to as a running back who appears to be crashing through brick walls. He initially clashed with Vermeil and didn't take kindly to the back-up role to Holmes.

Vermeil preached patience to the up-and-comer, preferring the veteran Holmes, who had established the Chiefs' record for rushing yards in 2002 (with 1,615) and then set the NFL record (since eclipsed) for most touchdowns in a season, with 27 in 2003. Johnson saw action in six games as a rookie, rushing 20 times for 85 yards and one touchdown.

CAREER HIGHLIGHTS

- Drafted 27th overall by Kansas City in 2003.
- Holds Chiefs records for rushing yards in one season (1,750 in 2005) and rushing yards in one game (211 yards at Houston on November 20, 2005).
- Averaged 150.1 rushing yards per game in his nine starts in 2005.
- Was Pro Bowl selection in 2005.
- Selected *Associated Press* All Pro in 2005.

He played in 10 games the following season, making three starts. But his determination drew attention to his explosive potential. He rushed for 581 yards and nine touchdowns on 120 carries, then added two more TDs from 22 catches for 278 yards.

When Holmes, a three-time Pro Bowl selection, sustained head and neck trauma in 2005, Johnson immediately emerged in his own right.

Johnson was born into football: his father, Larry Sr., played one season in the NFL before turning to coaching. Larry Sr. is the defensive line coach for Joe Paterno with Penn State's Nittany Lions.

Larry Jr.'s career at Penn State saw him engage in multiple roles, including returning kickoffs and punts. He started 18 games of the 46 he played at Penn State and finished with 2,953 rushing yards, earning fifth place on the school's all-time rushing list. His 2,087 rushing yards in his final season shattered the Penn State record (1,567 by Lydell Mitchell in 1971).

CINCINNATI BENGALS

RUDI JOHNSON

AS FANS IN CINCINNATI's Paul Brown Stadium chant "ROO-DEE! ROO-DEE!" Bengals running back Rudi Johnson is in his element. After he had set the Bengals' record with 1,454 yards rushing in 2004, he hadn't concealed his desire to seek a new contract with the franchise.

Once the deal was done, Johnson, the Bengals and the huge following of long-suffering Bengals fans who had come to love him were thrilled. Johnson didn't disappoint them. He shattered his club record for rushing yards with 1,458 yards in 2005.

At 5′10″ and 225 pounds, he doesn't come across as an overpowering runner. But give him the ball and then watch him challenge foes. He knows where the end zone is—something he found often during his two years at Butler County Community College in Kansas.

Johnson scored 35 touchdowns in 1999. His seven-touchdown, 373-yard rushing performance in Butler's 49–35 Junior College Championship over Dixie was, in today's parlance, "sick." Shifting to Auburn for one more year of collegiate ball, he set the Tigers' record with 324 carries while his 1,567 rushing yards rank second in Auburn College's history to none other than Bo Jackson (1,786 in 1985).

IN THE HUDDLE

Rudi Johnson and Pittsburgh Steelers middle linebacker James Farrior grew up together in Ettrick, Virginia. Johnson is proud to join his friend in the off-season to work with youth at Farrior's football camp.

Despite being the Player of the Year in the Southeastern Conference, Johnson wasn't selected in the 2001 NFL draft until the fourth round. While he calls making the NFL his greatest achievement, establishing himself required two years of limited game.

An injury (a quad strain) made Johnson a scratch in the first three games of 2003, but once he got into the lineup, there was no denying him. He came within 43 yards of a 1,000-yard season and was one game shy of tying the club record of five 100-yard rushing games, and his nine touchdowns were second on the club.

Healthy and in the lineup for all 16 games in 2004, Johnson shattered the club's season marks for carries (361) and rushing yards (1,454) while finding the house for 12 TDs. In his first two seasons on the Bengals' roster, Johnson had been part of 6–10 and 2–14 records. In his first two seasons as a starter, the Bengals were on their way to respectability, finishing 8–8 each time.

But the breakthrough for the Bengals occurred in 2005 when they won the AFC North with an 11–5 record. QB Carson Palmer and the Johnsons — Rudi and receiver Chad — powered an offense that averaged 26.3 points per game, fourth in the NFL. The Bengals rushed for 1,910 yards and Rudi Johnson accounted for another record-breaking total (1,458) while scoring 12 TDs.

When Palmer went down on the second snap, he took in the Wild Card game against the Pittsburgh Steelers. Rudi Johnson kept the Bengals' hopes alive. His 20-yard TD late in the first quarter put Cincinnati in front 10–0. Johnson was the game's top rusher with 13 carries for 56 yards, but as the Pittsburgh defense dug in, the Steelers' offense turned things around in their favor.

So the Bengals' 2005 season ended that day. In light of how they had advanced, however, the Bengals gave their fans reason to believe long-term success has finally arrived in Cincy. ROO-DEE Johnson is one of the major reasons they feel this way.

CHICAGO BEARS

THOMAS JONES

REARED IN THE coal-mining environment of Big Stone Gap, Virginia, Thomas Jones knows all too well about the hardships of that life. His parents, Thomas Sr. and Betty, worked in the coal mines for a time, but they have been able to go on to other things, since two of their sons are running backs in the NFL. Thomas is with the Chicago Bears and Julius, the Dallas Cowboys.

Julius came out of Notre Dame to land a position in the Dallas backfield. He posted rushing seasons of 819 yards (seven touchdowns) in eight games as a rookie in 2004 and 993 yards (five touchdowns) in 13 games during 2005.

Against a backdrop of high expectations following his collegiate career at Virginia, Thomas has gone from being called a bust with the Arizona Cardinals to being a productive Bear in Chicago—with one season in between with the Tampa Bay Buccaneers.

He started only six of the first 30 games he played over his first two NFL seasons, rushing for 373 and 380 yards. He burst into the NFC rushing lead in 2002, but injuries restricted him to nine games with 511 rushing yards. His average yardage per carry of 3.3, 3.4 and 3.7 hardly befitted a first-round draft pick.

The Cardinals unloaded Jones to the

Buccaneers on June 13, 2003, for wide receiver Marquise Walker. Although he started three of 16 games with the Bucs, his second-half performance of 548 yards rushing pushed him to 627 for the season. During a game against the Green Bay Packers on November 16, 2003, Jones busted loose with runs of 61 and 51 yards. That was the first time a Buccaneers running back had twice rushed for 50 or more yards in one game.

The Bears signed Jones as a free agent on March 4, 2004, and he finally found a home, proving he could handle the starter's role. He rushed for a career-high 948 yards and supplied 427 more yards on pass receptions. His 56 catches broke the Bears' record, held by the great Walter Payton, for most receptions by a running back.

Jones' 1,375 combined yards in 2004 represented 36 percent of the Bears' offense, a figure bettered in the NFL that year only by fellow Virginia alumnus Tiki Barber of the New York Giants (44 percent).

Resting on his laurels was hardly something Jones could ponder. That became especially clear on NFL draft day in 2005, when the Bears selected highly regarded running back Cedric Benson of the Texas Longhorns in the fourth overall spot.

Benson never really got out of the starting blocks to challenge for the number one running back slot in 2005, however, because he was a contract holdout and then suffered a knee injury. Jones, meanwhile, continued to put up yardage for the offensively challenged Bears, shattering the 1,000-yard rushing mark for the first time (finishing with 1,335, for ninth in the NFL). His pass-reception yardage (143) and pass receptions (26) were down from 2004. But his number of carries increased by 74 to a career best of 314. He also rushed for a personal high of nine TDs, up two from the previous season.

IN THE HUDDLE

Tiki Barber's rushing record of 3,389 yards from 1993 to 1996 at Virginia didn't last long. Thomas Jones came in and left Virginia in 2000 with 3,998 yards rushing.

Jones then added 80 yards on 20 carries in the Bears' loss to the Carolina Panthers in the NFC Divisional Playoffs. In a game driven by production, Jones will still have to fend off suitors for his job.

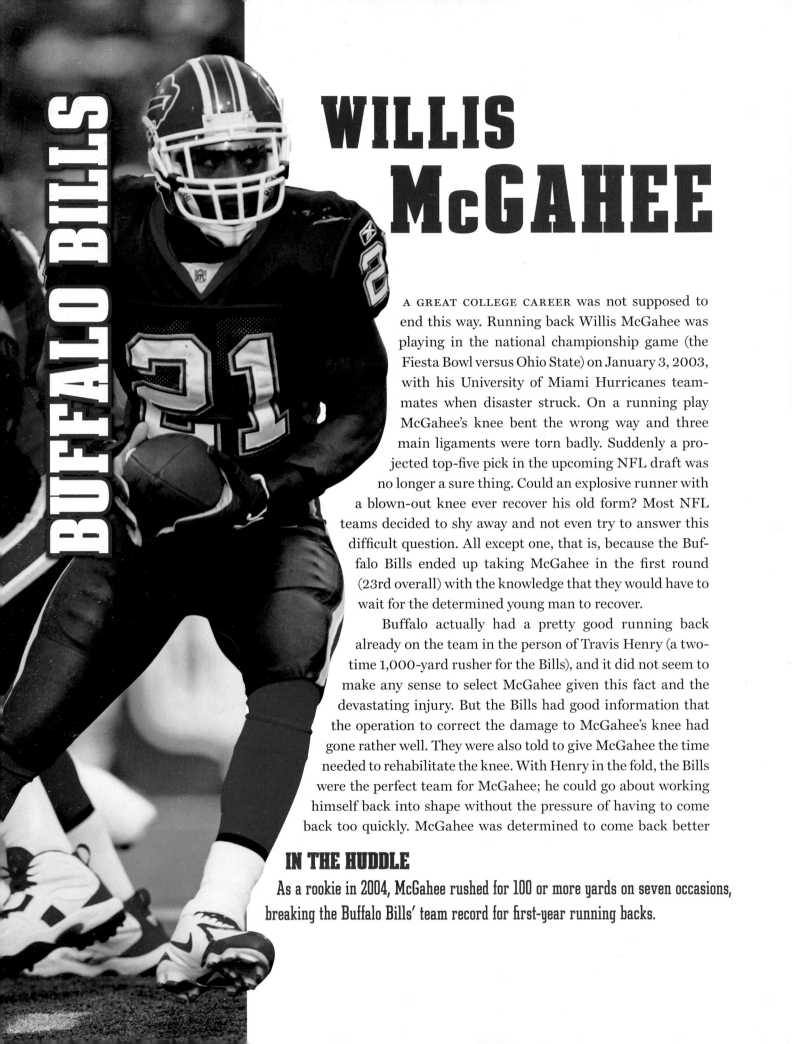

BUFFALO BILLS

WILLIS McGAHEE

A GREAT COLLEGE CAREER was not supposed to end this way. Running back Willis McGahee was playing in the national championship game (the Fiesta Bowl versus Ohio State) on January 3, 2003, with his University of Miami Hurricanes teammates when disaster struck. On a running play McGahee's knee bent the wrong way and three main ligaments were torn badly. Suddenly a projected top-five pick in the upcoming NFL draft was no longer a sure thing. Could an explosive runner with a blown-out knee ever recover his old form? Most NFL teams decided to shy away and not even try to answer this difficult question. All except one, that is, because the Buffalo Bills ended up taking McGahee in the first round (23rd overall) with the knowledge that they would have to wait for the determined young man to recover.

Buffalo actually had a pretty good running back already on the team in the person of Travis Henry (a two-time 1,000-yard rusher for the Bills), and it did not seem to make any sense to select McGahee given this fact and the devastating injury. But the Bills had good information that the operation to correct the damage to McGahee's knee had gone rather well. They were also told to give McGahee the time needed to rehabilitate the knee. With Henry in the fold, the Bills were the perfect team for McGahee; he could go about working himself back into shape without the pressure of having to come back too quickly. McGahee was determined to come back better

IN THE HUDDLE

As a rookie in 2004, McGahee rushed for 100 or more yards on seven occasions, breaking the Buffalo Bills' team record for first-year running backs.

than ever, and even though he had to miss the entire 2003 season, it was well worth the effort.

During the 2004 season, McGahee slowly but surely began to assert himself in the Bills' starting lineup. He started 11 games and rushed for 1,128 yards on 284 carries, making former Pro Bowler Henry expendable by the end of the season (he was traded to the Titans for a draft choice). Not overly large at 6´ and 228 pounds, McGahee has basically become the main weapon for the Bills' offense. If he's not going, Buffalo's chances of winning any game are greatly reduced. He has a sort of slide-and-glide style that makes defenders miss, and once he breaks into the open he can go all the way. McGahee can slash through the line and loves to make the quick cutback to get into the defensive backfield. He had a good nose for the goal line (13 touchdowns along the ground in '04) and he can run over defenders if he has to.

To start the 2005 season, the Bills decided to turn the offense over to a rookie quarterback.

While J.P. Losman showed some promise, he was clearly too inexperienced to take the team far. Backup Kelly Holcomb stepped in for a while but the 5–11 Bills came to rely on McGahee's running even more. The Buffalo back was a little up and down during the season (a season total of 1,247 yards along the ground in 325 attempts), but he showed he could listen and learn. After a rather poor performance against Tampa Bay, McGahee was criticized by the coaching staff for not hitting the holes fast enough. Rather than sulk, McGahee looked closely at film and tried to correct his errors. He came out with a good performance against Atlanta (140 yards on 27 carries) and showed he was going to respond in a positive way.

McGahee needs to work on his consistency, but he wants to be the best back in the NFL. It will be interesting to see how new coach Dick Jauron handles the somewhat temperamental running back. Still, the Bills may yet say they made one of their best moves ever by taking a chance on McGahee.

PITTSBURGH STEELERS

WILLIE PARKER

THE LAST GAME of the 2004 National Football League season saw the Pittsburgh Steelers visit Orchard Park for a game against the Buffalo Bills. The game had little meaning for the Steelers, who had the best record in the AFC all wrapped up, but it was vital for the Bills, who needed a win to secure a play-off spot. Coach Bill Cowher decided to rest many of his starters, which gave many of the backup Steelers a chance to show what they could do. One player who took complete advantage of this opportunity was running back Willie Parker, who rushed for 102 yards and helped his team to a 29–24 victory. Such a performance was not expected from the little-used Parker, but it showed

IN THE HUDDLE

As a junior at Clinton High School (in North Carolina), Willie Parker led his team to the state 2-A title with 1,329 yards rushing and 20 touchdowns.

the Steelers that they had a hidden gem on their bench.

Actually few people knew of Parker at all, and perhaps the only reason the Steelers signed the free-agent running back was that he was known to Dan Rooney Jr., the son of the very respected Pittsburgh owner. Many NFL players have forged excellent careers despite not being drafted, but the Steelers were not quite sure what they had in the 5′10″, 209-pound back. Parker was not even a regular on his college team at North Carolina, gaining 181 yards on 28 carries as a senior. He was used on a rotating basis for the most part, and he was not the coaches' favorite because he did not want to become a power back. Perhaps that is why Parker was overlooked, but Rooney was familiar with his potential. More than a few NFL teams regret the error of their ways now that Parker has established himself as a quality running back.

While Parker is not the big, bruising back the Steelers have become accustomed to recently (like Jerome Bettis and Duce Staley at 255 and 242 pounds, respectively), Parker has the speed to get outside and make the big run. He also shows a good amount of power when he has to run inside and does not let his lack of bulk hold him back. Once he gets through the line, Parker shows a good burst of acceleration and the ability to turn a corner. The Steelers have been a running team since Cowher took over the team, and he loves running backs who can produce. As the 2005 season began, Parker showed he was ready to be the main back by running for 161 yards against Tennessee and then for 111 versus the Texans in the second week of the season.

Parker is more likely to excel when he is spelled off by the other capable backs who are available to Cowher. This will keep Parker fresher and get him used to the hard pace of the NFL a little more easily. With the Steelers being a team that relies on the run as much as they do, the possibility of injury increases with each carry. But Parker likes to consider himself the patient type, so he is unlikely to push too hard for more carries. When he does get his hands on the ball, you can be sure it will have a great impact on the game, and that's what the Steelers have come to expect from the surprising Parker.

Parker was at his best when he ripped off a Super Bowl–record 75-yard touchdown run to give his team a 14–3 lead against the Seattle Seahawks. Once he burst through the line, no Seattle player was going to catch him. The Steelers won the game 21–10, and Parker earned his first ever Super Bowl ring. At only 25 years of age, there may be more championships in the future for this running back on the rise.

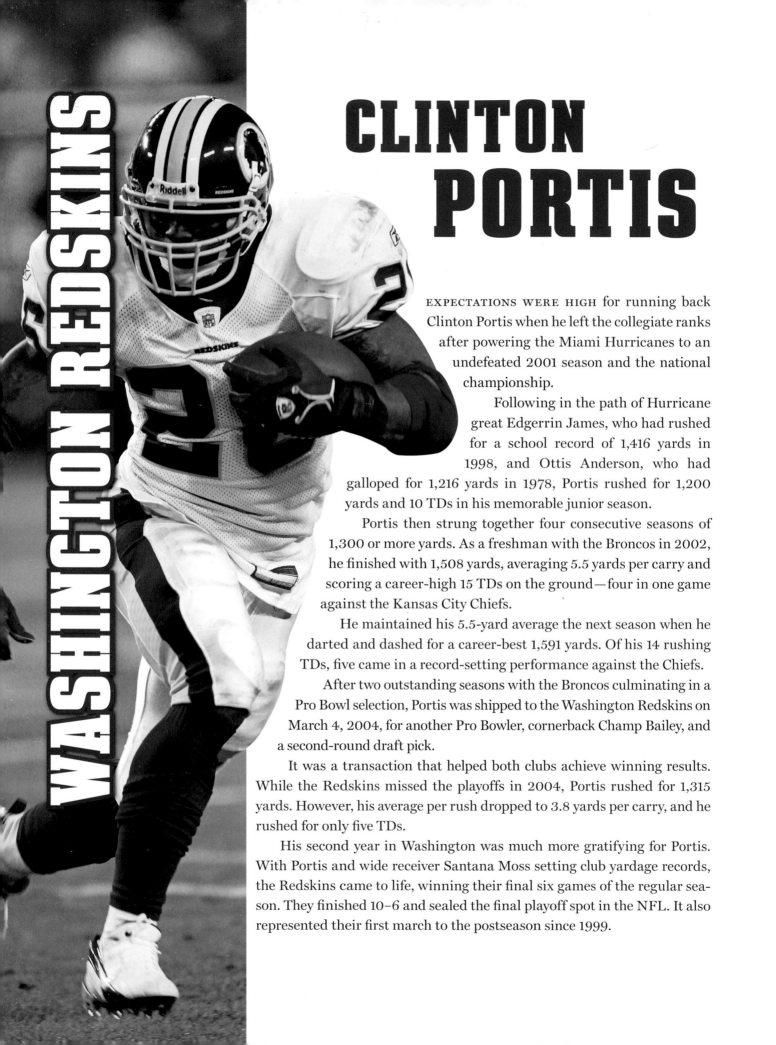

WASHINGTON REDSKINS

CLINTON PORTIS

EXPECTATIONS WERE HIGH for running back Clinton Portis when he left the collegiate ranks after powering the Miami Hurricanes to an undefeated 2001 season and the national championship.

Following in the path of Hurricane great Edgerrin James, who had rushed for a school record of 1,416 yards in 1998, and Ottis Anderson, who had galloped for 1,216 yards in 1978, Portis rushed for 1,200 yards and 10 TDs in his memorable junior season.

Portis then strung together four consecutive seasons of 1,300 or more yards. As a freshman with the Broncos in 2002, he finished with 1,508 yards, averaging 5.5 yards per carry and scoring a career-high 15 TDs on the ground—four in one game against the Kansas City Chiefs.

He maintained his 5.5-yard average the next season when he darted and dashed for a career-best 1,591 yards. Of his 14 rushing TDs, five came in a record-setting performance against the Chiefs.

After two outstanding seasons with the Broncos culminating in a Pro Bowl selection, Portis was shipped to the Washington Redskins on March 4, 2004, for another Pro Bowler, cornerback Champ Bailey, and a second-round draft pick.

It was a transaction that helped both clubs achieve winning results. While the Redskins missed the playoffs in 2004, Portis rushed for 1,315 yards. However, his average per rush dropped to 3.8 yards per carry, and he rushed for only five TDs.

His second year in Washington was much more gratifying for Portis. With Portis and wide receiver Santana Moss setting club yardage records, the Redskins came to life, winning their final six games of the regular season. They finished 10–6 and sealed the final playoff spot in the NFL. It also represented their first march to the postseason since 1999.

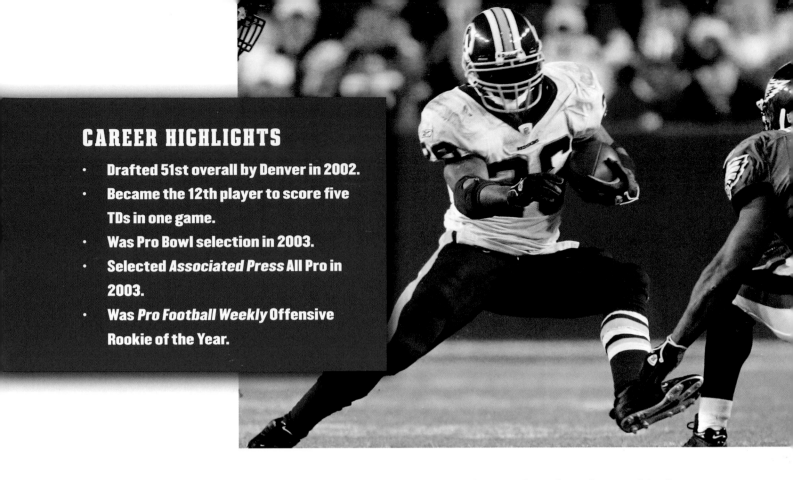

Portis then scored one TD but was limited to 53 yards rushing on 16 carries in the Wild Card win at Tampa Bay and was thoroughly contained (41 yards on 17 carries) in the Divisional Playoff loss at Seattle. Still, Washington left 2005 with ample reason for optimism.

Portis carried a career-high 352 times for 1,516 yards and 11 TDs. Needing a victory at Philadelphia in Week 17 to gain their playoff ticket and eliminate the rival Dallas Cowboys, the Redskins received a two-touchdown, 112-yard performance from Portis.

His brilliant 22-yard TD run in the fourth quarter put the Redskins up 24–20 in a game they won 31–20. Emotions ran high in this contest, and they filtered into the stands, where Portis' mother, Rhonnel Hearn, allegedly punched a woman who'd dumped beer on her during that fourth quarter. His mother was moved from the end-zone location to the Redskins' sideline for a portion of that game.

Portis is extremely close to his mother. He was extremely proud to have her as his date during his high-school prom. He also acknowledges the influence of Edgerrin James, who passed the torch to Portis at Miami before launching his exceptional career with the Indianapolis Colts.

IN THE HUDDLE

Clinton Portis was also a track star at Gainesville High School. He clocked 10.6 seconds in the 100 meters and participated in two significant state relays—setting a record 40.8 seconds in the 4 x 100 meters and winning the state championship in the 4 x 400 meters.

Off the field, Portis has a fondness for aquariums and sleek cars. In an interview with *Sports Illustrated*, he said he bought a Ferrari after signing his contract with the Redskins. But in the same interview he also admitted that surviving a car crash in 2001, which also involved Hurricane teammates Jarrett Payton and Clint Hurtt, had changed his outlook and approach to life.

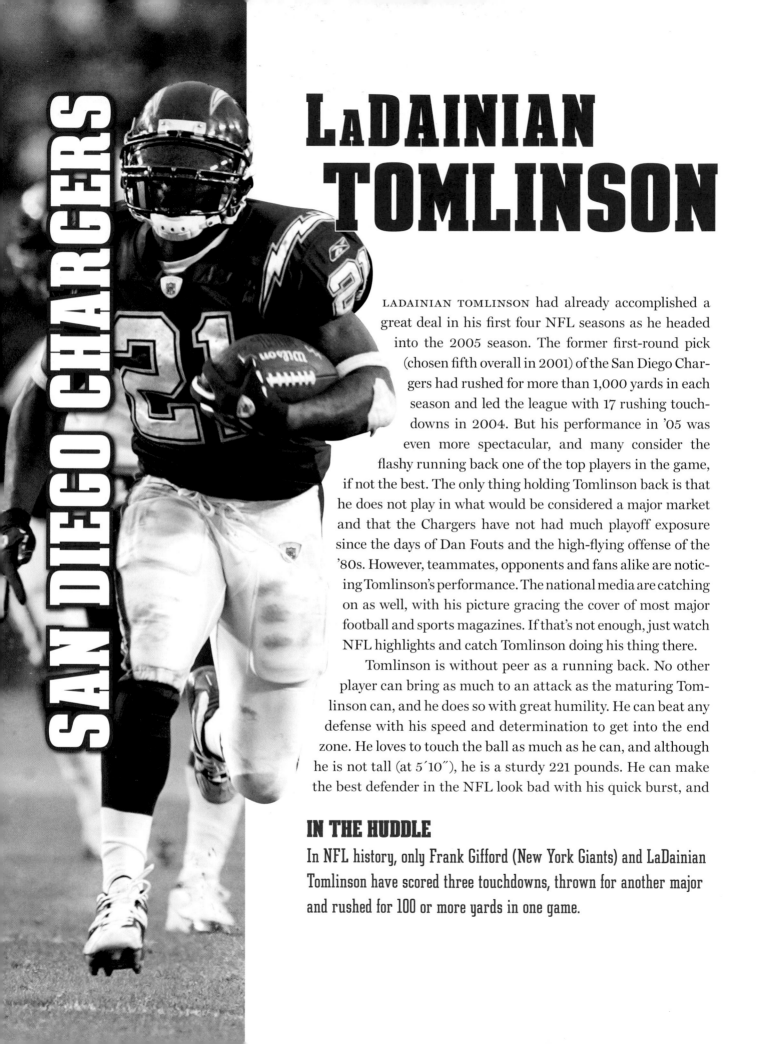

SAN DIEGO CHARGERS

LaDAINIAN TOMLINSON

LADAINIAN TOMLINSON had already accomplished a great deal in his first four NFL seasons as he headed into the 2005 season. The former first-round pick (chosen fifth overall in 2001) of the San Diego Chargers had rushed for more than 1,000 yards in each season and led the league with 17 rushing touchdowns in 2004. But his performance in '05 was even more spectacular, and many consider the flashy running back one of the top players in the game, if not the best. The only thing holding Tomlinson back is that he does not play in what would be considered a major market and that the Chargers have not had much playoff exposure since the days of Dan Fouts and the high-flying offense of the '80s. However, teammates, opponents and fans alike are noticing Tomlinson's performance. The national media are catching on as well, with his picture gracing the cover of most major football and sports magazines. If that's not enough, just watch NFL highlights and catch Tomlinson doing his thing there.

Tomlinson is without peer as a running back. No other player can bring as much to an attack as the maturing Tomlinson can, and he does so with great humility. He can beat any defense with his speed and determination to get into the end zone. He loves to touch the ball as much as he can, and although he is not tall (at 5´10″), he is a sturdy 221 pounds. He can make the best defender in the NFL look bad with his quick burst, and

IN THE HUDDLE

In NFL history, only Frank Gifford (New York Giants) and LaDainian Tomlinson have scored three touchdowns, thrown for another major and rushed for 100 or more yards in one game.

CAREER HIGHLIGHTS

- Drafted fifth overall by San Diego in 2001 from Texas Christian University.
- Has rushed for more than 1,000 yards in each of his five NFL seasons.
- Has scored 74 career touchdowns (as of 2005).
- Holds San Diego all-time club record for most career yards rushing (7,361).

he is also instinctive. As tough an inside runner as there is, Tomlinson's character is unquestioned, and he is considered a leader on the team. He believes that he is now experienced enough that the game is slowing down for him, allowing Tomlinson to read the defenses better than ever. He also realizes he is in the prime of his career and wants to make the most of it.

The '05 schedule was a difficult one for the Chargers, and they started the season 0–2. But a Sunday night contest against the visiting New York Giants saw the San Diego club begin to play better. Tomlinson led the way with three touchdown runs and threw for another on a halfback option play as the Chargers won the game 49–24. The workhorse back had more than 100 yards rushing and caught five passes to round out his evening. The win over New York gave the Chargers a needed boost in confidence and they defeated Super Bowl champion New England the following week on the road, with a surprising 41–17 win. During a 27–14 win over the Oakland Raiders, Tomlinson ran, caught and threw for a touchdown, making him only the seventh player in NFL history to accomplish this feat. Another contest versus another New York team may have been the best performance of Tomlinson's career to date when he scored four touchdowns (three runs, one catch) and had 107 rushing yards in the contest, which saw the Chargers hang on to beat the Jets 31–26 at East Rutherford, New Jersey.

The Chargers play in one of the toughest divisions along with tough teams like Denver and Kansas City, and a late-season loss to the Chiefs ended their playoff hopes and gave them a record of 9–7. Tomlinson was slowed down by a fractured rib late in the year, but he still finished the '05 season with 20 touchdowns scored (a team record) while rushing for 1,462 yards on 339 carries. He also caught 51 passes for another 373 yards to keep him an all-round threat. With talent like Tomlinson and tight end Antonio Gates on offense, the Chargers certainly have a team with the ability to make the rest of the league stand up and take notice.

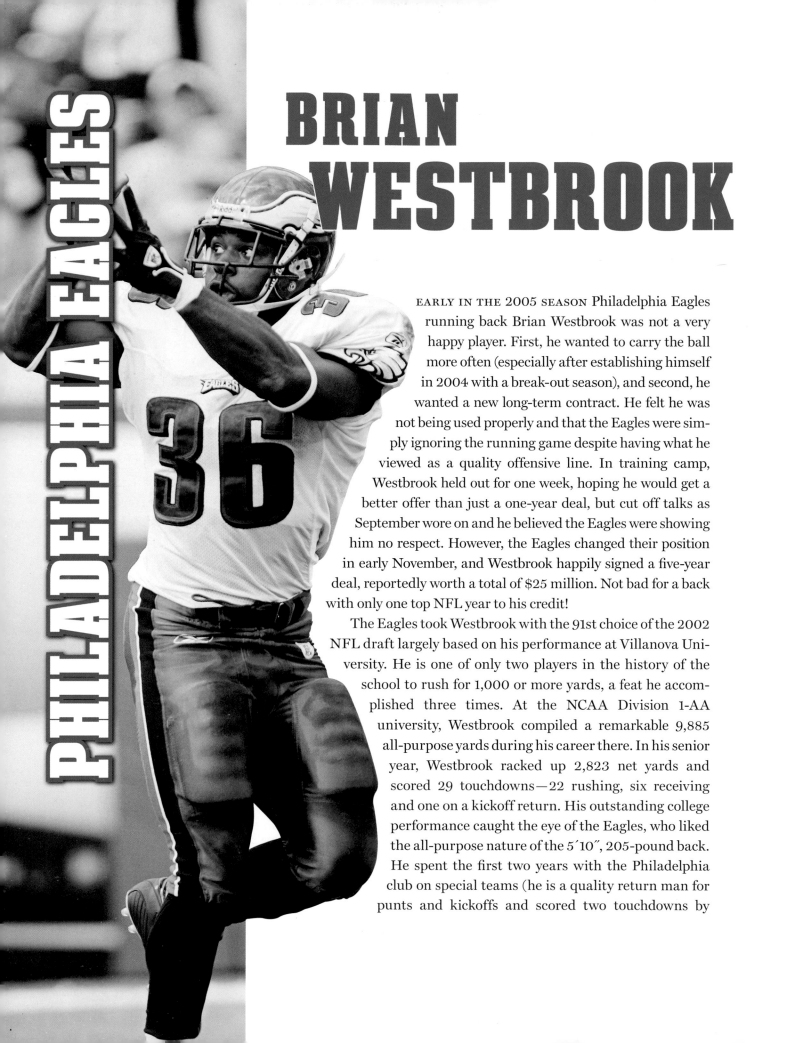

BRIAN WESTBROOK

PHILADELPHIA EAGLES

EARLY IN THE 2005 SEASON Philadelphia Eagles running back Brian Westbrook was not a very happy player. First, he wanted to carry the ball more often (especially after establishing himself in 2004 with a break-out season), and second, he wanted a new long-term contract. He felt he was not being used properly and that the Eagles were simply ignoring the running game despite having what he viewed as a quality offensive line. In training camp, Westbrook held out for one week, hoping he would get a better offer than just a one-year deal, but cut off talks as September wore on and he believed the Eagles were showing him no respect. However, the Eagles changed their position in early November, and Westbrook happily signed a five-year deal, reportedly worth a total of $25 million. Not bad for a back with only one top NFL year to his credit!

The Eagles took Westbrook with the 91st choice of the 2002 NFL draft largely based on his performance at Villanova University. He is one of only two players in the history of the school to rush for 1,000 or more yards, a feat he accomplished three times. At the NCAA Division 1-AA university, Westbrook compiled a remarkable 9,885 all-purpose yards during his career there. In his senior year, Westbrook racked up 2,823 net yards and scored 29 touchdowns—22 rushing, six receiving and one on a kickoff return. His outstanding college performance caught the eye of the Eagles, who liked the all-purpose nature of the 5´10˝, 205-pound back. He spent the first two years with the Philadelphia club on special teams (he is a quality return man for punts and kickoffs and scored two touchdowns by

returning punts all the way in 2003). Then in '03 he started eight games. However, it was in the '04 campaign that he got to show what he could do with the ball as a starter in 12 contests. With Westbrook in the backfield, the Eagles finally made it to the Super Bowl.

Some NFL observers believe Westbrook plays bigger than his 205-pound frame. He has proven to be tough and durable and not an easy tackle by any means. Westbrook can beat tacklers one on one, which means the defense has to surround him to contain the shifty back. Get him the ball in the open field and he can take it a long way. Westbrook's main strength is his versatility: he shows equal ability to run and to catch the ball out of the backfield. In '04 Westbrook led all NFL backs with 73 catches (for 703 yards and six touchdowns) and still found time for 812 yards along the ground (on 177 carries with three TDs). He showed a good initial burst and made the cuts all good running backs are known for. The defense has to be aware of where he lines up at all times,

which led quarterback Donovan McNabb to say that Westbrook is the Eagles' best weapon on the attack. He is not the preferred back when the Eagles are near the opponents' goal line (they like beefier runners in close), and he is not the best blocker in the league, but he may overcome both these deficiencies with more experience.

As the '05 season continued Westbrook once again was at his best coming out of the backfield.

IN THE HUDDLE

Villanova retired Brian Westbrook's sweater number 20 in honor of his great performance at the university.

He made 61 receptions for 616 yards and four touchdowns while rushing for 617 yards on 156 carries with three scores. However, a serious foot injury cut his season to just 12 games, and the Eagles trailed off to finish 6–10, out of the playoffs. No doubt the Eagles are hoping for a return to good health for Westbrook if they are going back to the playoffs in 2006.

OUT THERE ON THEIR

RE

OWN — AND COUNTED ON TO MAKE THE BIG CATCH

CEIVERS!

NEW ENGLAND PATRIOTS

DEION BRANCH

THE FACT THAT he ranks 21st in reception yards with 998 and is in a tie for 16th in receptions with 78 (2005 regular season) really doesn't tell the complete story for wide receiver Deion Branch. Neither does a reflection upon his regular-season totals since breaking into the NFL in 2002.

Time after time, the wide receiver for the New England Patriots has been the big-play weapon that quarterback Tom Brady and the Patriots have relied upon. Even when the Patriots' NFL record 10-game postseason winning streak came to an end at Denver on January 14, 2006, the Brady-to-Branch combo went down firing away.

Branch had game-highs of eight receptions for 153 yards and longest reception gain of 73 yards. The 153 yards against the Broncos set another club record for Branch. Speedy, smart and skilled, the 5´9˝ 193-pounder just keeps bettering the standards he establishes.

He'd gained 143 receiving yards in Super Bowl XXXVIII. He came close to that number the following year with 133 yards in Super Bowl XXXIX, when he picked up the Pete Rozelle Trophy as the game's MVP.

Branch had played in eight postseason games through the loss to the Broncos and he'd eclipsed 100 receiving yards four times. His playoff total of 629 receiving yards stands as a record for the Patriots, bumping Troy Brown's 597 total down a notch. Branch's stellar achieve-

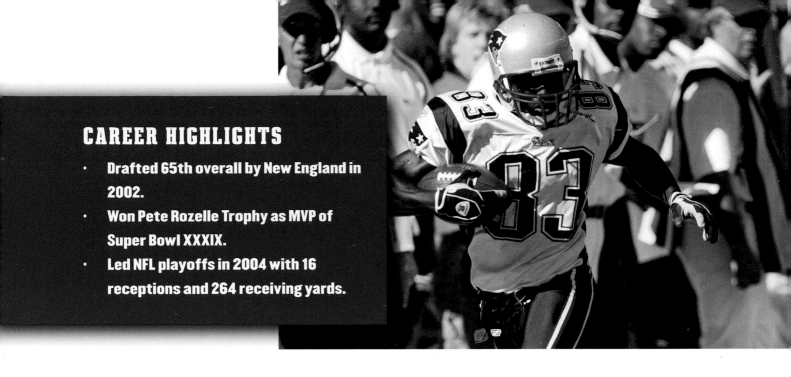

ments, however, might come as a surprise to some who remember the smallish youngster who at first had difficulty latching on to a football spot at Monroe High School in Albany, Georgia.

Coaches feared that Branch, who was 5′6″ at the time, would crumble with the pounding, but he wasn't about to yield to such notions.

He had quickness and toughness to go along with his ability to hang on to any ball thrown in his area. He became a high-school star and carried on to the next step by signing for two years with Jones County Junior College in Mississippi.

When he committed himself to upgrading his marks through his sophomore season, his academic performance improved. This allowed him to transfer to Louisville, where he became only the second player in that school's history with multiple 1,000 receiving–yard seasons. Perhaps as a prelude to relishing the bigger games, his final game at Louisville came in the Liberty Bowl, where he caught six passes for 88 yards, including a 34-yard TD, in the victory over BYU.

Branch broke in with the Patriots in 2002. Even though he missed the last three games of the season because of injury, among AFC rookies he placed second in receptions (43) and third in receiving yards (489 yards).

The following season he led the Patriots in receptions (57) and in receiving yards (803), capping his statistical upgrades with his 10-reception performance at the Super Bowl. After playing only nine games in 2004, when he caught 35 passes for 454 yards, Branch's brilliant Super Bowl—and another championship for the Patriots—earned him more accolades.

IN THE HUDDLE

Deion Branch became the fourth wide receiver to be selected as the Super Bowl's MVP. He won this honor in Super Bowl XXXIX.

In 2005, Branch established career-highs for pass receptions and receiving yards as Tom Brady's favorite target. Branch has evolved into an esteemed receiver, but, outside the game, he's dealt with a pressing family issue. His twin sons, who are now four years old, were born prematurely, and one of them still requires round-the-clock medical attention.

Branch's religious beliefs have helped him cope with this ordeal, and he remains committed to the game of football.

NEW YORK GIANTS

PLAXICO BURRESS

IN MANY WAYS Plaxico Burress is a dream wide receiver. He's listed at 6´5˝ and 226 pounds, and the game of football comes easily to Burress, who can catch any ball thrown near him. He possesses the speed needed to get deep and can be a defensive back's worst nightmare when there is a fight for the ball. Burress can be very physical and he knows how to get the proper body position on just about any defender. His outstanding play at Michigan State led the Pittsburgh Steelers to select him eighth overall in the 2000 NFL draft, and they expected him to dominate.

However, it did not quite work out that way, despite four good seasons (261 catches for 4,164 yards in a conservative run-first offense) in Pittsburgh. When his contract was up, Burress began to look around for a new team. Based on his talent a plethora of teams should have been interested in his services, yet few clubs were curious about him. Luckily he signed with the New York Giants, and both sides are pretty happy with the new arrangement.

Burress wore out his welcome with the Steelers by showing a lack of dedication to his craft and his team. He missed a mini camp in 2004 (to honor the passing of his mother, he claimed) and came to be seen as a bit of a problem in the locker room. Whether or not this was true, it did become the perception around the league, and so the offers to sign were not there. However, the Giants were looking to rebound after a poor season in '04 (a 6–10 record) and wanted to give their young quarterback, Eli Manning, a big target at wide receiver who also could go deep. They

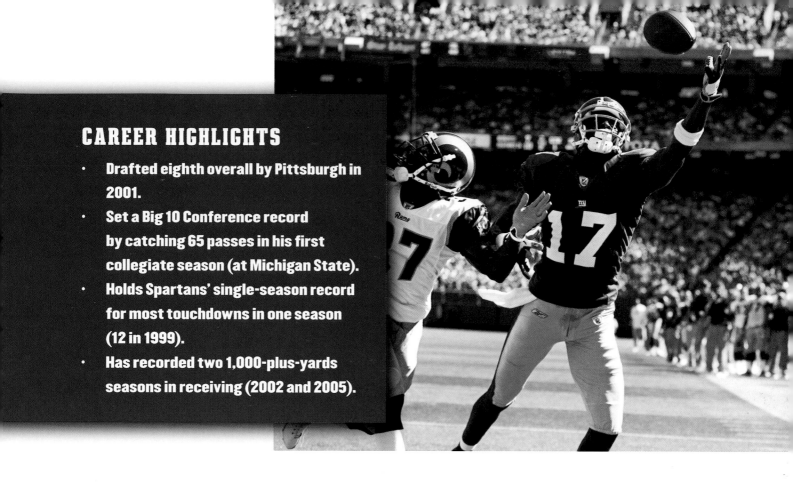

believed that a no-nonsense coach like Tom Coughlin would be good for a player who had not always displayed great maturity. Eventually Giants general manager Ernie Accorsi signed Burress to a six-year contract worth $25 million (after some heated negotiations), and the New York club is very pleased with the deal.

When he joined the Giants, Burress was more prepared than ever to excel in the NFL. He trained with a number of veteran players who showed him he was not as ready as he once thought. Burress realized he had to work harder once the defenses in the NFL were wise to his talents. He is in better condition and uses his large body to good advantage; his reading of the defense is sharper, too.

Burress is still not perfect. He has got into Coughlin's bad books on at least a couple of occasions (he was benched for a brief period), but he has developed a great on-field rapport with Manning. The still-learning pivot seems to have a good grasp of how to best use Burress and when to get him the ball. Burress' arrival has opened up more opportunities for other receivers like Amani Toomer and Jeremy Shockey, diversifying the Giants' attack.

A 10-catch game (for 204 yards) against the St. Louis Rams was the best individual performance of Burress' career to date, and he caught a touchdown against Denver in the seventh week of the '05 campaign to help his team eke out a crucial 24–23 victory. During that game Broncos cornerback Champ Bailey took three penalties while trying to cover Burress. Burress also had a 61-yard TD reception against division rival Philadelphia to put the final nail in the Eagles' coffin for a 27–17 Giants win.

In short, Burress was doing everything expected of him (he finished the season with 76 catches for 1,214 yards and seven touchdowns), and it looks as if he enjoys playing in a large market like New York. Sometimes a change of venue works wonders.

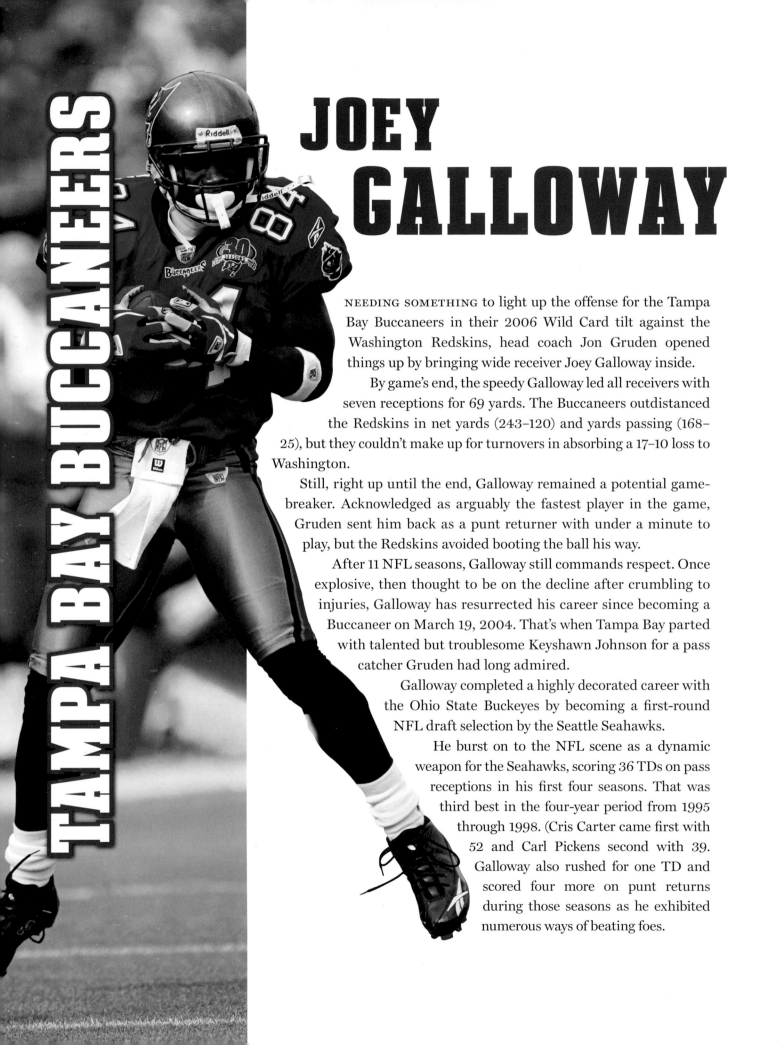

JOEY GALLOWAY

NEEDING SOMETHING to light up the offense for the Tampa Bay Buccaneers in their 2006 Wild Card tilt against the Washington Redskins, head coach Jon Gruden opened things up by bringing wide receiver Joey Galloway inside.

By game's end, the speedy Galloway led all receivers with seven receptions for 69 yards. The Buccaneers outdistanced the Redskins in net yards (243–120) and yards passing (168–25), but they couldn't make up for turnovers in absorbing a 17–10 loss to Washington.

Still, right up until the end, Galloway remained a potential game-breaker. Acknowledged as arguably the fastest player in the game, Gruden sent him back as a punt returner with under a minute to play, but the Redskins avoided booting the ball his way.

After 11 NFL seasons, Galloway still commands respect. Once explosive, then thought to be on the decline after crumbling to injuries, Galloway has resurrected his career since becoming a Buccaneer on March 19, 2004. That's when Tampa Bay parted with talented but troublesome Keyshawn Johnson for a pass catcher Gruden had long admired.

Galloway completed a highly decorated career with the Ohio State Buckeyes by becoming a first-round NFL draft selection by the Seattle Seahawks.

He burst on to the NFL scene as a dynamic weapon for the Seahawks, scoring 36 TDs on pass receptions in his first four seasons. That was third best in the four-year period from 1995 through 1998. (Cris Carter came first with 52 and Carl Pickens second with 39. Galloway also rushed for one TD and scored four more on punt returns during those seasons as he exhibited numerous ways of beating foes.

He'd exceeded 1,000 yards received three times and finished just short (987) once during those first four seasons. A contract dispute limited him to eight games in 1999, four of them starts, and his production suffered—335 yards on 22 receptions, with four TDs.

But his Seattle exit was set and he was traded to the Cowboys on February 12, 2000. Galloway's hopes of starting anew and returning to the elite level among receivers were dashed in his first game with Dallas. He tore the anterior cruciate ligament in his left knee during the fourth quarter against the Philadelphia Eagles, and his season was over.

Galloway's return the following year coincided with the retirement of Troy Aikman. The Cowboys endured consecutive 5–11 seasons before finishing 10–6 in 2003, the first season under head coach Bill Parcells.

But the numbers produced by Galloway never came close to his totals in Seattle. He had receiving-yard seasons of 699, 908 and 672, combining for 11 TD receptions in those campaigns.

After catching one pass in his first game with Tampa Bay, he sustained a groin injury that kept him out of the next six games. He returned with a vengeance, scoring six TDs over the last five games—five on receptions and one on a punt return.

He carried that performance over into 2005 where, initially with Brian Griese and then with Chris Simms, Galloway put up career bests with 83 receptions and 1,287 receiving yards. His TD receptions marked the third time in his career that he reached double figures in that category and the first time since 1998.

Galloway became the go-to guy, particularly on third downs. With Simms starting 10 of 11 games in 2005 plus the Wild Card playoff game, Galloway showed his veteran leadership by taking the youngster under his wing and constantly communicating with him.

It was the beginning of a solid QB-to-receiver relationship.

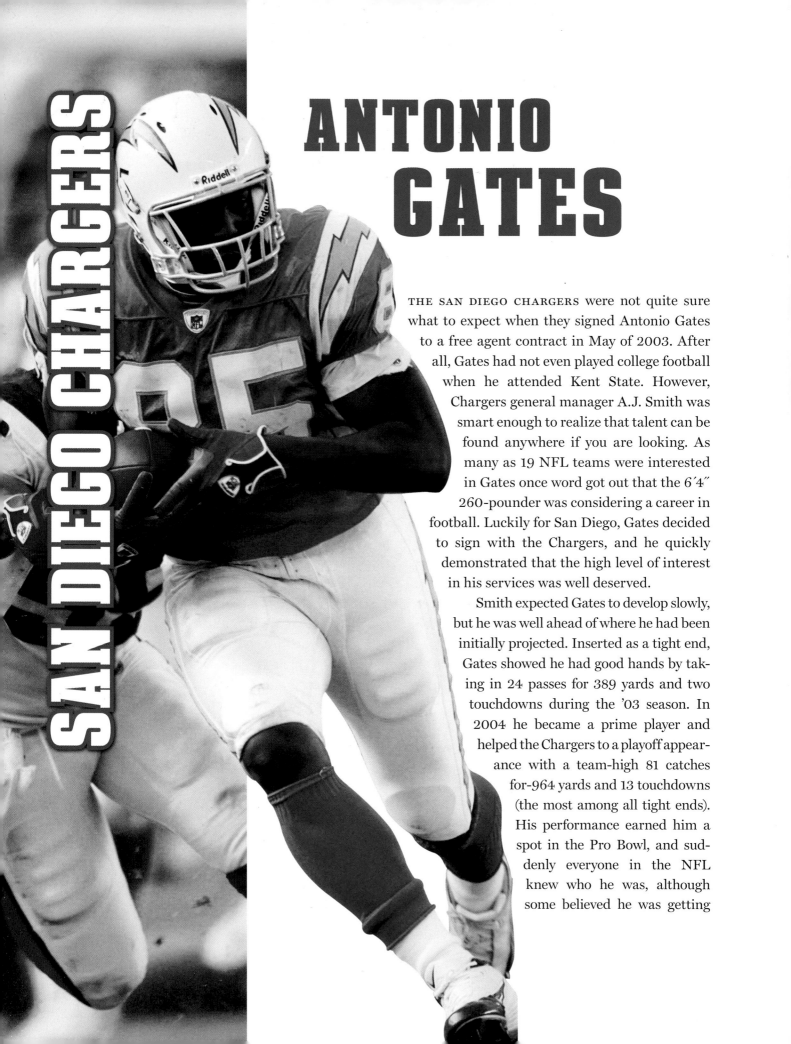

SAN DIEGO CHARGERS

ANTONIO GATES

THE SAN DIEGO CHARGERS were not quite sure what to expect when they signed Antonio Gates to a free agent contract in May of 2003. After all, Gates had not even played college football when he attended Kent State. However, Chargers general manager A.J. Smith was smart enough to realize that talent can be found anywhere if you are looking. As many as 19 NFL teams were interested in Gates once word got out that the 6´4˝ 260-pounder was considering a career in football. Luckily for San Diego, Gates decided to sign with the Chargers, and he quickly demonstrated that the high level of interest in his services was well deserved.

Smith expected Gates to develop slowly, but he was well ahead of where he had been initially projected. Inserted as a tight end, Gates showed he had good hands by taking in 24 passes for 389 yards and two touchdowns during the '03 season. In 2004 he became a prime player and helped the Chargers to a playoff appearance with a team-high 81 catches for-964 yards and 13 touchdowns (the most among all tight ends). His performance earned him a spot in the Pro Bowl, and suddenly everyone in the NFL knew who he was, although some believed he was getting

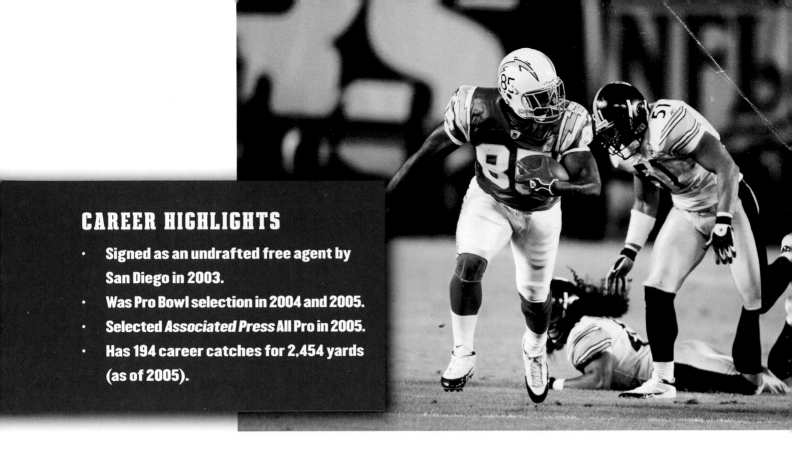

the benefit of playing alongside running back LaDainian Tomlinson. Gates quite rightly pointed out that he was consistent for 16 games, but he knew he would not sneak up on opponents in 2005.

Gates is a complete package of size, speed and skill. He is quick off the line and shows soft hands while hauling in passes from quarterback Drew Brees (who considered the tight end his "go-to guy" when he put the ball in the air). Gates is still learning to play his position and is getting better at reading defenses. Being a former basketball player (a star in this sport when he attended Kent State) has helped Gates to get his body in the right spot to ward off defenders, and he knows how to make room for himself down the field.

Once he gets his hands on the ball, Gates, with his large size and determination, becomes difficult to bring down. He is also developing his blocking skills, and that is important to the Chargers, who want to spring their main weapon in Tomlinson as often as possible.

Even though Gates was relatively new to stardom, it did not stop a nasty contract dispute with the Chargers prior to the start of the '05 season. A new deal was finally signed just before the beginning of the regular season, but the team decided to suspend him for one game for failing to report on time (San Diego had lost their season opener at home to Dallas without Gates in the lineup).

But Gates knows he has to work hard to prove he was not a flash in the pan, and the second game of the year saw him catch six passes for 80 yards in a loss to Denver. It was Gates' first game of the year, and he showed that he was in fact dedicated to improving his performance. He had a 108-yard game against New England, caught 10 passes for 145 yards versus the Kansas City Chiefs and made 13 receptions (a career high to date) against the Miami Dolphins. In all, Gates made 89 catches for 1,101 yards during the '05 campaign.

The Chargers are in one of the most competitive divisions in the NFL, and they need Gates to be one of their best players if they are to succeed and get back to the playoffs.

DALLAS COWBOYS

TERRY GLENN

FROM HIS FIRST START as a pro on September 8, 1996, at Buffalo, wide receiver Terry Glenn clicked with quarterback Drew Bledsoe during a season when the New England Patriots marched all the way to the Super Bowl. In 2005, that pair was together once more when Bledsoe joined the Dallas Cowboys.

Completing the reunion of former Patriots was Cowboys head coach Bill Parcells, who had guided New England to New Orleans for the NFL Championship Game in 1997, a 35–21 loss to the Green Bay Packers.

Glenn hails from Columbus, Ohio, where he instinctively developed a passion for the Ohio State Buckeyes. The explosive wide receiver played in the shadows of Joey Galloway and Chris Sanders before garnering national acclaim in his third and final year with the Buckeyes.

With Ohio State records of 64 receptions, 1,411 yards and 17 touchdowns, Glenn earned the Fred Biletnikoff Award as the nation's top collegiate receiver. The Patriots used their first-round selection in 1996 to pick Glenn, and he played 15 games—all starts—in his phenomenal rookie season.

Glenn's first reception (from Bledsoe) went for nine yards. Later in that game against the Bills, Glenn snared a 37-yard toss from Bledsoe for his first NFL touchdown. Setting an NFL rookie record for most receptions in one season (90), Glenn finished with 1,132 yards to rank 11th in the NFL.

IN THE HUDDLE

Terry Glenn can relate to soft-drink vendors in stadiums, because in his youth he sold sodas at Ohio State football games.

Injuries limited his effectiveness during the next two seasons, but he returned for a career-best 1,147 yards in 1999. Two seasons later, when the Patriots won their first Super Bowl, Glenn's season was marred by league and team suspensions, while Bledsoe was the backup to Tom Brady.

After a season with the Green Bay Packers, Glenn was brought to the Cowboys by Parcells in 2003. Questions arose about Glenn's mental toughness and declining production, particularly in 2004, when he played only six games because of a nagging foot injury.

However, he became a vital deep-threat weapon for the Cowboys in 2005 when he surpassed the 1,000-yard mark for the third time—all with Bledsoe. Glenn compiled 1,136 yards with a career-best seven TDs. His 18.3-yard average from 62 receptions was not only a personal best, it led the NFL in 2005.

Overcoming adversity and silencing the doubters, Glenn became the first Cowboys receiver with four 100-yard receiving games since Michael Irvin in 1997.

In a dramatic Week 14 win over the Kansas City Chiefs, Glenn and Bledsoe shocked the defense with a successful 71-yard flea-flicker for a TD—the wide receiver's longest reception since 1998. Glenn then surprised defenders once more when he ran six yards for the first rushing TD of his NFL career.

Another of his finest moments came in Week 16 when, despite dislocating his right thumb, Glenn made the highlight reels with a one-handed catch for the winning TD against Carolina. The victory kept the Cowboys in the playoff hunt.

At 31 and with 10 NFL seasons under his belt, Glenn proved he's still a top receiver, finishing 11th in receiving yards. The one-time Buckeye can still get the job done, especially if the QB throwing the ball his way happens to be Drew Bledsoe. And now Dallas has Terrell Owens in the fold as well.

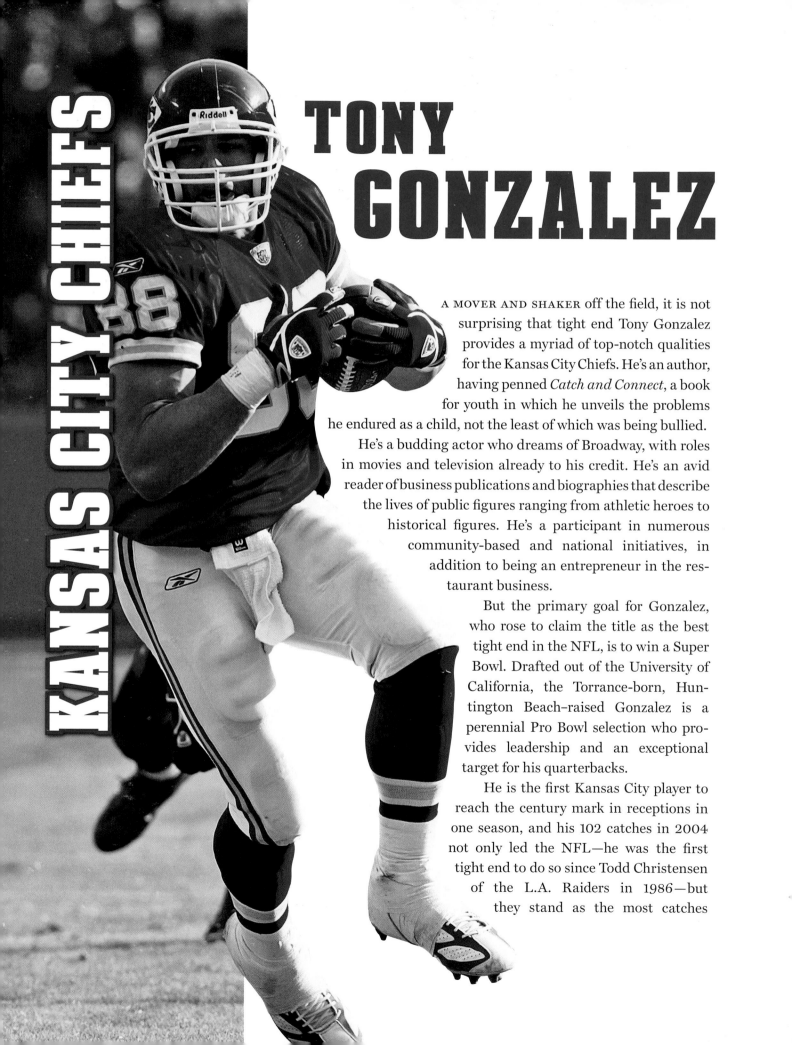

TONY GONZALEZ

KANSAS CITY CHIEFS

A MOVER AND SHAKER off the field, it is not surprising that tight end Tony Gonzalez provides a myriad of top-notch qualities for the Kansas City Chiefs. He's an author, having penned *Catch and Connect*, a book for youth in which he unveils the problems he endured as a child, not the least of which was being bullied. He's a budding actor who dreams of Broadway, with roles in movies and television already to his credit. He's an avid reader of business publications and biographies that describe the lives of public figures ranging from athletic heroes to historical figures. He's a participant in numerous community-based and national initiatives, in addition to being an entrepreneur in the restaurant business.

But the primary goal for Gonzalez, who rose to claim the title as the best tight end in the NFL, is to win a Super Bowl. Drafted out of the University of California, the Torrance-born, Huntington Beach–raised Gonzalez is a perennial Pro Bowl selection who provides leadership and an exceptional target for his quarterbacks.

He is the first Kansas City player to reach the century mark in receptions in one season, and his 102 catches in 2004 not only led the NFL—he was the first tight end to do so since Todd Christensen of the L.A. Raiders in 1986—but they stand as the most catches

in one season by a tight end…period. MacArthur Lane, with 66 receptions in 1976, was the only other member of the Chiefs to lead the NFL in passes caught in a season.

Gonzalez is already the all-time leader for the Chiefs in receptions, with 648, and in reception yards, with 7,810. He caught at least one pass in each of Kansas City's 16 games in 2005 to establish the club record of receptions in 84 consecutive games.

After his remarkable 2004 totals, many viewed his statistics in 2005 (78 receptions for 905 yards with two TDs) as indicators that his hold as "best" tight end in the NFL is now swinging to Antonio Gates of the San Diego Chargers.

Gonzalez expressed frustration in 2005 that he didn't participate more in Kansas City's offense. But the totals for receptions and yards ranked third and fifth, respectively, among his personal-best seasons. Still, with 24 fewer catches and 353 fewer reception yards, Gonzalez longed to see the ball more often.

Number 88 has become a Kansas City fixture since the Chiefs traded up five spots with the Houston Oilers in 1997 in order to ensure Gonzalez would be theirs. After starring in football and basketball at Huntington Beach High School, Gonzalez continued to excel in those sports while at Cal.

With Steve Mariucci as his football coach, he tied for the collegiate lead in catches (46) and led in receiving yards (with 699) in his junior—and final—NCAA season. That year, he was also part of Cal's strong performance on the court as his school reached the NCAA's Sweet 16.

Gonzalez claimed a spot with the Chiefs in 1997, playing all 16 games with no starts. However, beginning in 1998 and through 2005, he started 127 consecutive games. A fan favorite from the outset who uses his 6′4″ frame to make some incredible lunging catches, Gonzalez was selected as Kansas City's top rookie in 1997.

IN THE HUDDLE

Tony Gonzalez and nine-time Pro Bowl quarterback Warren Moon, who ended his brilliant pro career with the Chiefs in 2000, are partners in a restaurant in Newport Beach, California.

Over the years, Gonzalez has developed a trademark way of celebrating after scoring touchdowns. Combining his proficiency in football and basketball, he enthusiastically slam-dunks the football over the crossbar. It's a sight Chiefs fans expect to see for many more years.

INDIANAPOLIS COLTS

MARVIN HARRISON

WIDE RECEIVER Marvin Harrison has done just about everything a football player can do in a career, and he still has plenty of time to go in the National Football League. The 10-year veteran (who will turn 34 before the start of the 2006 campaign) holds a variety of team records for the Indianapolis Colts. (He might end up holding a number of league records, too.) However, a Super Bowl championship still proves to be elusive for the star wideout. The Colts won a league-high 14 games during the 2005 season, but another disappointment in the playoffs (a loss to Pittsburgh at home) kept the Indianapolis club from the big game one more time. Harrison is signed through to 2011, which gives him a chance to get his ring with the Colts if they can keep the team as competitive as it's been over the last years.

Harrison was selected by the Colts in 1996 (a great year for receivers) after attending the University of Syracuse. He caught 64 passes for 836 yards and eight touchdowns as an NFL rookie and has never looked back. Harrison has generally performed with little fanfare, preferring to do his job in a more business-like manner. He's not a flashy type (especially for a wide receiver), but Harrison's statistics are astounding. His career totals show 927 receptions for 12,331 yards and 110 touchdowns, reflecting a receiver who runs precise routes, displays a good work ethic, and has deceptive speed and extraordinary hands. He has no hot dog in him (and is normally mild-mannered), but he knows how to play in traffic and makes the necessary body adjustments easily. Not the biggest wide receiver in the

IN THE HUDDLE

Many of the NFL's top receivers of the 2005 season came out of the 1996 draft. These include Marvin Harrison, along with Calvin Muhammad, Joe Horn, Terrell Owens, Eric Moulds, Eddie Kennison, Bobby Engram, Amani Toomer, Terry Glenn and Keyshawn Johnson.

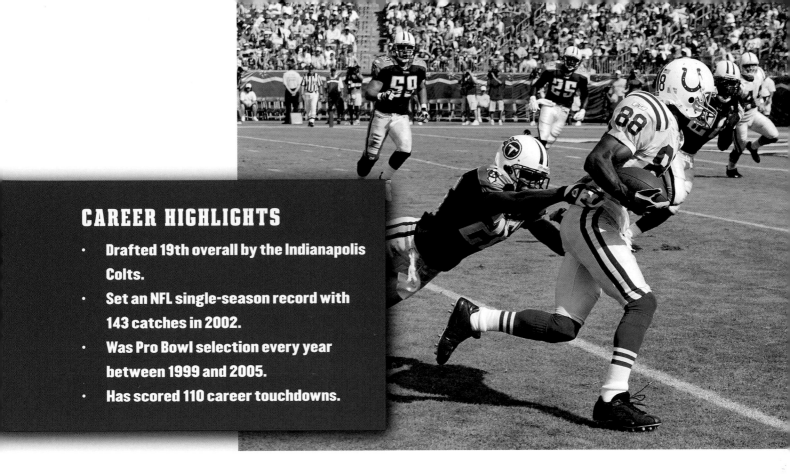

NFL at 6′ and 175 pounds, Harrison is still quite capable of taking the ball away from any defender. He can also make a defender miss a tackle and take the ball all the way to the house. Naturally Harrison has not done it all on his own, but he has spent time developing a special chemistry with star quarterback Peyton Manning. It's a special relationship that will one day land both of them in the Pro Football Hall of Fame.

During the '05 season Harrison had six games where he had 100 or more yards in receiving and caught 12 touchdown passes (including his 100th career major). He caught a total of 82 passes, which is far off his record-setting 143 receptions of 2002 but still was good enough to rank him in 13th place among all NFL receivers in '05. Harrison has pushed himself by refusing to be easily satisfied. Although he wants to make every catch he can, there are other receivers (such as Reggie Wayne and Brandon Stokley) on the Colts who are contributing to the attack. In fact, Wayne caught one more pass than Harrison

during the season (albeit for fewer yards and only five TDs), an indicator that a changing of the guard may be at hand for the Colts at the receiver position. However, it was Harrison who was selected to play in the Pro Bowl for the '05 season.

The Colts built their offense around the triumvirate of Harrison, Manning and running back Edgerrin James (who now is with Arizona). General manager Bill Polian tried his best to keep the trio together, but he knew that would be difficult given the constraints of a salary cap. All three players are high achievers, and no one is more focused than Harrison, who understands it's all about the team winning. He also takes the time to keep himself in top condition, and believes that he is capable of playing many more years because he feels so young. It will be up to the Colts to keep the talent level high so that Harrison and Manning can one day walk away with the title they have yearned for during the past seven seasons.

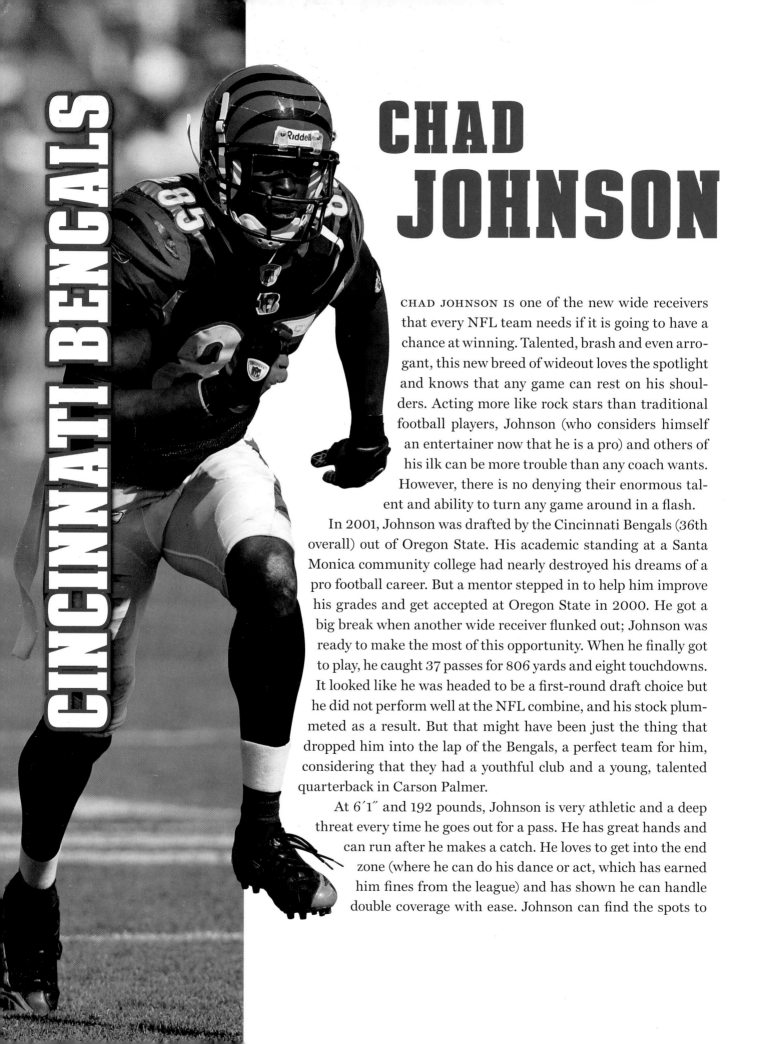

CINCINNATI BENGALS

CHAD JOHNSON

CHAD JOHNSON IS one of the new wide receivers that every NFL team needs if it is going to have a chance at winning. Talented, brash and even arrogant, this new breed of wideout loves the spotlight and knows that any game can rest on his shoulders. Acting more like rock stars than traditional football players, Johnson (who considers himself an entertainer now that he is a pro) and others of his ilk can be more trouble than any coach wants. However, there is no denying their enormous talent and ability to turn any game around in a flash.

In 2001, Johnson was drafted by the Cincinnati Bengals (36th overall) out of Oregon State. His academic standing at a Santa Monica community college had nearly destroyed his dreams of a pro football career. But a mentor stepped in to help him improve his grades and get accepted at Oregon State in 2000. He got a big break when another wide receiver flunked out; Johnson was ready to make the most of this opportunity. When he finally got to play, he caught 37 passes for 806 yards and eight touchdowns. It looked like he was headed to be a first-round draft choice but he did not perform well at the NFL combine, and his stock plummeted as a result. But that might have been just the thing that dropped him into the lap of the Bengals, a perfect team for him, considering that they had a youthful club and a young, talented quarterback in Carson Palmer.

At 6´1˝ and 192 pounds, Johnson is very athletic and a deep threat every time he goes out for a pass. He has great hands and can run after he makes a catch. He loves to get into the end zone (where he can do his dance or act, which has earned him fines from the league) and has shown he can handle double coverage with ease. Johnson can find the spots to

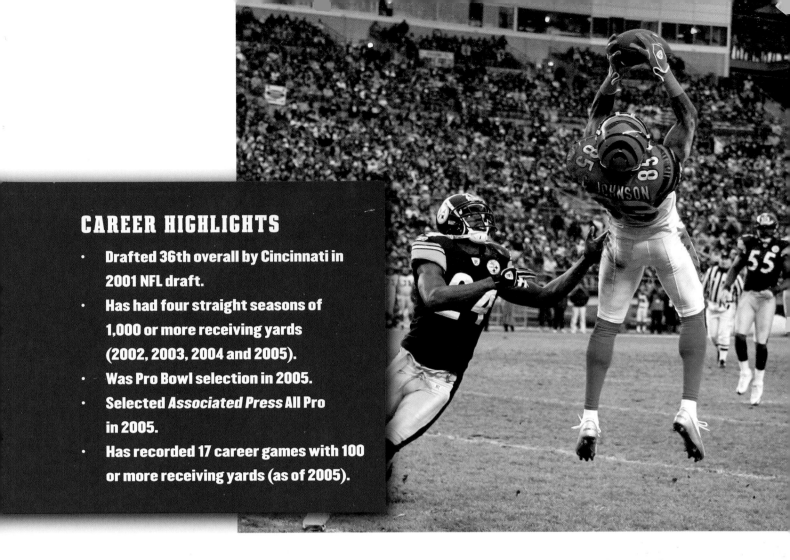

CAREER HIGHLIGHTS

- Drafted 36th overall by Cincinnati in 2001 NFL draft.
- Has had four straight seasons of 1,000 or more receiving yards (2002, 2003, 2004 and 2005).
- Was Pro Bowl selection in 2005.
- Selected *Associated Press* All Pro in 2005.
- Has recorded 17 career games with 100 or more receiving yards (as of 2005).

get open and has developed an excellent on-field rapport with Palmer. He started slowly as a rookie in '01. However, since the 2002 season, he has never been below 1,000 receiving yards. In 2003 and 2004, he caught 90 and 95 passes, respectively, and gained all the notoriety he desired as a football player. Johnson had a tendency to drop passes he should have caught. But that trait seems to be declining with experience, although he needs to give more when he is not the featured player, according to some experts.

Johnson does not seem to let the critics bother him at all and remains focused on getting the Bengals into the playoffs, even if he has to do it kicking and screaming. During the 2005 season, Johnson put up by his locker a list of defensive backs he planned to humiliate in each and every game. For the most part, he was able to give defensive backs headaches all season long, with 97 catches for a club record of 1,432 yards. The Cincinnati club finally made the playoffs, fulfilling one of Johnson's major objectives.

IN THE HUDDLE

At one time Chad Johnson worked in a store in a mall. In 2003 Chad Johnson signed a five-year $26-million-dollar contract with Cincinnati!

The question now is whether or not he can mature enough off the field to keep his focus on getting his team to the Super Bowl—the ultimate stage for this grand performer. When it comes to dealing with Chad Johnson, this might be the greatest challenge facing Bengals coach Marvin Lewis.

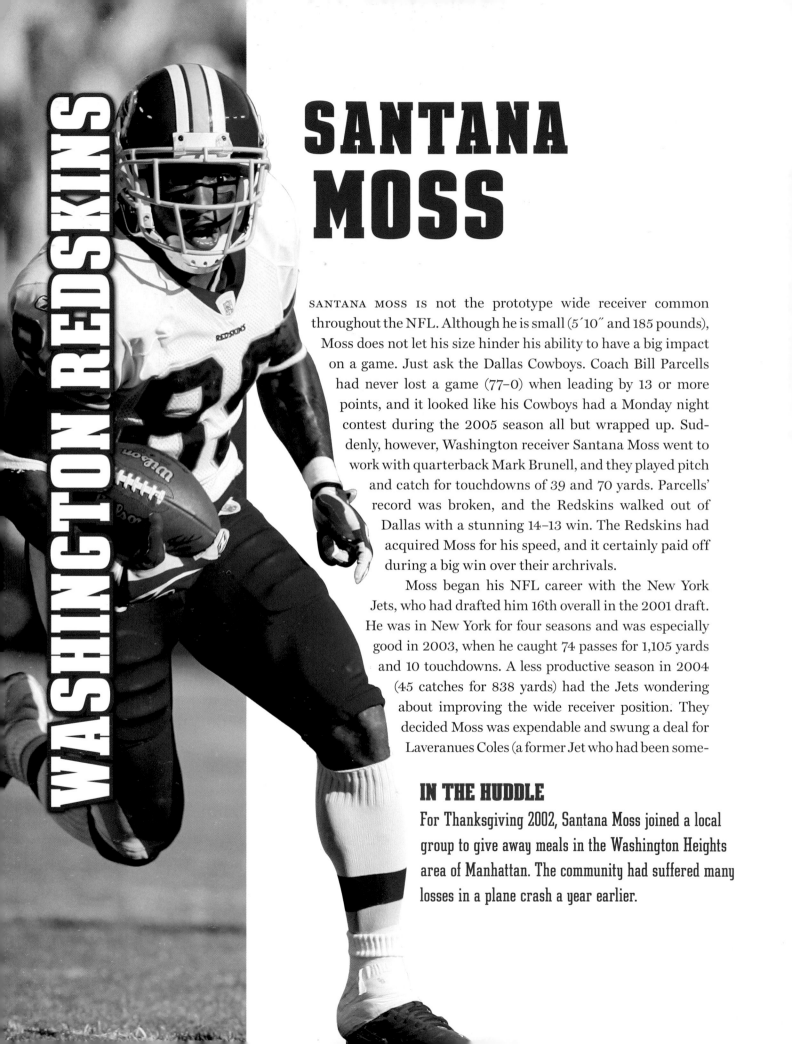

WASHINGTON REDSKINS

SANTANA MOSS

SANTANA MOSS IS not the prototype wide receiver common throughout the NFL. Although he is small (5´10˝ and 185 pounds), Moss does not let his size hinder his ability to have a big impact on a game. Just ask the Dallas Cowboys. Coach Bill Parcells had never lost a game (77–0) when leading by 13 or more points, and it looked like his Cowboys had a Monday night contest during the 2005 season all but wrapped up. Suddenly, however, Washington receiver Santana Moss went to work with quarterback Mark Brunell, and they played pitch and catch for touchdowns of 39 and 70 yards. Parcells' record was broken, and the Redskins walked out of Dallas with a stunning 14–13 win. The Redskins had acquired Moss for his speed, and it certainly paid off during a big win over their archrivals.

Moss began his NFL career with the New York Jets, who had drafted him 16th overall in the 2001 draft. He was in New York for four seasons and was especially good in 2003, when he caught 74 passes for 1,105 yards and 10 touchdowns. A less productive season in 2004 (45 catches for 838 yards) had the Jets wondering about improving the wide receiver position. They decided Moss was expendable and swung a deal for Laveranues Coles (a former Jet who had been some-

IN THE HUDDLE
For Thanksgiving 2002, Santana Moss joined a local group to give away meals in the Washington Heights area of Manhattan. The community had suffered many losses in a plane crash a year earlier.

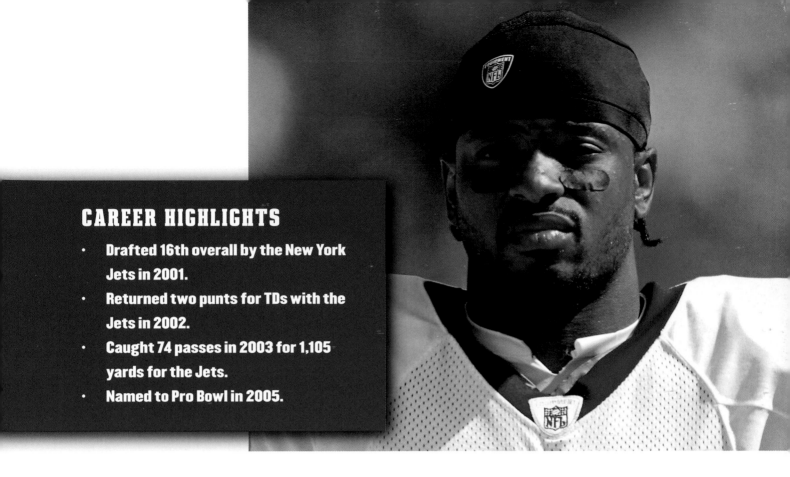

thing of a mentor to Moss when the two were together in New York). It was a move the Jets likely regretted as the 2005 season progressed and Moss showed he was an all-round player. Get him the ball and watch him make a spectacular play (against the Kansas City Chiefs he took a short screen pass and ran 78 yards for a TD). His moves cause the opposition to miss the elusive Moss, and his very competitive nature drives him to the end zone. Moss is not just fast, because that alone will not keep him in the league. He has learned to run disciplined pass patterns at full speed, and his great hands allow him to grab many balls that might otherwise elude a smaller receiver. Moss does not worry about his lack of height, and the Redskins seem to have figured out how to use him best.

From the time he was about 12 years old, Moss figured football would be his future. The native of Miami, Florida, was able to see the Dolphin players who stayed at a hotel near his home. He would often wave as they drove by and pic-

tured himself in their shoes in the future. A coach at Moss' elementary school sensed his potential and encouraged him. Moss practiced and played football every chance he had before and after school. Visualizing his goal helped Moss get to a major college (the University of Miami) and then to a starring role on the Hurricanes team. He was also a top kick returner during his college career. In addition to his football exploits for the Hurricanes (he had 1,604 all-purpose yards and 11 touchdowns in 2000), he was an excellent track-and-field competitor. Those skills helped him to become a better football player as well.

Washington coach Joe Gibbs admires Moss' ability to react to the ball once it is up in the air. He also loves the sheer speed the wideout brings to the Redskins offense. Moss has also shown a good work ethic and a desire to excel in practice. His performance during the '05 season (the best of his career) has made Moss a team leader, and his big play style makes him one of the most exciting players in the NFL.

NEW YORK GIANTS

JEREMY SHOCKEY

IF EVER A SURNAME suited the individual, Jeremy Shockey is appropriately named. The notoriously quotable tight end for the New York Giants has shocked and created headlines since joining the NFL in 2002.

He has been in the tabloid gossip columns. He's been referred to as a modern-day Joe Namath because he does not shy away from the constant bright lights of Broadway. Shockey has mingled with and dated some extremely attractive ladies from the world of modeling and entertainment. He has mouthed off about everything from social issues to the foibles of coaches and players. He's fought with teammates.

Shockey is a football talent who wears his heart on his sleeve.

He was raised by his mother, Lucinda, in Ada, Oklahoma, a city of 16,000 in the southeastern part of the state. When the Oklahoma Sooners showed a lack of interest in Shockey because he hadn't yet grown enough to suit them, he went to Northeast Oklahoma A&M for a year. After he had bulked up and put up some eye-catching numbers, the Sooners came calling, but Shockey told them to take a hike. He went to the Miami Hurricanes in 2000 and won the national title with them in 2001.

IN THE HUDDLE

Jeremy Shockey is the first member of the New York Giants since the great Lawrence Taylor (1981-82) to gain Pro Bowl selection in each of his first two NFL seasons.

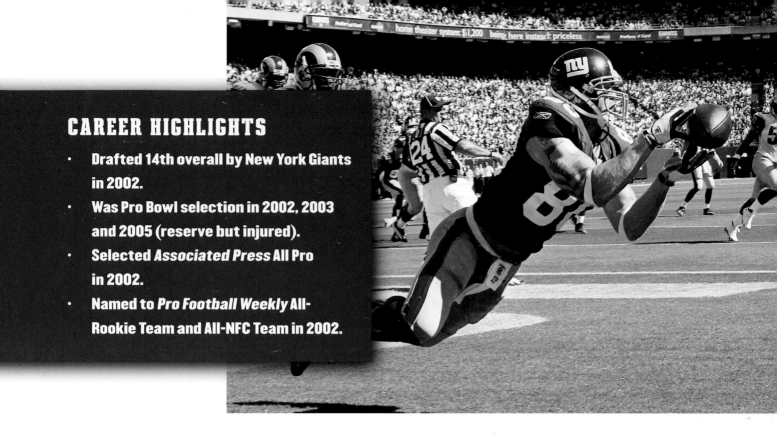

The Giants came away impressed with Shockey's gung-ho mind-set during a pre-draft interview with him. They even swapped spots with the Tennessee Titans and added a fourth-round pick in the 2002 NFL draft to ensure they'd get Shockey at number 14.

When the draft was over, Shockey and his representatives boldly predicted this guy would make it in the Big Apple. At 6´5˝ and 252 pounds, Shockey was a nice target for QB Kerry Collins, and soon he not only won over teammates, he became a fan darling and a media dream.

He topped all NFL tight ends and NFL freshmen in 2002 with 74 catches for 894 yards. He became the first rookie tight end to play in the Pro Bowl since Keith Jackson of the Philadelphia Eagles in 1988. On the final day of the season at Philadelphia, Shockey firmly established him as a clutch performer. He out-muscled Brian Dawkins for the game-tying TD, and the Giants clinched a postseason spot when they won in overtime.

His first playoff experience was a series of highs (he scored one touchdown) and lows (he dropped another). The 49ers, with a miracle come-back at San Francisco, turned a 24-point deficit in the third quarter into a 39–38 win. Shockey got into it with some of the fans and allegedly tossed a cup of ice—he insists it was water—into the stands. He also made an obscene gesture and was fined in both instances by the NFL.

From 48 catches for 535 yards and two TDs in his injury-plagued 2003, he jumped to 61 receptions, 666 yards and six TDs in another play-off-missing season in 2004. But with quarterback Eli Manning showing more poise in his sophomore season, the offense came to life in 2005.

Shockey caught 65 passes for 891 yards and a career-high seven TDs. He played through a chest/shoulder injury that he picked up against the Vikings on November 13 but missed the final regular-season game against Oakland because of a high ankle sprain. He was less than 100 percent when the Giants were humbled by the Panthers in the Wild Card game.

It was a devastating conclusion after so much had gone right for the Giants in the season. Given his swagger, Shockey will use this setback as motivation for next time.

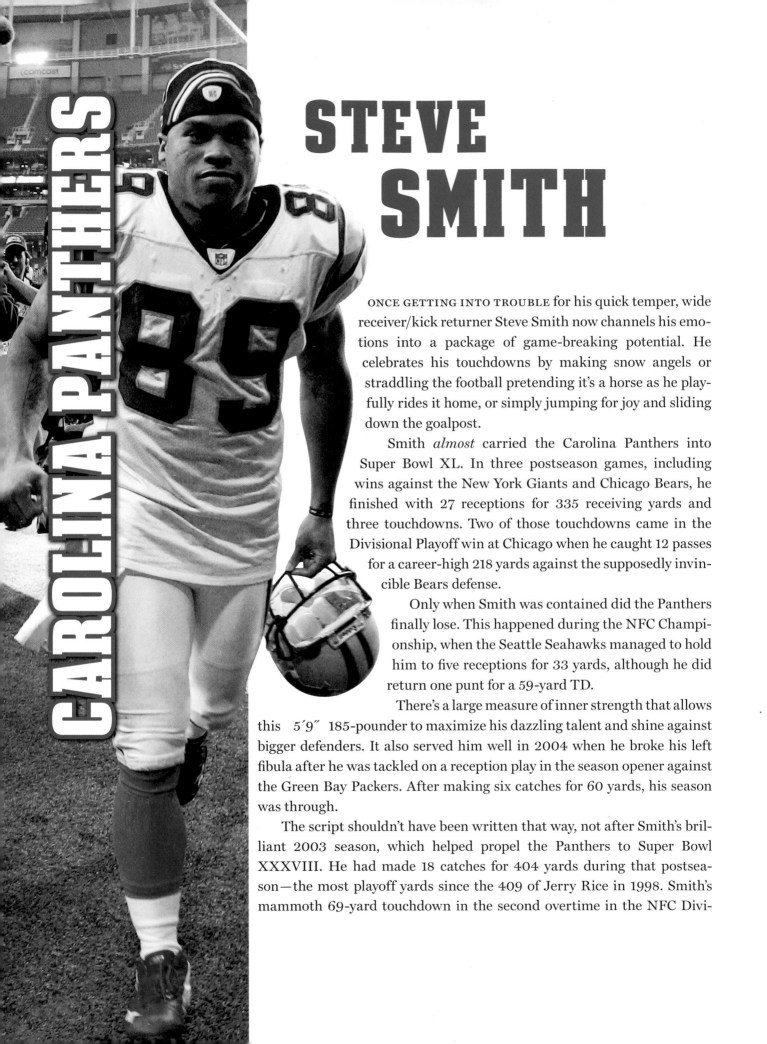

STEVE SMITH

ONCE GETTING INTO TROUBLE for his quick temper, wide receiver/kick returner Steve Smith now channels his emotions into a package of game-breaking potential. He celebrates his touchdowns by making snow angels or straddling the football pretending it's a horse as he playfully rides it home, or simply jumping for joy and sliding down the goalpost.

Smith *almost* carried the Carolina Panthers into Super Bowl XL. In three postseason games, including wins against the New York Giants and Chicago Bears, he finished with 27 receptions for 335 receiving yards and three touchdowns. Two of those touchdowns came in the Divisional Playoff win at Chicago when he caught 12 passes for a career-high 218 yards against the supposedly invincible Bears defense.

Only when Smith was contained did the Panthers finally lose. This happened during the NFC Championship, when the Seattle Seahawks managed to hold him to five receptions for 33 yards, although he did return one punt for a 59-yard TD.

There's a large measure of inner strength that allows this 5´9˝ 185-pounder to maximize his dazzling talent and shine against bigger defenders. It also served him well in 2004 when he broke his left fibula after he was tackled on a reception play in the season opener against the Green Bay Packers. After making six catches for 60 yards, his season was through.

The script shouldn't have been written that way, not after Smith's brilliant 2003 season, which helped propel the Panthers to Super Bowl XXXVIII. He had made 18 catches for 404 yards during that postseason—the most playoff yards since the 409 of Jerry Rice in 1998. Smith's mammoth 69-yard touchdown in the second overtime in the NFC Divi-

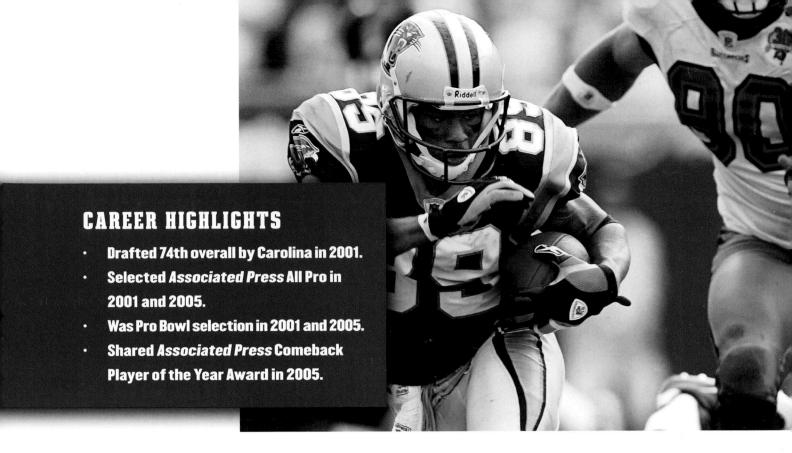

sional Playoff at St. Louis ranked as the longest TD to end a postseason game in NFL history.

In March of 2004, he had even signed a contract extension. Instead it would be a long road back for Smith. But return he did, and he did so in a spectacular fashion. Smith completed the 2005 regular season tied with Arizona's Larry Fitzgerald for the NFL lead with 103 receptions; he tied with Marvin Harrison of Indianapolis with 12 TD receptions and paced the NFL outright with 1,563 receiving yards. He also ranked fourth in the NFL with a punt-return average of 10.6 yards.

With a record of 11–5, the Panthers matched their mark of 2003 and drastically improved from 7–9 in 2004. They qualified for the playoffs, second to Tampa Bay in the NFC South.

Smith earned his second Pro Bowl and *Associated Press* All Pro selections, this time as a wide receiver after making it as a kick returner in 2001. In 2005 he also shared the *Associated Press'* NFL Comeback Player of the Year Award with Tedy Bruschi of the New England Patriots.

From the moment Smith stepped onto an NFL field to play for keeps, there was something special about him. He'd spent two years at Santa Monica Junior College before heading to the University of Utah. His kickoff and punt-returning totals were noteworthy, as were his versatility and resiliency.

IN THE HUDDLE

Steve Smith sees himself serving as a coach for youth sports at some time in the future. He's already tested the waters by coaching the soccer team that his son, Peyton, plays on.

The Panthers selected Smith in the third round of the 2001 NFL draft and he rubber-stamped his credentials instantly: he took his first NFL kickoff at Minnesota on September 9, 2001, and returned it 93 yards for a touchdown—the first touchdown in the 2001 NFL season.

Smith has since gone on to set numerous return and receiving records for the Panthers—with many more yet to be celebrated as only he can do before he wraps up his career.

PITTSBURGH STEELERS

HINES WARD

IN THE END, there was no way the Pittsburgh Steelers were going to let wide receiver Hines Ward walk away. As the start of the 2005 season loomed, the Steelers rewarded the man who was poised to become the franchise's all-time leading receiver with a four-year deal that could see Ward earn a total of $25.8 million. Even Ward seemed a little surprised that the Steelers went as far as they did. It's still not quite the landmark deal other receivers have signed, but Ward saw himself wearing the black and gold of the Steelers for the rest of his career. It's not likely to be a deal either side will regret.

Pittsburgh drafted the 6′, 215-pound receiver in the third round of the NFL draft in 1998 (92nd overall), and many experts thought Ward would never play in the league. The Steelers were probably not certain either and took wide receivers in the first round of the draft in 1999 (Troy Edwards) and in 2000 (Plaxico Burress). However, neither of those players is still in Pittsburgh, while Ward continues to thrive there. In the four seasons prior to the '05 campaign, Ward had 1,000 or more receiving

IN THE HUDDLE

Hines Ward was born on March 8, 1976, in Seoul, South Korea, to a black American father and a Korean mother. Ward's photo appeared in virtually all the South Korean newspapers as the Super Bowl MVP participated in the Steelers' victory parade.

yards and totaled 505 career catches. Not bad numbers for a player who was told he would not likely be a starter and who plays on a team that tends to emphasize the running game. Ward defied the odds by becoming one of the best all-round receivers in the entire NFL. He does not have great speed, but he knows how to get open and is ultra-competitive on the field. Ward lacks the height of many of his peers. However, he makes up for it with excellent hands and the elusive moves needed to get open.

Another trait that distinguishes Ward is his willingness to block for the Steelers running backs. He seems to relish laying out a good hit to spring a teammate as much as he does hauling in a pass. Veteran linebacker Steve Foley recalled recently that he was welcomed to the NFL in his rookie year (when he was with Cincinnati) by Ward, who caught him with a blind-side hit when the Steelers were running a reverse. Foley said he knew then that he was playing in the big leagues. Naturally this style of play makes Ward one of the most popular members of the team, and the loyal Steelers fans would have been more than upset if Ward was not in the fold for the long term. Fans are not likely to forget that Ward has averaged 95 catches over the past four seasons or that he had a

career-high 12 touchdowns in 2002. His numbers were down a little in 2004, when he had 80 catches and four TDs, but he was still named to the Pro Bowl.

Ward wanted to improve on his performance for the '05 season, and he did that with solid games, despite missing some time because of injuries. He had scored six majors by the third week of the season, including an 85-yard TD against the champion Patriots (although the Steelers lost that game). Ward also had a touchdown pass against the Bengals in the seventh week of the year, despite playing through pain; he then sprung running back Willie Parker for another TD with a great block—a typical Ward performance. He finished the '05 season with 69 catches for 975 yards and 11 touchdowns through the air.

The Steelers needed to win three road games to make it to the Super Bowl in Detroit. They managed to pull off the feat, with Ward making his biggest contribution during the championship game played in Detroit. He was named MVP of the Super Bowl after making five receptions for 123 yards and one TD (on a catch he made from the pass thrown by fellow receiver Antwaan Randle El). It was a fitting end to a great season for the Steelers' number one receiver.

LARGE MEN WHO PROTECT

OFFENSIVE

THE QUARTERBACK AND OPEN THE HOLES

LINEMEN!

PITTSBURGH STEELERS

ALAN FANECA

DURING THE 2004 NFL season, the Pittsburgh Steelers became the first team in 20 years to run the ball 60 percent of the time on offense. Given that there is more passing in the league than ever before, that was quite a startling number. But the Steelers love to pound the ball along the ground. They churn out the wins behind a great offensive line that is anchored by perennial All Pro guard Alan Faneca. The 6′5″, 307-pound lineman plays the game with an edge, and he leads the Pittsburgh running backs through the holes and into the open field.

The Steelers selected the bruising guard 26th overall in 1998 after his career at Louisiana State. He was an outstanding player in college (a first-team All-American in 1997) and allowed only one sack during his final year. As a rookie in '98 he got an opportunity to show what he could do when injuries struck starters Will Wolford and Jim Sweeney. Faneca never looked back, and at the age of 28, he is just approaching the prime of his career with five trips to the Pro Bowl already under his belt. He is a superb run blocker by taking the proper angles, and, when he has to, Faneca has no

difficulty getting down the field to crush a defensive back. He shows good vision and an awareness that helps him with pass blocking (he played a little at the left tackle position as well) when the Steelers decide to put the ball in the air.

Early in the 2005 season, the Steelers were being challenged by the upstart Cincinnati Bengals. However, the Pittsburgh club rolled up 221 yards along the ground and beat their division rivals rather easily by a score of 27–13. After the game, Faneca commented that the Steelers simply imposed their will on the young Bengals and beat them along the line of scrimmage. It was the kind of performance that has become Faneca's trademark. The Steelers rolled up 2,223 yards

along the ground in '05, the third-best mark in the AFC. After an 11–5 record during the season,

IN THE HUDDLE

Alan Faneca was once named the offensive AFC Player of the Week (which is very unusual for an offensive lineman) for his outstanding blocking during a game against the Cincinnati Bengals in the 2003 season.

the Steelers won four straight playoff games, including the fifth Super Bowl in franchise history. It was the first championship for Faneca in his NFL career.

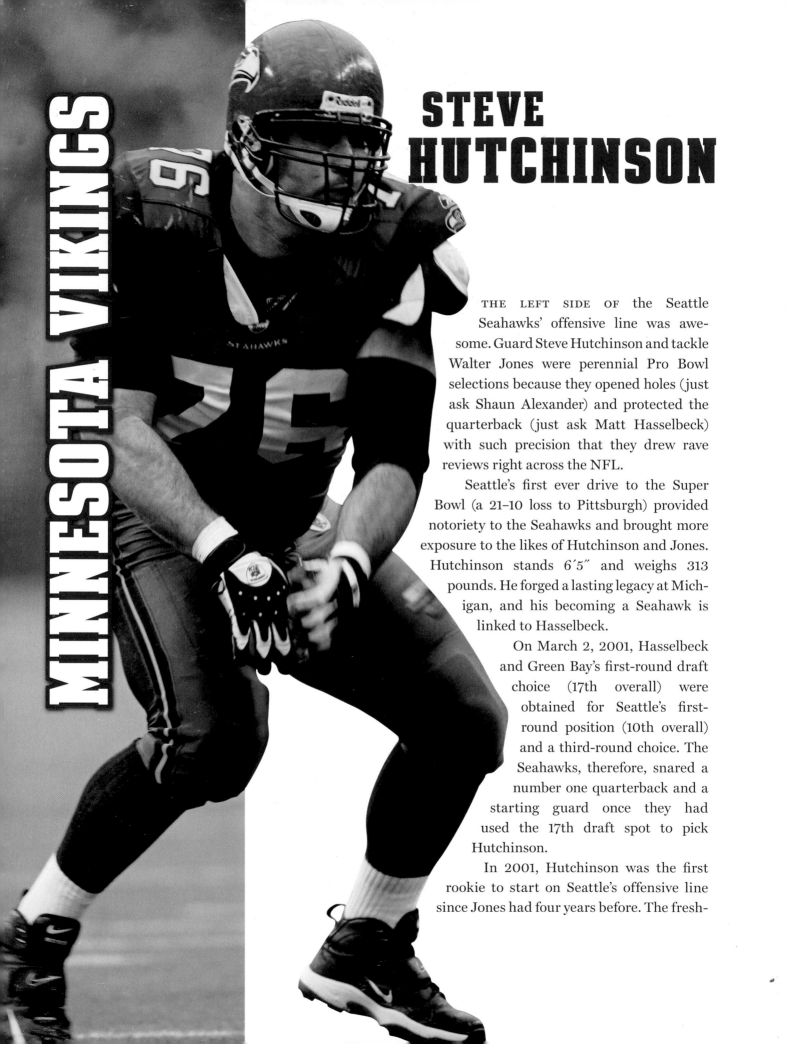

MINNESOTA VIKINGS

STEVE HUTCHINSON

THE LEFT SIDE OF the Seattle Seahawks' offensive line was awesome. Guard Steve Hutchinson and tackle Walter Jones were perennial Pro Bowl selections because they opened holes (just ask Shaun Alexander) and protected the quarterback (just ask Matt Hasselbeck) with such precision that they drew rave reviews right across the NFL.

Seattle's first ever drive to the Super Bowl (a 21–10 loss to Pittsburgh) provided notoriety to the Seahawks and brought more exposure to the likes of Hutchinson and Jones. Hutchinson stands 6′5″ and weighs 313 pounds. He forged a lasting legacy at Michigan, and his becoming a Seahawk is linked to Hasselbeck.

On March 2, 2001, Hasselbeck and Green Bay's first-round draft choice (17th overall) were obtained for Seattle's first-round position (10th overall) and a third-round choice. The Seahawks, therefore, snared a number one quarterback and a starting guard once they had used the 17th draft spot to pick Hutchinson.

In 2001, Hutchinson was the first rookie to start on Seattle's offensive line since Jones had four years before. The fresh-

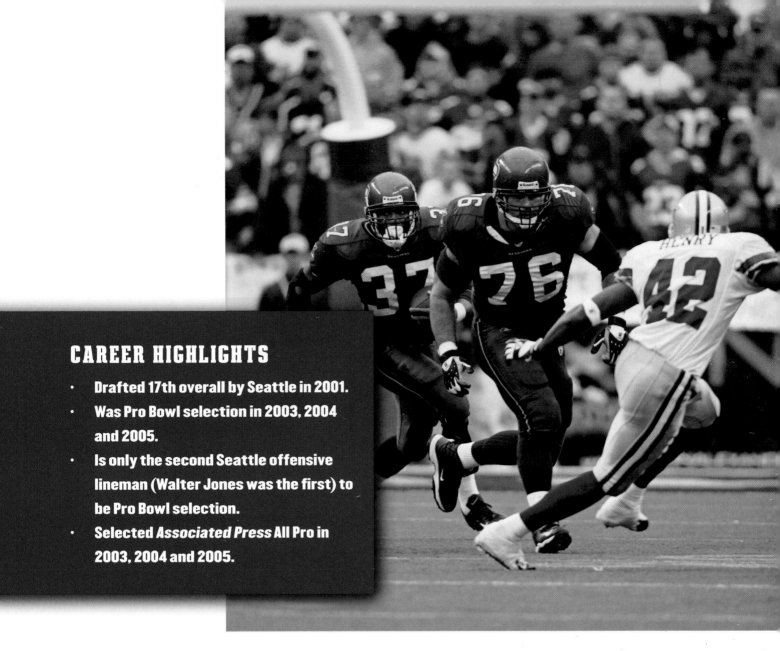

CAREER HIGHLIGHTS

- Drafted 17th overall by Seattle in 2001.
- Was Pro Bowl selection in 2003, 2004 and 2005.
- Is only the second Seattle offensive lineman (Walter Jones was the first) to be Pro Bowl selection.
- Selected *Associated Press* All Pro in 2003, 2004 and 2005.

man played all 16 games as the Seahawks' offense provided an omen of great things to come.

A broken leg sidelined Hutchinson for all but four games in 2002. However, he returned and achieved Pro Bowl status in 2003. Two years later, he factored big time in Alexander's rise to number one rusher in the NFL and in his record-setting performance for TDs in a season. As Alexander chalked up the yardage he required to overtake Tiki Barber for the rushing title in 2005, it was Hutchinson who acted as the calculator. The big guard counted down the yards, proving that he took as much pride in the accomplishment as Alexander did. But following the best season in Seahawks history, Hutchinson signed with the Vikings as a free agent.

IN THE HUDDLE

Seahawks' fans appreciated the work of offensive linemen Steve Hutchinson and Walter Jones so much that those players' jerseys were displayed prominently in Seattle-area stores, right alongside those of Matt Hasselbeck and Shaun Alexander. It is rare for offensive linemen to be so popular.

SEATTLE SEAHAWKS

WALTER JONES

IT'S NO SECRET why the Seattle Seahawks have one of the best running attacks in the NFL. The key to any good ground game begins with a solid offensive line, and Seattle's group of starters along the O-Line is perhaps the top one in the league. Veteran center Robbie Tobeck was aided by the likes of Chris Gray, Steve Hutchinson, Sean Locklear and backup Floyd Womack. They formed the core of an athletic unit that exhibited good chemistry. The offensive line led the Seahawks to their first ever Super Bowl appearance, with Seattle rushing for 2,457 yards during the 2005 season (the second highest total in the NFC). There is little doubt that the star of the group is tackle Walter Jones, a first-round choice of the Seahawks in 1997 (sixth overall).

A graduate of the football program at Florida State, Jones is as consistent and dominant as any-

IN THE HUDDLE

Since entering the NFL in 1997, Walter Jones has missed only seven games (four due to injuries and three due to a contract dispute) and has started every game in six seasons ('98, '99, '00, '01, '03 and '04). He started 15 of 16 games in 2005.

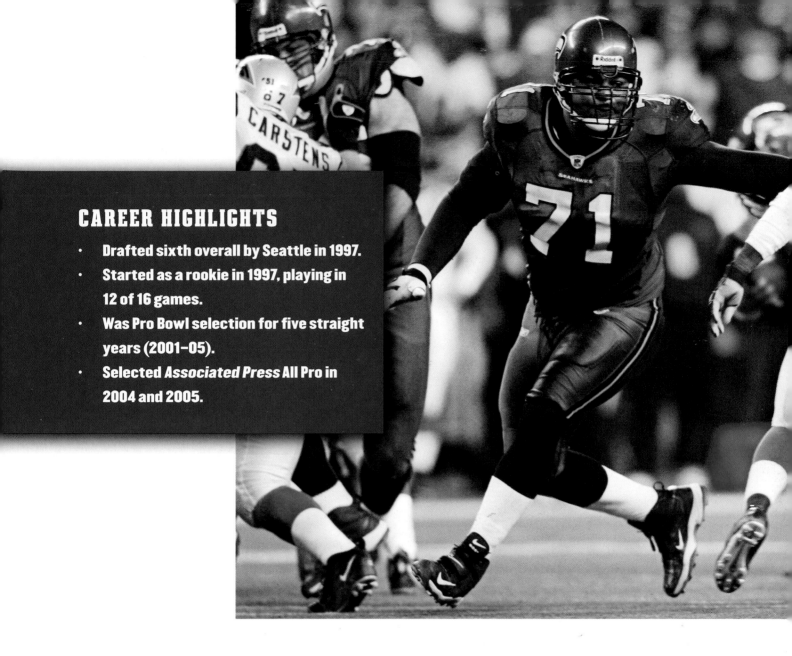

one who plays the most crucial position along the offensive line. The 6´5˝, 315-pound Jones moves very efficiently for a man of his size, and there is nothing a defensive lineman can throw at him that Jones cannot handle. He uses his long arms to keep defenders away from the pocket and is considered a top pass blocker. Jones is seen as more of a finesse blocker than a smash-mouth hitter, but he rarely allows a sack. It has been suggested that Jones could be meaner in his approach, but when a running back like Shaun Alexander rushes for 141 yards as he did in a game against the Houston Texans during the 2005 season (the Seahawks accumulated a total of 324 yards along the ground), it appears that Jones is doing just fine.

Jones and guard Hutchinson (now with Minnesota) formed a very effective tandem on the left side of the line for the Seahawks and gave the team a strong identity. In fact, the Seahawks designated Jones as their franchise player, a strong indicator that they think very highly of the five-time Pro Bowl player. If Jones works at his physical conditioning, there is no reason why he cannot continue to be one of the best tackles in the NFL for years to come.

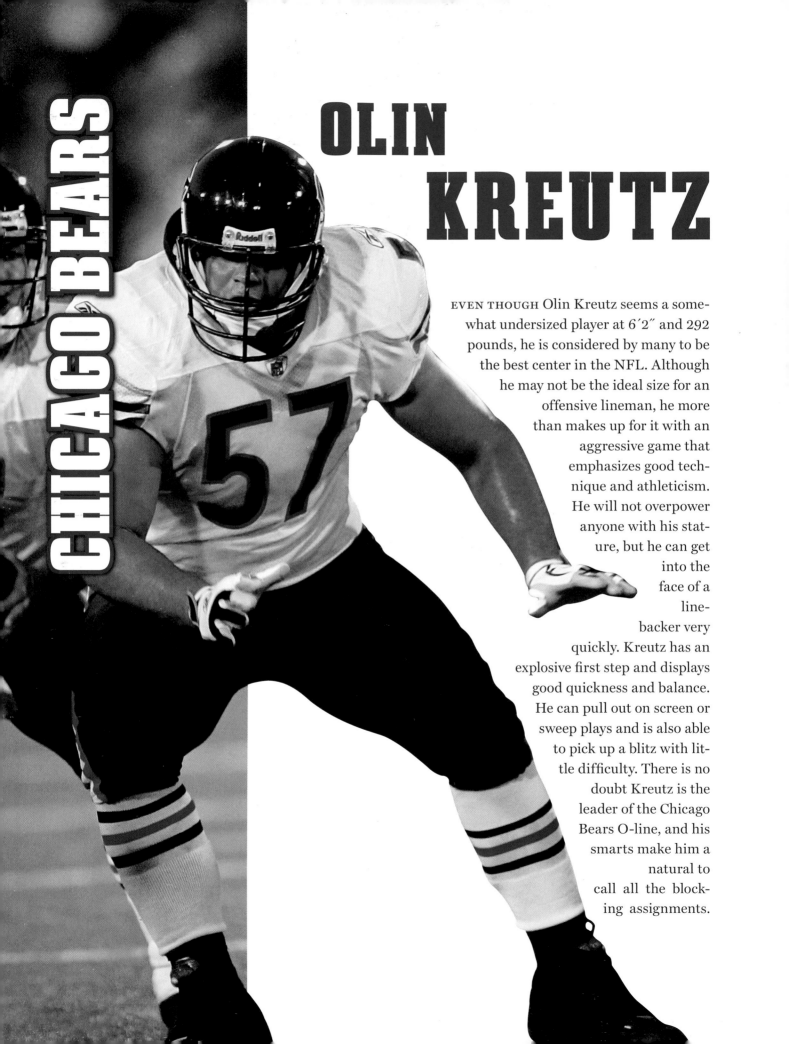

CHICAGO BEARS

OLIN
KREUTZ

EVEN THOUGH Olin Kreutz seems a somewhat undersized player at 6´2˝ and 292 pounds, he is considered by many to be the best center in the NFL. Although he may not be the ideal size for an offensive lineman, he more than makes up for it with an aggressive game that emphasizes good technique and athleticism. He will not overpower anyone with his stature, but he can get into the face of a linebacker very quickly. Kreutz has an explosive first step and displays good quickness and balance. He can pull out on screen or sweep plays and is also able to pick up a blitz with little difficulty. There is no doubt Kreutz is the leader of the Chicago Bears O-line, and his smarts make him a natural to call all the blocking assignments.

CAREER HIGHLIGHTS

- Drafted by the Chicago Bears 64th overall in 1998.
- Earned All-American status at Washington University in 1997.
- Made his first NFL start versus Green Bay on December 27, 1998.
- Was Pro Bowl selection in 2003 and 2005.

He is a very fierce, feisty competitor and always gives his best effort.

Kreutz attended the University of Washington and was named an All-American after his junior year—a season that saw him start every game for the Huskies—and he was graded as the best lineman on the team by the coaches. He decided to enter the NFL draft after his junior year and the Bears selected him in the third round in 1998. He played in nine games as a rookie, but the next season saw him become the Bears' regular center. He has been a mainstay of the team ever since.

The Bears were not expected to do much in 2005. However, they surprised everyone with an 11–5 record, good for first place in the NFC North. Chicago lost their starting quarterback (Rex Grossman) early in the year but made the most of the skills of young pivot Kyle Orton. A strong running game (led by the unheralded Thomas

IN THE HUDDLE

Olin Kreutz is a native of Honolulu, Hawaii, and was named the senior captain of his high-school team at St. Louis High School in Honolulu.

Jones), spearheaded by the blocking of Kreutz and the others along the line, allowed the Bears to keep the ball along the ground and then rely on their defense to grind out the victories. Good old-fashioned Bears football!

DENVER BRONCOS

TOM NALEN

TOM NALEN IS the anchor of an offensive line for the Denver Broncos that prefers to let performance do all the talking for the unit. Even though the 6′3″ 286-pounder is often pitted against much larger players, he remains one of the NFL's most exceptional centers.

He was a leading force in Denver, rushing for 2,539 yards in 2005—the second-best total in the NFL and the second most in Broncos history. In 2003, the Broncos rushed for 2,629 yards and Nalen was named NFL Offensive Lineman of the Year.

The O-line assisted Mike Anderson in rushing for 1,014 yards in 2005 (after he had 1,487 yards as a rookie in 2000). It also assisted Tatum Bell in rushing for 921 yards. In addition it protected quarterback Jake Plummer effectively, yielding 23 QB sacks, three off the league lead belonging to Indianapolis.

Nalen helped Terrell Davis become the fourth player in NFL history to exceed 2,000 rushing yards in a season (2,008 in 1998), and Nalen has provided openings for Clinton Portis, yet another 1,000-yard rusher.

IN THE HUDDLE

Tom Nalen has a desire to enter law enforcement once his playing days are over. Some of his off-field hobbies include golf, movies and playing Sega video games.

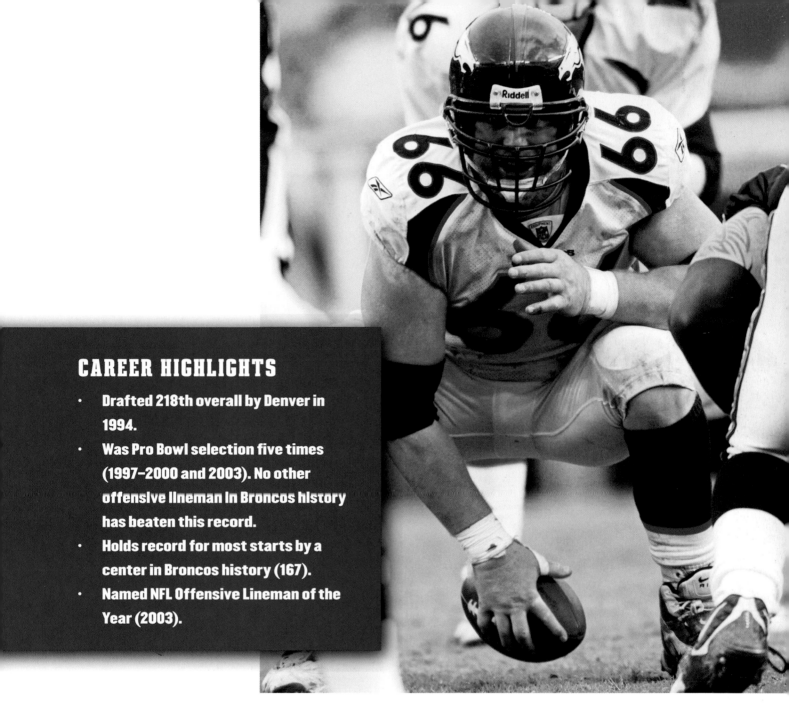

CAREER HIGHLIGHTS

- Drafted 218th overall by Denver in 1994.
- Was Pro Bowl selection five times (1997–2000 and 2003). No other offensive lineman in Broncos history has beaten this record.
- Holds record for most starts by a center in Broncos history (167).
- Named NFL Offensive Lineman of the Year (2003).

The respect Nalen has earned is reflected in an ESPN fan poll to select the Ultimate Super Bowl 40-Man Roster to commemorate Super Bowl XL in 2006. Nalen was the only active player listed among the 11 names provided on a ballot that included Mike Webster, Jeff Bostic, Bart Oates and Ray Mansfield.

The thumbnail sketch of Nalen recognizes his part in two Super Bowl wins. Nalen's blocking was a factor in Davis' 157-yard, three-touchdown game over Green Bay in Super Bowl XXXII, and his blocking also kept Atlanta from gaining any sacks in Super Bowl XXXIII.

Nalen, who hails from Foxborough, Massachusetts, is firmly committed to the Broncos, a point he emphasized in February 2005. That's when receiver Rod Smith, safety John Lynch, Plummer and Nalen—all core players for the Broncos—restructured their contracts to provide more cap room.

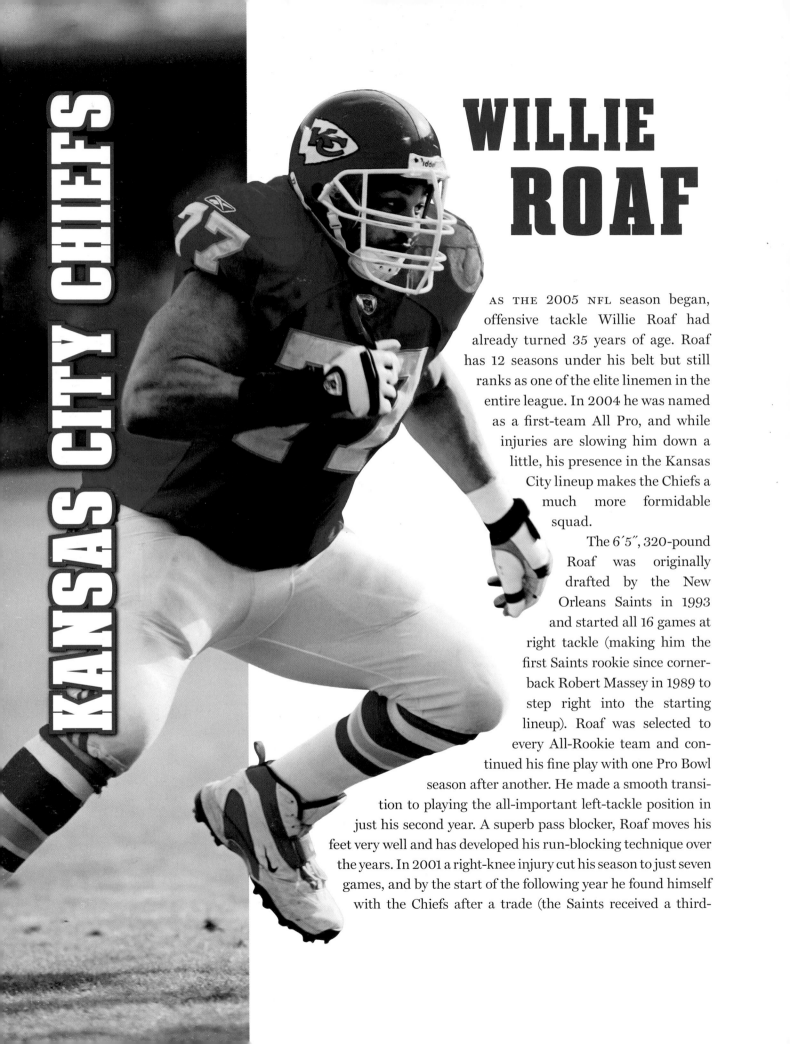

KANSAS CITY CHIEFS

WILLIE ROAF

AS THE 2005 NFL season began, offensive tackle Willie Roaf had already turned 35 years of age. Roaf has 12 seasons under his belt but still ranks as one of the elite linemen in the entire league. In 2004 he was named as a first-team All Pro, and while injuries are slowing him down a little, his presence in the Kansas City lineup makes the Chiefs a much more formidable squad.

The 6′5″, 320-pound Roaf was originally drafted by the New Orleans Saints in 1993 and started all 16 games at right tackle (making him the first Saints rookie since corner-back Robert Massey in 1989 to step right into the starting lineup). Roaf was selected to every All-Rookie team and continued his fine play with one Pro Bowl season after another. He made a smooth transition to playing the all-important left-tackle position in just his second year. A superb pass blocker, Roaf moves his feet very well and has developed his run-blocking technique over the years. In 2001 a right-knee injury cut his season to just seven games, and by the start of the following year he found himself with the Chiefs after a trade (the Saints received a third-

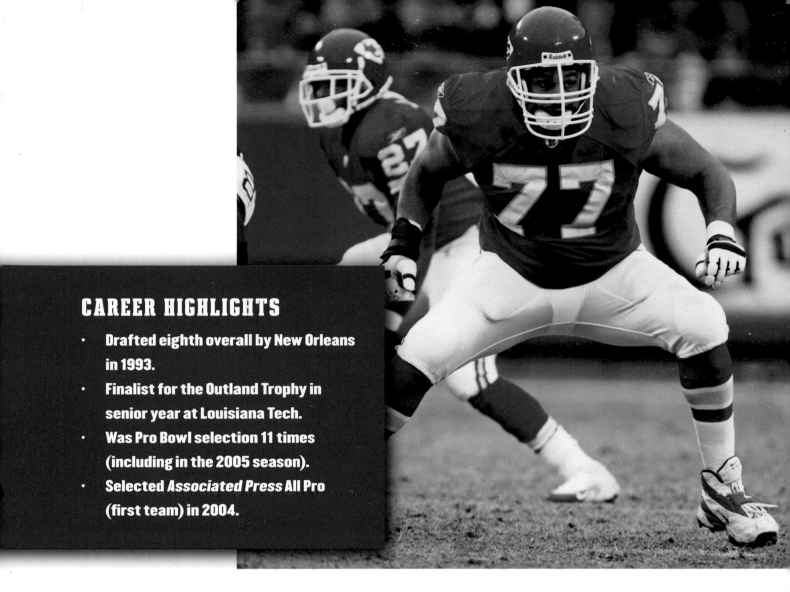

round pick in return). Roaf immediately paid dividends for Kansas City by earning another appearance in the Pro Bowl, and the Chiefs racked up 467 points (leading the NFL in 2002) and set a club record with 6,000 yards of offense.

He also played in all 16 games in both 2003 (a playoff year for the Chiefs) and 2004, and his Pro Bowl nominations have now reached a total of 10. The 2005 campaign saw Roaf deal with a nagging hamstring injury (he was able to start 10 games), but he was a welcome sight when he got into the lineup. Coach Dick Vermeil said the team was inspired just seeing the big man out at practice. The team scored 28 points in a win over Washington and rolled up 462 yards of offense in whipping the Miami Dolphins 30–20 with Roaf in the starting lineup. When the Chiefs' O-line is intact (the others in '05 included center Casey Wiegman, guards Brian Walters and Will

IN THE HUDDLE

Willie Roaf made a guest appearance on HBO's hit show *Arliss*.

Shields and right tackle Jordan Black), Kansas City is capable of beating any team in the NFL. Roaf was named to the Pro Bowl starting lineup, but the Chiefs missed the postseason despite a 10–6 record. Roaf believes he can play a couple more seasons if he is managed properly, which means he has to save everything for the games.

KICKERS WHO COME THROUGH IN THE CLUTCH

SPECIAL

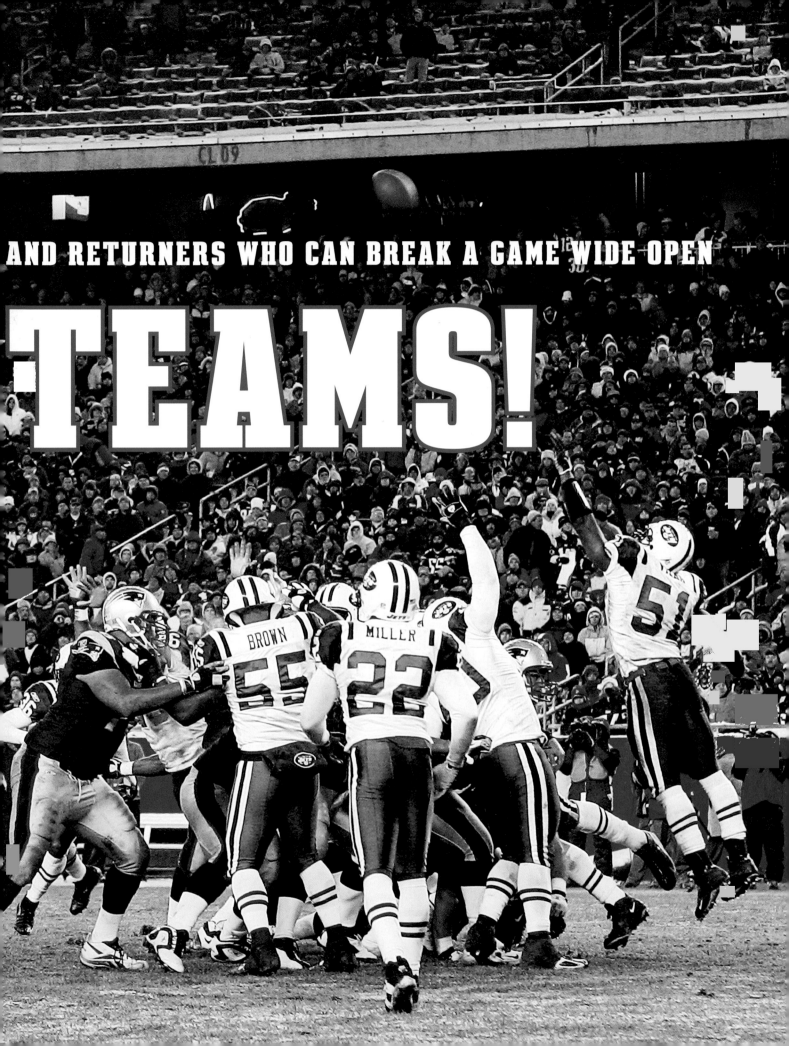

AND RETURNERS WHO CAN BREAK A GAME WIDE OPEN

TEAMS!

KANSAS CITY CHIEFS

DANTE HALL

KANSAS CITY CHIEFS kick returner Dante Hall is one of the smallest players in the NFL at 5′8″ and 187 pounds, but he is also one of the most dangerous. Although he may be short, Hall is solidly built and an explosive runner. His good vision allows him to pick and weave his way up the field on a return, and Hall's ability to bust a game wide open is legendary. The native of Chesapeake, Virginia, is so elusive that he can run backward trying to avoid tacklers and then turn a corner to get into open field. With his enormous skill set, Hall is also able to be used in the Chiefs' passing game, and he excels when the field is stretched on a screen pass or running a reverse. Versatile return men are hard to come by, so the Chiefs are lucky to have one as good as Hall.

Kansas City selected Hall with the 153rd pick of the 2000 NFL draft after a college career at Texas A&M. It was there that Hall totaled 4,707 all-purpose yards with 24 touchdowns and caught the eye of the pro scouts. He started slowly for the Chiefs (getting into only five games) in the 2000 season, and Kansas City decided to place him with the Scottish Claymores of NFL Europe for some seasoning (as a kick returner and wide receiver). He did well there and then came back to the Chiefs for 13 games in 2001. He started to make an impact during the 2002 season when he played in all 16 games and touched the ball 117 times for a total yardage of 2,120. He added two touchdowns on punt returns, one TD on a kickoff return and three as a pass receiver. His all-round perfor-

CAREER HIGHLIGHTS

- Drafted 153rd overall by Kansas City in 2000.
- Holds Chiefs' single-season record for most kickoff returns (68) and yards (1,718), established in 2004.
- Selected *Associated Press* All Pro in 2003.
- Was only one of three players to return a punt and kickoff for a TD in 2002.

mance earned him a spot in the Pro Bowl for the first time.

Hall's play reached new heights in 2003 when he scored a kick-return TD in four consecutive games (and he added one more major score on a kick return during the playoffs). He was named the AFC's Special Teams Player of the Week for each of those games, becoming the first player to earn that award for four straight weeks. He also established a team record for one season by averaging 16.3 yards on punt returns, and Hall made another trip to the Pro Bowl. By the 2004 season, he was no longer a secret weapon, and although his reception total went down to 25 (from 40 in '03), Hall led the entire NFL with 68 kickoff returns for a league-leading 1,718 yards (while scoring two touchdowns on those returns). Since he's a threat to score anytime he touches the ball, the Chiefs hoped to incorporate Hall

more into their offense as the 2005 season got under way, although it would be as a third or fourth wide receiver.

In the '05 campaign, Hall returned kickoffs for 1,560 yards (including one for 96 yards and a touchdown), although his spectacular plays

IN THE HUDDLE

Dante Hall holds the NFL single-season record for most kick returns for a touchdown, with four, a mark he set in 2004.

occurred a little less often. He contributed 2,283 yards of total offense, including 34 catches for 436 yards and five TDs when he played the wide receiver position. Hall's versatility must be respected by the opposition, and his skills make the Chiefs' attack very dangerous whenever he is out on the field.

TENNESSEE TITANS

PACMAN JONES

THE ROOKIE NFL season for Adam (Pacman) Jones was full of headlines. Initially, they pertained to his holdout from the Tennessee Titans and then to his brush with the law in the Nashville area.

Titans fans didn't take too kindly at the outset to the superbly skilled, speedy and agile cornerback/kickoff-punt returner. But once the season progressed, Jones won support his way.

When he dazzled the Texans with a 52-yard punt return for a touchdown at Houston in Week 14, Jones didn't forget Jeff Fisher. The Titans' head coach was en route to a dejecting 4–12 season, but Jones brought him the football. It was a token of the rookie's appreciation for Fisher's sticking by him throughout his ordeals on and off the field.

In fact, Jones had rejoined his teammates in Houston the night before facing the Texans, having returned from Atlanta, where he'd attended the funeral of a close friend who had been shot as well as the funeral of an aunt who had died earlier that week.

Jones' life story involves triumph over extreme adversity. He grew up in the Atlanta projects. Fatherless at the age of four, he considered himself fortunate to be raised by his mother, Deborah, and grandmother Chris-

tine, both strong guiding lights. Jones became the first member of his family to attend college, and the only game he'd miss while starring at West Virginia was to attend his grandmother's funeral after she died of cancer.

The Titans liked the versatility of the 5´10˝ Jones so much that they made him the first defensive player selected in the 2005 NFL draft. To commemorate his grandmother, on the day of the draft Jones wore a T-shirt with her picture on it.

Jones has said the NFL player he followed as a youngster was the brash and talented Deion Sanders, who excelled in his career because he backed up all his talk with consistent prime-time performances.

Fisher eased Jones into the lineup to start 2005, given the rookie's lost time due to the holdout. Jones finished his first pro season with 44 tackles and nine assists. He returned 43 kickoffs for 1,127 yards, with his average KO return of 26.2 yards ranking fourth in the NFL. Five of his kickoff returns exceeded 40 yards,

with 85 his longest. His 29 punt returns averaged 9.4 yards, good enough for ninth in the NFL. He returned four punts in excess of 20 yards, with his 52-yard score in Houston ranking as his finest.

Some view his stature as a detriment to his position, but he believes his quickness and reach more than make up for this. Blessed with potential, Jones didn't do himself any favors by taking

IN THE HUDDLE

Young Adam Jones was nicknamed Pacman by his mother because he attacked his baby bottle like the Pac-Man video game character.

two personal foul penalties within three plays in the final game of the season.

Fisher benched him immediately, and although Jones apologized the following day, his head coach said he must become less of a distraction to the team in future. The Titans have invested heavily in Jones. The rest is up to him.

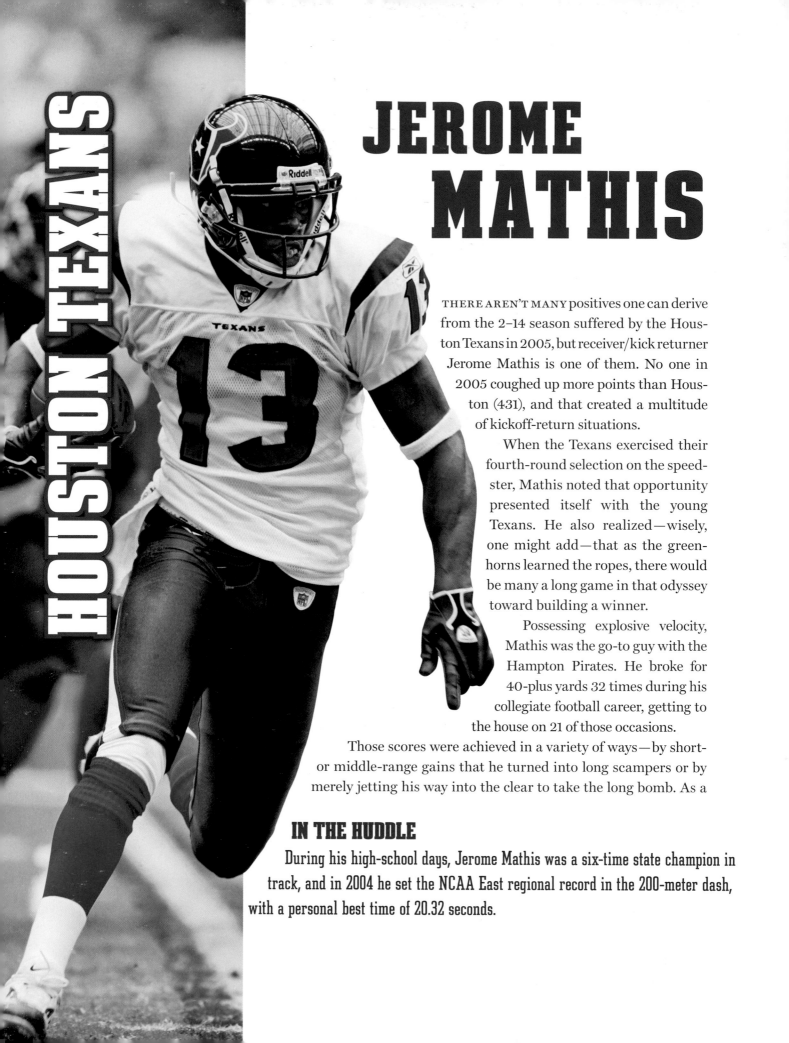

HOUSTON TEXANS

JEROME MATHIS

THERE AREN'T MANY positives one can derive from the 2–14 season suffered by the Houston Texans in 2005, but receiver/kick returner Jerome Mathis is one of them. No one in 2005 coughed up more points than Houston (431), and that created a multitude of kickoff-return situations.

When the Texans exercised their fourth-round selection on the speedster, Mathis noted that opportunity presented itself with the young Texans. He also realized—wisely, one might add—that as the greenhorns learned the ropes, there would be many a long game in that odyssey toward building a winner.

Possessing explosive velocity, Mathis was the go-to guy with the Hampton Pirates. He broke for 40-plus yards 32 times during his collegiate football career, getting to the house on 21 of those occasions. Those scores were achieved in a variety of ways—by short- or middle-range gains that he turned into long scampers or by merely jetting his way into the clear to take the long bomb. As a

IN THE HUDDLE

During his high-school days, Jerome Mathis was a six-time state champion in track, and in 2004 he set the NCAA East regional record in the 200-meter dash, with a personal best time of 20.32 seconds.

receiver, he averaged 129.74 yards per game in 35 games for the Pirates and averaged 26.6 yards—an NCAA record—with six TDs on 62 kickoff returns.

His times in pre-draft testing were eye-popping: 4.28 seconds in the 40-yard dash, 2.51 seconds over 20 yards, and 1.53 seconds over 10. At 5'11" and 172 pounds, his frame isn't imposing, but his game-breaking potential is.

Scratched from Houston's first two games of 2005, he made his NFL debut by returning five kickoffs for 130 yards at Cincinnati on October 2. Three weeks later, he electrified the home crowd, despite a 38–20 loss to Indianapolis, when he returned seven kickoffs for a Texans record 266 yards (fifth most all-time in the NFL), including the first kickoff-return TD in Texans history.

The following week, he was voted the AFC's Special Teams Player of the Week after his deft running paved the way for Houston's first win of the season, 19–16 over Cleveland. Mathis returned five kickoffs for 177 yards (35.4-yard average) against Cleveland.

Three weeks later the Texans absorbed another one-sided home loss against the Chiefs (45–17), but Mathis once again erupted for 266 kickoff-return yards, highlighted by a 99-yard TD—the longest return in Texans annals.

He was the only player to score two kickoff-return TDs in 2005, leading all rookies with a 28.6-yard average on kickoff returns, second to Buffalo's Terrence McGee, who had a 30.2-yard average. Mathis returned 54 kickoffs for 1,542 yards.

In the wake of the difficult season for the Texans, number 13's package of excitement in the 12 games he played did attract attention from fans, coaches and players. Despite his late addition to the NFL.com fan ballot, Mathis earned Pro Bowl selection as the AFC's kick-return specialist.

Given the tools he possesses, it likely won't be his last.

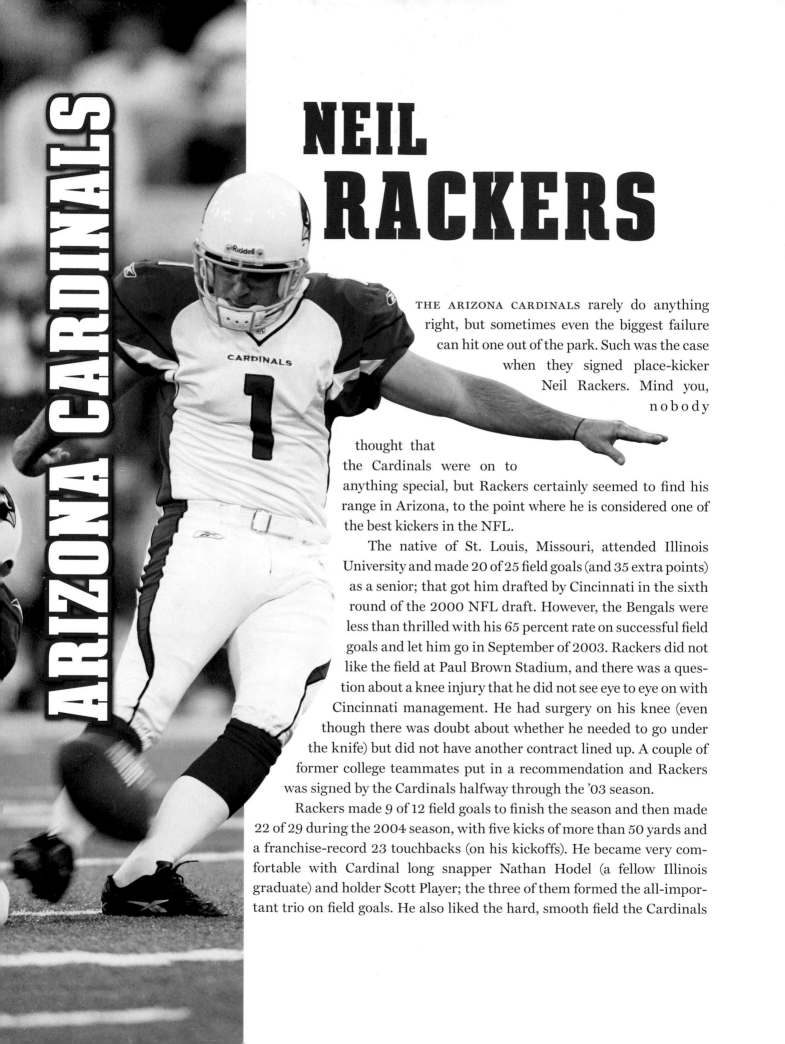

ARIZONA CARDINALS

NEIL RACKERS

THE ARIZONA CARDINALS rarely do anything right, but sometimes even the biggest failure can hit one out of the park. Such was the case when they signed place-kicker Neil Rackers. Mind you, nobody thought that the Cardinals were on to anything special, but Rackers certainly seemed to find his range in Arizona, to the point where he is considered one of the best kickers in the NFL.

The native of St. Louis, Missouri, attended Illinois University and made 20 of 25 field goals (and 35 extra points) as a senior; that got him drafted by Cincinnati in the sixth round of the 2000 NFL draft. However, the Bengals were less than thrilled with his 65 percent rate on successful field goals and let him go in September of 2003. Rackers did not like the field at Paul Brown Stadium, and there was a question about a knee injury that he did not see eye to eye on with Cincinnati management. He had surgery on his knee (even though there was doubt about whether he needed to go under the knife) but did not have another contract lined up. A couple of former college teammates put in a recommendation and Rackers was signed by the Cardinals halfway through the '03 season.

Rackers made 9 of 12 field goals to finish the season and then made 22 of 29 during the 2004 season, with five kicks of more than 50 yards and a franchise-record 23 touchbacks (on his kickoffs). He became very comfortable with Cardinal long snapper Nathan Hodel (a fellow Illinois graduate) and holder Scott Player; the three of them formed the all-important trio on field goals. He also liked the hard, smooth field the Cardinals

CAREER HIGHLIGHTS

- Drafted 169th overall by Cincinnati in 2000.
- Signed as a free agent by Arizona in 2003.
- Kicked a career-best 55-yard field goal in 2004 season.
- Kicked six field goals in one game versus San Francisco in 2005.

play on, claiming it can give him a 10-yard boost when everything is just right. With his confidence soaring, Rackers entered the 2005 season ready to have the best year of his career.

The 6´, 200-pound kicker was having a dream season in '05 prior to an injury in early December. His season was perfect until he missed a field goal against Jacksonville on November 27, but he still made 40 of 42 FGs on the season for the still-hapless Cardinals (5–11 on the year) to go along with 20 PATs. Six of his kicks were 50 yards or better (54 was the longest), and coach Dennis Green would not hesitate to use the strong-legged kicker whenever they got close to his range. In a game against the San Francisco 49ers that was played in Mexico City, Rackers left an impression by hitting six of six field goals, leading his team to a 31–14 victory. He finished with a total of 140 points, good for

second place in NFL scoring among kickers. Rackers would like to make a 60-yard-plus kick, and there is little doubt he will get it done in this range sooner or later. The NFL record of 63 yards may well be in jeopardy. Rackers' excellent record since joining Arizona was rewarded with a long-

IN THE HUDDLE

Neil Rackers set an NFL record for most field goals in one season in 2005, when he had 40. His mark was one better than Olindo Mare (Miami in 1999) and Jeff Wilkins (St. Louis in 2003), who had previously shared the record with 39.

term contract that will see his pay go as high as $4.5 million per year by 2009. It's likely to be a very good investment for the Cardinals, and they could use more of them if they are to improve their lot in the NFL.

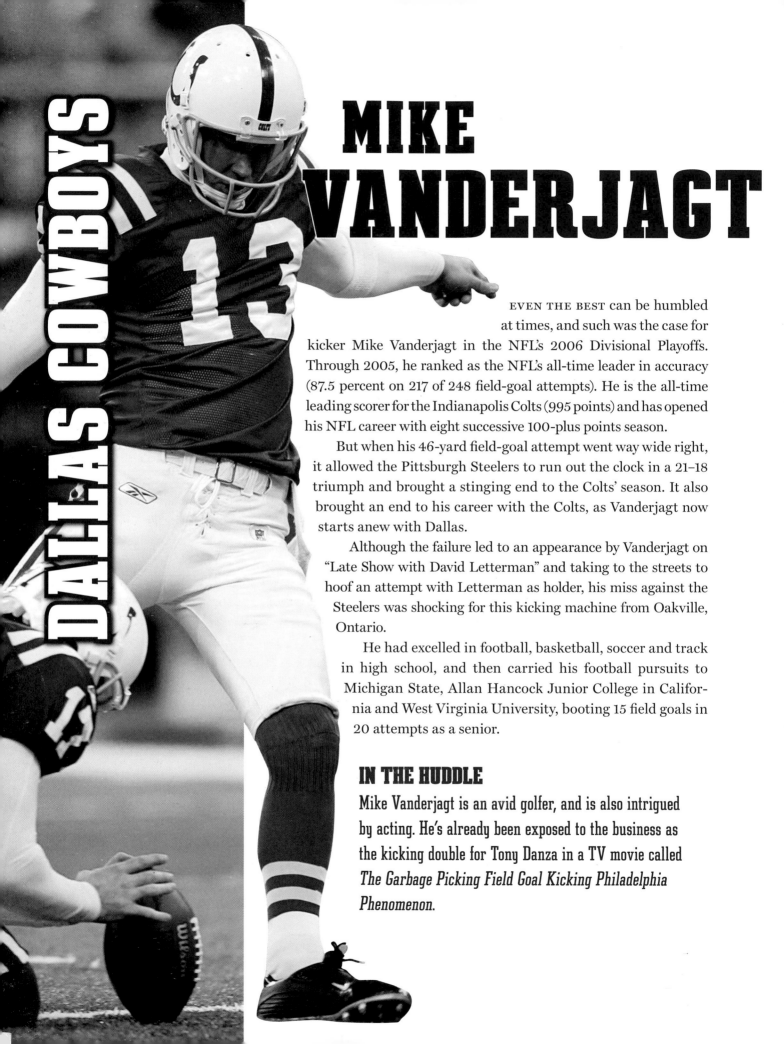

MIKE VANDERJAGT

DALLAS COWBOYS

EVEN THE BEST can be humbled at times, and such was the case for kicker Mike Vanderjagt in the NFL's 2006 Divisional Playoffs. Through 2005, he ranked as the NFL's all-time leader in accuracy (87.5 percent on 217 of 248 field-goal attempts). He is the all-time leading scorer for the Indianapolis Colts (995 points) and has opened his NFL career with eight successive 100-plus points season.

But when his 46-yard field-goal attempt went way wide right, it allowed the Pittsburgh Steelers to run out the clock in a 21–18 triumph and brought a stinging end to the Colts' season. It also brought an end to his career with the Colts, as Vanderjagt now starts anew with Dallas.

Although the failure led to an appearance by Vanderjagt on "Late Show with David Letterman" and taking to the streets to hoof an attempt with Letterman as holder, his miss against the Steelers was shocking for this kicking machine from Oakville, Ontario.

He had excelled in football, basketball, soccer and track in high school, and then carried his football pursuits to Michigan State, Allan Hancock Junior College in California and West Virginia University, booting 15 field goals in 20 attempts as a senior.

IN THE HUDDLE

Mike Vanderjagt is an avid golfer, and is also intrigued by acting. He's already been exposed to the business as the kicking double for Tony Danza in a TV movie called *The Garbage Picking Field Goal Kicking Philadelphia Phenomenon.*

He tried to latch on to several Canadian Football League clubs without much luck except for two games with Saskatchewan in 1993. His breakthrough occurred in 1996 when he served as kicker/punter for the Toronto Argonauts—Grey Cup champions under the brilliant quarterbacking of Doug Flutie.

Vanderjagt's ticket to the NFL finally came in 1998 with the Colts. He achieved the third-best field-goal percentage of any rookie or first-year player in the NFL with 87.1 (27 of 31). He was also perfect on point-after attempts (23 of 23).

The following season, Vanderjagt booted himself into the Colts' record book with 26 consecutive field goals to end 1999. At 6′5″ and 211 pounds, Vanderjagt kept the momentum building. He exuded a brashness and confidence, backed by a strong leg that made field-goal attempts—short or long—good far more often than not.

On December 23, 2003, Vanderjagt kicked his 41st consecutive regular-season field goal to erase the NFL record set by Gary Anderson. It was a 43-yard boot that gave Indianapolis a 20–17 win at Houston in the final game of the season. His line for the 2003 season: 37 of 37 on field goals, 46 of 46 on PATs.

After starting the next season with a field goal in New England, his next three-point attempt (from 48 yards) against the Patriots missed—and Vanderjagt's record streak ended at 42 on September 9, 2004.

Off the field, the ever-quotable Vanderjagt has twice caused a stir. During an interview with The Score Television Network in Canada after the 2002 season, he took Colts quarterback Peyton Manning to task for lacking emotion and criticized head coach Tony Dungy for being too placid. Eventually Vanderjagt apologized, but neither Manning nor Dungy was amused by the incident.

Then, during the 2005 playoffs, Vanderjagt irked the Patriots when he said they were ripe for the taking. The Patriots used that comment as an incentive and defeated the Colts 20–3 en route to another Super Bowl season.

Yes, Vanderjagt does speak his mind. But his remarks are usually supported by a kicking game unmatched in NFL history. That's why his few miscues always stand out.

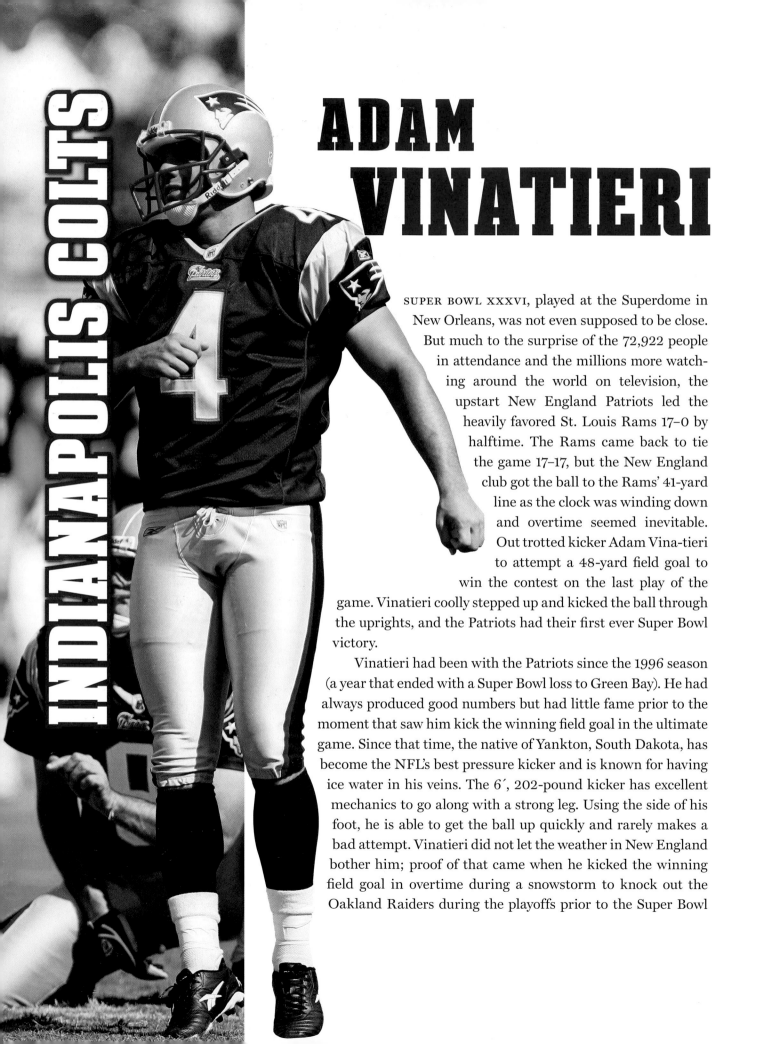

INDIANAPOLIS COLTS

ADAM VINATIERI

SUPER BOWL XXXVI, played at the Superdome in New Orleans, was not even supposed to be close. But much to the surprise of the 72,922 people in attendance and the millions more watching around the world on television, the upstart New England Patriots led the heavily favored St. Louis Rams 17–0 by halftime. The Rams came back to tie the game 17–17, but the New England club got the ball to the Rams' 41-yard line as the clock was winding down and overtime seemed inevitable. Out trotted kicker Adam Vina-tieri to attempt a 48-yard field goal to win the contest on the last play of the game. Vinatieri coolly stepped up and kicked the ball through the uprights, and the Patriots had their first ever Super Bowl victory.

Vinatieri had been with the Patriots since the 1996 season (a year that ended with a Super Bowl loss to Green Bay). He had always produced good numbers but had little fame prior to the moment that saw him kick the winning field goal in the ultimate game. Since that time, the native of Yankton, South Dakota, has become the NFL's best pressure kicker and is known for having ice water in his veins. The 6´, 202-pound kicker has excellent mechanics to go along with a strong leg. Using the side of his foot, he is able to get the ball up quickly and rarely makes a bad attempt. Vinatieri did not let the weather in New England bother him; proof of that came when he kicked the winning field goal in overtime during a snowstorm to knock out the Oakland Raiders during the playoffs prior to the Super Bowl

win in New Orleans. In short, Vinatieri seems to thrive under pressure, and he is a model of consistency.

Vinatieri's teammates love having such a reliable kicker. They know he can kick a game-winning FG in the first week of the season and do likewise in the Super Bowl. (He had a second Vince Lombardi Trophy–winning kick). During Super Bowl XXXVIII in Houston, when the Patriots edged Carolina 31–29 on a kick by Vinatieri with just four seconds to play.) Quarterback Tom Brady knew he just had to get inside the other team's 50-yard line to give his club a chance to steal a victory, which provided him with many more options when he was trying to run a late-game offense.

Vinatieri's calmness in the face of a storm gives his team and coach great confidence in his abilities to get off a successful kick in the clutch. Early in the 2005 season, the Vinatieri legend grew as he drilled a 48-yard field goal through the uprights to knock off the Steelers 23–20 right in Pittsburgh in the third week of the year. That kick marked the 18th time Vinatieri had knocked through a game-winning kick in his career. Two weeks later Vinatieri broke the hearts of the hometown Falcons fans when he kicked another game winner to edge Atlanta 31–28.

IN THE HUDDLE

Adam Vinatieri was never drafted by an NFL team and began his professional career with the Amsterdam Admirals of the World League in 1996.

The Patriots had a rather difficult year in 2005, but they still managed to post a 10–6 record, good enough to finish first in the AFC East, with Vinatieri managing an even 100 points on the season. New England was bounced from the playoffs by Denver, and Vinatieri then signed with Indianapolis during the off-season.

DEFENSIVE

BACKS!

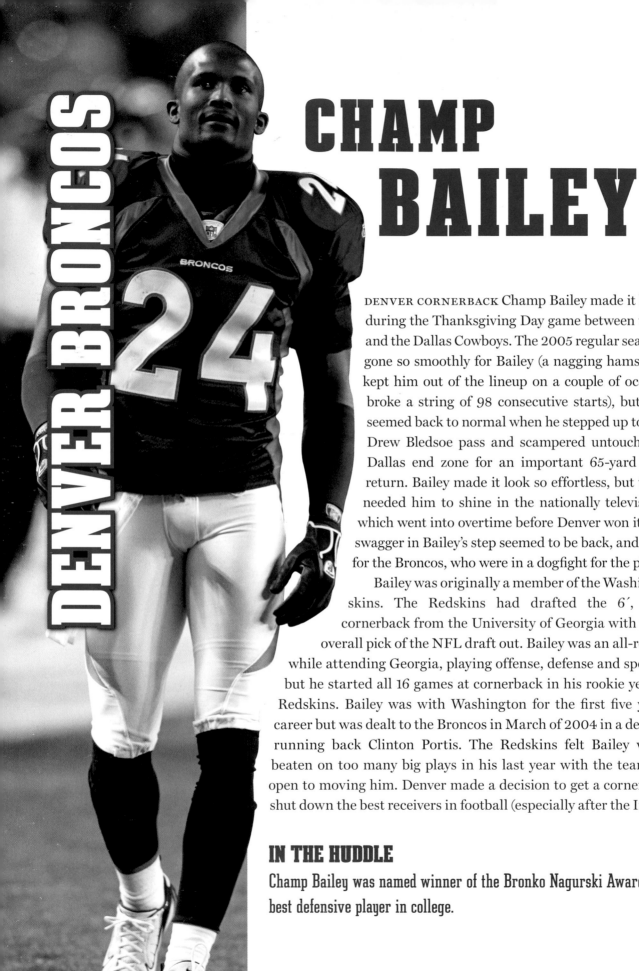

DENVER BRONCOS

CHAMP BAILEY

DENVER CORNERBACK Champ Bailey made it look so easy during the Thanksgiving Day game between the Broncos and the Dallas Cowboys. The 2005 regular season had not gone so smoothly for Bailey (a nagging hamstring injury kept him out of the lineup on a couple of occasions and broke a string of 98 consecutive starts), but everything seemed back to normal when he stepped up to intercept a Drew Bledsoe pass and scampered untouched into the Dallas end zone for an important 65-yard touchdown return. Bailey made it look so effortless, but the Broncos needed him to shine in the nationally televised contest, which went into overtime before Denver won it 24–21. The swagger in Bailey's step seemed to be back, and just in time for the Broncos, who were in a dogfight for the playoffs.

Bailey was originally a member of the Washington Redskins. The Redskins had drafted the 6´, 192-pound cornerback from the University of Georgia with the seventh overall pick of the NFL draft out. Bailey was an all-round threat while attending Georgia, playing offense, defense and special teams, but he started all 16 games at cornerback in his rookie year with the Redskins. Bailey was with Washington for the first five years of his career but was dealt to the Broncos in March of 2004 in a deal involving running back Clinton Portis. The Redskins felt Bailey was getting beaten on too many big plays in his last year with the team and were open to moving him. Denver made a decision to get a corner who could shut down the best receivers in football (especially after the Indianapolis

IN THE HUDDLE

Champ Bailey was named winner of the Bronko Nagurski Award (1999) as best defensive player in college.

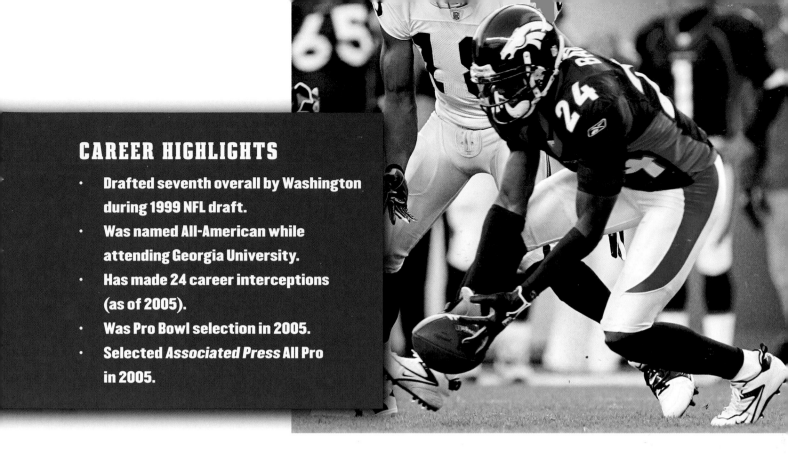

- Drafted seventh overall by Washington during 1999 NFL draft.
- Was named All-American while attending Georgia University.
- Has made 24 career interceptions (as of 2005).
- Was Pro Bowl selection in 2005.
- Selected *Associated Press* All Pro in 2005.

Colts stung them badly in the playoffs during a 41–10 rout in the 2003 playoffs). They were fully prepared to give up a quality running back like Portis to make the deal happen.

Although he does not have the great size typically needed to cover the top wide receivers, Bailey makes up for it with great athletic ability, and he is a sure tackler. He has good recovery speed when someone gets in behind him, and his ball-handling skills are first-rate. Bailey is adequate against running plays, but it's clear his strength is in stopping the pass. The Broncos had such faith in him that they gave Bailey a seven-year $63-million-dollar deal when they acquired him prior to the '04 season. Many consider him one of the best corners in the entire league (he was an All Pro selection for the 2004 season), while a smaller group thinks Bailey has slipped since his early days as a Redskin (the Colts still got the best of Denver again in the '04 playoffs, this time by a 49–24 score). Time will tell if the Broncos overpaid for Bailey (they introduced rookie corners on the team in '05), but he is considered a good team leader and a player with lots of character.

The Broncos made the playoffs with a 13–3 record, good for first place in the AFC West. Bailey helped lead the way to the postseason once again with eight interceptions and 64 solo tackles, despite missing two games. He further proved his value to the team by picking off a Tom Brady pass during a playoff game against the defending champions and took it back 99 yards when it looked like the Patriots were about to take over the contest. Bailey's return set up a touchdown, which helped end New England's hope for a third straight Super Bowl. Denver lost the AFC Championship Game at home to Pittsburgh, and Bailey did not have his finest performance that day. However, his outstanding season in '05 was recognized with a selection to the All Pro team and a spot on the Pro Bowl team.

Many would now consider Bailey the Broncos' most valuable player, a sentiment that is hard to argue against based on his performance since he joined the Denver club.

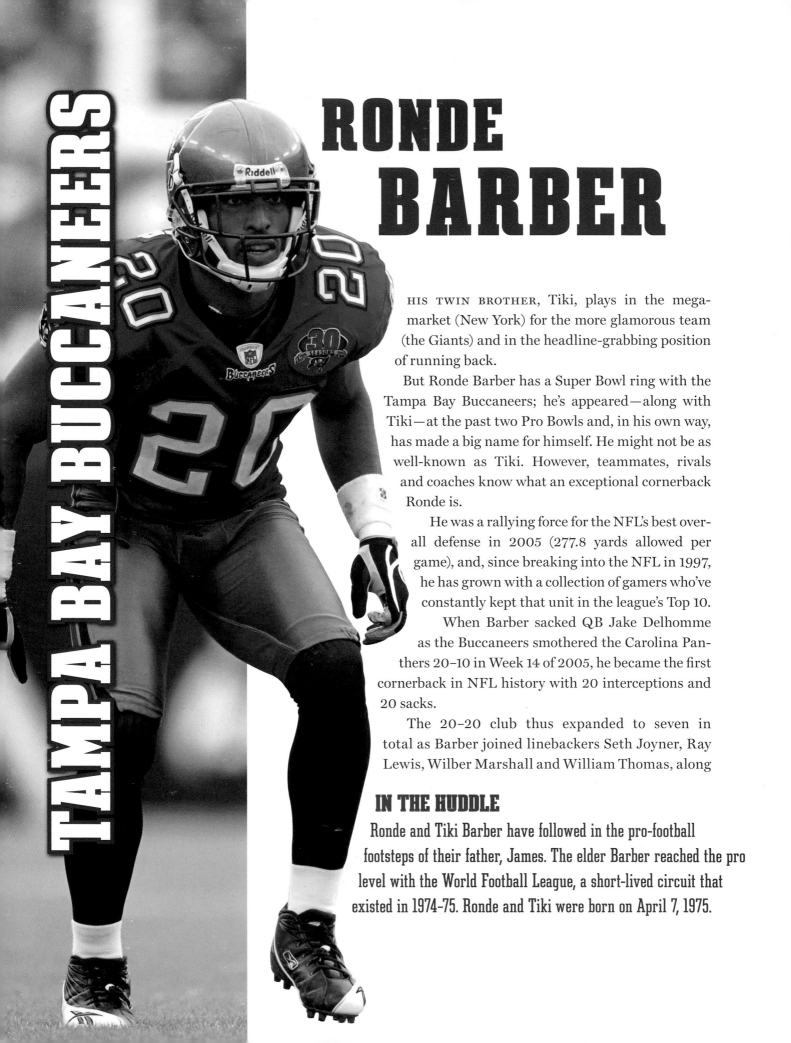

TAMPA BAY BUCCANEERS

RONDE BARBER

HIS TWIN BROTHER, Tiki, plays in the mega-market (New York) for the more glamorous team (the Giants) and in the headline-grabbing position of running back.

But Ronde Barber has a Super Bowl ring with the Tampa Bay Buccaneers; he's appeared—along with Tiki—at the past two Pro Bowls and, in his own way, has made a big name for himself. He might not be as well-known as Tiki. However, teammates, rivals and coaches know what an exceptional cornerback Ronde is.

He was a rallying force for the NFL's best over-all defense in 2005 (277.8 yards allowed per game), and, since breaking into the NFL in 1997, he has grown with a collection of gamers who've constantly kept that unit in the league's Top 10.

When Barber sacked QB Jake Delhomme as the Buccaneers smothered the Carolina Panthers 20–10 in Week 14 of 2005, he became the first cornerback in NFL history with 20 interceptions and 20 sacks.

The 20–20 club thus expanded to seven in total as Barber joined linebackers Seth Joyner, Ray Lewis, Wilber Marshall and William Thomas, along

IN THE HUDDLE

Ronde and Tiki Barber have followed in the pro-football footsteps of their father, James. The elder Barber reached the pro level with the World Football League, a short-lived circuit that existed in 1974-75. Ronde and Tiki were born on April 7, 1975.

with safeties LeRoy Butler and Rodney Harrison.

Hailing from Roanoke, Virginia, the Barber brothers remain close to this day and keep in contact with each other several times a week. They both attended the University of Virginia and starred for the Virginia Cavaliers, and they were both drafted in 1997—Tiki by the Giants 36th overall in the second round and Ronde by the Buccaneers 30 spots and one round later.

Ronde got into one NFL game in 1997 as opposed to 12 for Tiki. Ronde took hold as Tampa Bay's permanent right corner in 1998, and he has been a consistent force ever since.

A hard tackler, he combines an excellent sense of timing with his quickness and agility to put up consistent interception and sack numbers. He set a Buccaneers record with 10 interceptions in 2001 when he and Anthony Henry of the Cleveland Browns tied for the NFL lead. That was the first time that anyone in the NFL had reached double-digit interceptions since 1990, when Mark Carrier of the Chicago Bears did so.

Barber won numerous awards and honors for his all-star play in 2001. He was selected to play on the *Associated Press* All Pro Team (First Team), and on *Pro Football Weekly*'s All-NFL Team, as well as being named to the Pro Bowl. He was also named NFL Alumni Defensive Back of the Year.

A fractured thumb and a knee injury plagued him in 2002, but he still started all 16 games, although his interception total dropped by eight. He did earn selection to *Sports Illustrated*'s All Pro Team and made *Associated Press* All Pro (Second Team).

The crowning achievement awaited the Buccaneers that season as they won Super Bowl XXXVII over the Oakland Raiders. Barber prevailed in the NFC Championship Game at Philadelphia with three tackles, one sack, a forced fumble and a fourth-quarter interception off Donovan McNabb, which he converted into a 92-yard TD romp. The performance made Barber the NFC's Defensive Player of the Week.

Barber reached a career-high 79 tackles in 2003, but he surpassed that total with 83 in 2004 and the same number in 2005. Tampa Bay's defense held tough in the Wild Card playoff loss to the Washington Redskins, permitting a mere 120 yards and a puny 25 through the air.

Mistakes ruined that airtight performance, but the unit will keep the Buccaneers challenging. Barber ended 2005 with a total of 28 career interceptions, three off the club mark. As Tiki has injected his name into the Giants' record book, Ronde has blazed his own trail in the Buccaneers' annals.

PHILADELPHIA EAGLES

BRIAN DAWKINS

IF BRIAN DAWKINS is not the best safety in the NFL, he is very close. A member of the Philadelphia Eagles since his NFL career began in 1996, Dawkins has reached the point where his name is often mentioned when defensive stars are discussed. He was named to every All Pro team for his performance in the 2004 season (a year that saw him record 62 tackles with four interceptions). This earned him the recognition he deserves but often does not get because he is so consistent.

The 6´, 210-pound Dawkins was drafted out of Clemson University after he gained All-American status (234 career tackles in college) there. The Eagles selected the hard-hitting safety with the 61st selection of the '96 draft, and Dawkins started 13 games as a rookie (recording 53 tackles and three interceptions). The Philadelphia fans quickly learned that Dawkins, who is a mild-mannered family man off the field, is a high-intensity performer once the game begins. A hard-nosed player, he is one of the best blitzing safeties in the league and leaves everything on the field. He is considered a team leader (perhaps even more than the offensive stars on the club) and helps to guide young defensive players like Sheldon Brown and Lito Sheppard. Dawkins is very committed to training (sometimes joining the players on offense to get ready for the season) and shows a good example to his teammates.

The thing that makes Dawkins so dangerous to any receiver or quarterback who wants to challenge him is his great football instincts. He shows no significant weakness and his mistakes are few and far between. Dawkins has great range in the field (he is especially good in zone coverage) and can easily track a ball in the air. He makes the receiver pay for his catch and

can often knock the ball loose with a solid hit. By the end of the season, Dawkins usually leads the team in tackles, passes knocked down and interceptions, with the Eagles coming to expect that he will lead in all the important defensive categories. As a team leader, Dawkins has learned when he can push his teammates to greater heights, and this has helped the Eagles reach the NFC title game for four straight years (2002 to 2005) with one trip to the Super Bowl.

Dawkins has always believed that he can find a way to get the job done even in dire circumstances. In the first game of the 2005 season, for example, Dawkins had to take IV during the game against the Atlanta Falcons and then suffered back spasms. However, he still found a way to get back on the field to make a big stop on Atlanta quarterback Michael Vick (although the Falcons won the game 14–10). Injuries to key players set the Eagles back significantly during the '05 season, and they missed the playoffs. The hard-pressed Eagles defense gave up more points than was ever anticipated (including four games

IN THE HUDDLE

Being named to the "All-Madden team" is quite an honor for any player. Brian Dawkins earned that distinction in 2001, when former NFL coach and current TV analyst John Madden put him on his dream team.

of more than 30 points), but Philadelphia still has enough good players in the prime of their career to make a comeback in 2006. One of those leading the charge will be Dawkins, who, along with fellow safety Michael Lewis, still forms one of the best defensive tandems in the NFL.

CINCINNATI BENGALS

DELTHA O'NEAL

SOMETIMES ALL A talented athlete needs is a change of scenery to regain his form. Such was the case for the versatile and highly rated Deltha O'Neal. He recovered his Pro Bowl credentials once he was traded to the Cincinnati Bengals by the Denver Broncos.

After a standout career at the University of California, the cornerback attained Pro Bowl status in 2001 as a sophomore with the Broncos. But by 2003, he had fallen from the penthouse to head coach Mike Shanahan's doghouse.

That wasn't an easy time for O'Neal, who has admitted to being a hot dog from time to time. He was a player with an edge and a swag-

IN THE HUDDLE

A graduate of Milpitas (California) High School, O'Neal was not only an exceptional athlete, with a school-record 2,312 yards rushing, but also president of the student body in his senior year.

ger to support all his skills. But suddenly he had lost his confidence and was no longer wanted by the Broncos, who had selected him in the first round of the 2000 NFL draft.

It was a position O'Neal had earned following his success at Cal, where he became the school's leader in all-purpose yards (5,005) and interception yards (356). He was a versatile football player who scored his 12 TDs in five ways—five by interception returns, two by kickoff returns, two by rushing, two by receiving and one by punt return.

That resourcefulness was useful in his first NFL season as he became a kick/punt returner, special teams player and sometimes defensive player. *The Football News* picked him as an All-Rookie punt returner. He finished seventh in the AFC as a punt returner (averaging 10.4 yards) and sixth in kickoff returns (finishing with 1,102 yards).

He started all 16 games at the corner for the Broncos in 2001 and finished with nine interceptions, the second most interceptions in franchise history. Six of them came in October, including a four-interception game against Kansas City to tie the NFL record for most steals in a game. He was named the AFC's Defensive Player of October 2001.

He led the Broncos with five interceptions in 2002 but came up with only one in 2003, when he played 13 games and was inactive for the Broncos' postseason game. Throughout his four seasons with the Broncos, O'Neal remained the club's primary punt returner.

The Broncos and the Bengals completed a transaction on April 9, 2004, where O'Neal and Denver's 24th and 117th slots in the 2004 NFL draft went to Cincinnati for the number 17 choice.

The Bengals and head coach Marvin Lewis believed O'Neal could assist the club in its hopes to build a contender. O'Neal started 10 of the 12 games he played in 2004, with four interceptions for 60 yards and one TD. One of those picks was a 29-yard return off Jake Plummer in Cincinnati's win over Denver. Unable to control himself, O'Neal pointed his index finger in the air within view of Shanahan. It was a ploy that Lewis didn't like very much, but O'Neal felt vindicated and he had to let loose.

In 2005, when the Bengals qualified for the playoffs for the first time since 1991, O'Neal and Ty Law of the New York Jets tied for the NFL lead with 10 interceptions. With his steal of a Jeff Garcia pass during the second quarter of Cincinnati's 41–17 win at Detroit, O'Neal's 10th interception of the season shattered the Bengals' record of nine, which had been set by Ken Riley in 1976.

The Bengals finished 11–5 in 2005 to win the AFC North Division title before bowing out to the Pittsburgh Steelers in the Wild Card matchup. For O'Neal, it was a return to the upper echelon of ball-hawking defensive backs.

PITTSBURGH STEELERS

TROY POLAMALU

PITTSBURGH STEELERS SAFETY Troy Polamalu is a unique player, and not just because of his hairdo! Smallish at just 5´10˝ and 212 pounds, Polamalu can cover a receiver as a cornerback and can also deliver a walloping hit as a safety is supposed to. He has good speed and plays on great instinct, which allows him to line up all over the field. No quarterback is sure what Polamalu will do on any given play, and Steelers defensive coordinator Dick LeBeau gives him the freedom he needs to cause havoc by letting him play close to the line of scrimmage. On one play he might be a safety, on another he might be a linebacker, and on other occasions he can be a rush end! He can time a hit just perfectly to jar a ball loose, and he has a reputation as a defender whom the offense (especially anyone who

IN THE HUDDLE

Troy Polamalu tied an NFL record for safeties by recording three quarterback sacks in a game against Houston on September 18, 2005, during a 27-7 Pittsburgh victory.

might catch the ball) must be wary of at all times. Polamalu has a great enthusiasm for the game, which sometimes means he gambles too much, but more experience should take care of that problem. At the tender age of 24, Pola-malu has plenty of time to get better.

Polamalu is the consummate professional most of the time, but on occasion he can let his aggressiveness get the better of him. He will help up an opponent after delivering a crushing hit and quietly saunter back to the huddle. Not known as a trash talker, Polamalu is very intense when he lets his hair down on game day. On occasion he has crossed the line and earned some personal fouls, but he is working at staying on the right side of the rules. He has taken the time to study the other top safeties in the league because he does not want to fall behind his peers.

His efforts appear to be working, as evidenced by his performance in the 2004 season, when he led the Steelers with five interceptions and was tied for second in tackles when he had 97. The former USC graduate continued his good play during the 2005 campaign. For example, he returned a Green Bay fumble 77 yards for a touchdown in a 20–10 win and had an outstanding performance against San Diego in the fifth week of the season, with eight tackles and an assist in a 24–22 win.

Polamalu was raised by a single mother in Santa Ana, California. However, after visiting his football-playing cousin in Oregon, he asked his mother if he could stay with his uncle's family. Oregon provided a different sort of life, and his mother soon realized this would be best for Troy. He became a high-school football star in Oregon

CAREER HIGHLIGHTS

- Drafted 16th overall by the Pittsburgh Steelers in 2003.
- Was named an All-American twice while attending USC.
- Was Pro Bowl selection in 2004 and 2005.
- Selected *Associated Press* All Pro in 2005.
- Was a member of the Super Bowl XL winning team

but returned to his home state to attend Southern California, where he became a Trojan in 1999. He was named an All-American twice as a Trojan and was considered the best defensive back to play at the school since the days of Ronnie Lott. He had 278 career tackles while playing in college and returned three passes for touchdowns and blocked four punts during his time as a USC. His play caught the eye of the Steelers, who made him a first-round choice (16th overall in 2003), and he became a starter in 2004, earning his first appearance in the Pro Bowl.

Polamalu's performance in 2005 (91 total tackles, 73 solo) earned him a spot on the All Pro team and another nomination to the Pro Bowl. He continued his fine play in the postseason (he seemed to rattle Colts quarterback Peyton Manning to the point of distraction and made five solo tackles versus Denver); the tough Steeler defense was a big reason they made it all the way to Detroit for Super Bowl XL. A 21–10 victory over the Seattle Seahawks earned the Steelers their fifth Vince Lombardi Trophy. Polamalu and mates had held the Seattle attack in check for most of the game.

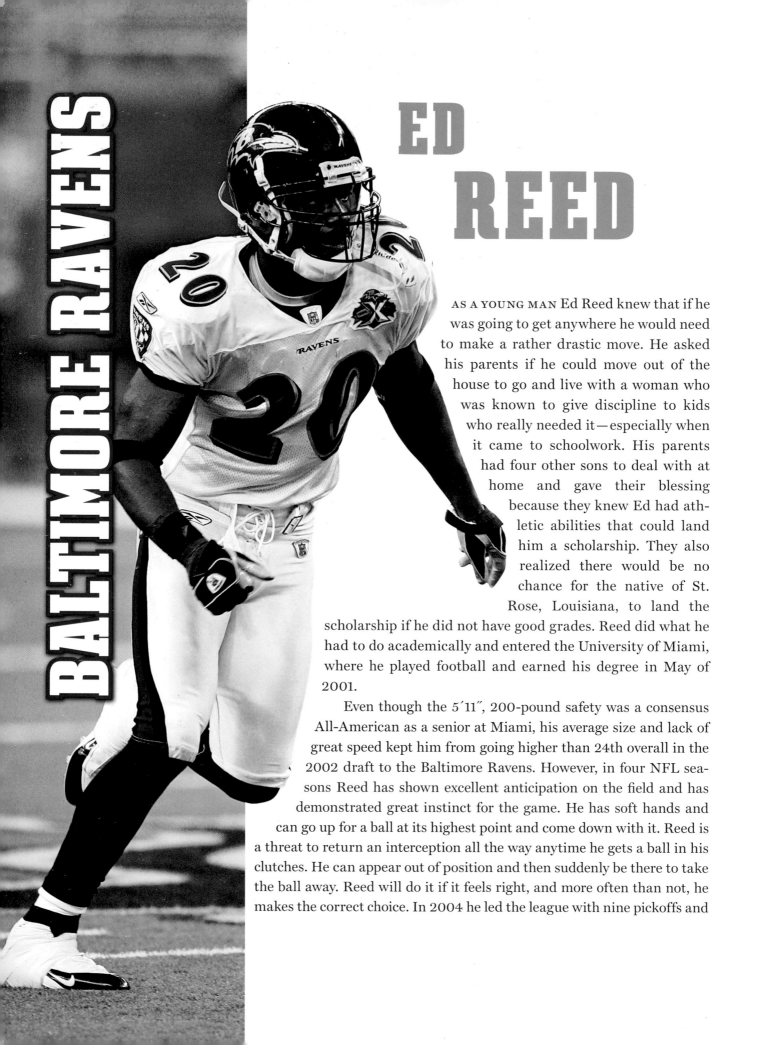

BALTIMORE RAVENS

ED REED

AS A YOUNG MAN Ed Reed knew that if he was going to get anywhere he would need to make a rather drastic move. He asked his parents if he could move out of the house to go and live with a woman who was known to give discipline to kids who really needed it—especially when it came to schoolwork. His parents had four other sons to deal with at home and gave their blessing because they knew Ed had athletic abilities that could land him a scholarship. They also realized there would be no chance for the native of St. Rose, Louisiana, to land the scholarship if he did not have good grades. Reed did what he had to do academically and entered the University of Miami, where he played football and earned his degree in May of 2001.

Even though the 5´11˝, 200-pound safety was a consensus All-American as a senior at Miami, his average size and lack of great speed kept him from going higher than 24th overall in the 2002 draft to the Baltimore Ravens. However, in four NFL seasons Reed has shown excellent anticipation on the field and has demonstrated great instinct for the game. He has soft hands and can go up for a ball at its highest point and come down with it. Reed is a threat to return an interception all the way anytime he gets a ball in his clutches. He can appear out of position and then suddenly be there to take the ball away. Reed will do it if it feels right, and more often than not, he makes the correct choice. In 2004 he led the league with nine pickoffs and

returned them for an NFL-record 358 yards. He made 89 tackles in the '04 season and earned the NFL's Defensive Player of the Year honors—only the third safety to earn the award in 34 years.

Reed has stayed humble during his rise to NFL stardom and has gained the respect of teammates and opponents alike. He is a great student of the game and has left an impression on top quarterbacks like Ben Roethlisberger (Pittsburgh) and Tom Brady (New England). Both are amazed at how often Reed is around the ball and marvel at his ability to cover the field so quickly. Quarterbacks can learn to avoid some cornerbacks, but there is no way they can get rid of Reed. The low-key Reed has developed his style around the notion that first he must listen, then learn, and finally lead. Coupled with former college teammate Ray Lewis at middle linebacker, it appears the Ravens have two of the best defensive stalwarts in the entire NFL.

The 2005 season was not kind to the 26-year-old Reed, as a high ankle sprain forced him to miss many games (he played in 10 games), and the entire Ravens club was ravaged by the injury bug, finishing the year with a mediocre 6–10 record. It was not the kind of season he was hoping to have after such an impressive performance in '04. The Ravens will likely be in store for some

IN THE HUDDLE

Ed Reed set an NFL record for longest interception return when he picked off a Cleveland pass and brought it back 106 yards for a touchdown on November 7, 2004.

changes prior to the start of the 2006 season (hopefully they will find an offense to take some of the pressure off the superb defense), but there is no doubt the very talented Reed will be a dominating force in the NFL for years to come.

MINNESOTA VIKINGS

DARREN SHARPER

FOOTBALL RUNS DEEP in the Sharper household. Harry Sharper's memorable days at Virginia State allowed him to attend training camp with the Kansas City Chiefs in 1971.

His sons—Jamie, who was born in 1974, and Darren, born a year later—were second-round NFL draft picks in 1997. Jamie, a linebacker out of Virginia, was drafted 34th overall by the Baltimore Ravens. He spent five seasons with the Ravens before playing three with the Houston Texans and then joined the Seattle Seahawks, playing eight games in 2005.

Darren, a free safety out of William and Mary, was drafted by Green Bay 26 picks after his brother was chosen by Baltimore. Since breaking into the defensive backfield with the Packers in 1997, Sharper has been one of the NFL's leading ball hawks.

Twice a Pro Bowl selection with the Packers, Sharper's first season with the rival Minnesota Vikings in 2005 also resulted in a trip to Hawaii. While some predicted his career was on the decline, Sharper proved otherwise.

He equaled a career high with nine interceptions—trailing only Deltha O'Neal of the Cincinnati Bengals and Ty Law of the New York Jets, who each had 10. He tied Champ Bailey of the Denver Broncos and Clinton Hart of the San Diego Chargers for the NFL lead with two interception-return touchdowns (thrilling plays of 92 and 88 yards).

Sharper was number one in interception-return yards with 276 (81 more than Law), and he set a personal best with three interceptions in one game at the Meadowlands, to ignite a 24–21 win over the New York Giants on November 13. In that game, the

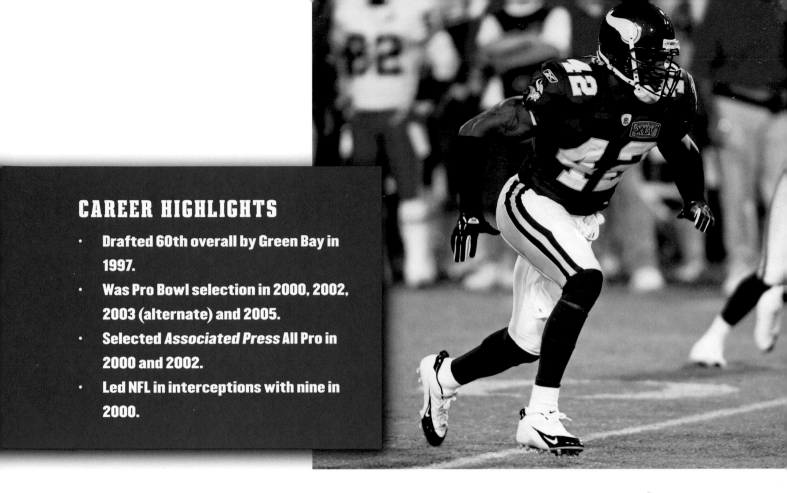

Vikings became the first NFL team to return an interception (Sharper), kickoff (Koren Robinson) and punt (Mewelde Moore) for TDs in the same game. Sharper's pick off Eli Manning and subsequent career-best 92-yard return set the stage for that wild accomplishment.

Sharper started to fill his NFL portfolio with big plays as a freshman. The first two passes he intercepted were returned for TDs—and he added a third TD that season on a fumble return, thereby setting a Packers rookie record and tying the club record for defensive TDs in a season. He was exceptional in helping the Packers to a second consecutive Super Bowl, although they eventually lost SB XXXII 31–24 to the Broncos.

In 2000, Sharper, with nine interceptions, became the first Packer to lead the NFL in that category since the great Willie Wood in 1962. Two years later, he was third in the NFL with seven interceptions but tops, with 233 yards, on interception returns.

A knee injury hampered Sharper's final season with The Pack, but he still managed to equal the club record with three defensive TDs in one season (two on interception returns, one on a fumble return). His four interceptions led the Packers, making it the fifth consecutive season he had paced Green Bay in that category, tying the club mark.

After eight solid seasons with the Packers that included four division titles, Sharper signed with the Vikings in March 2005. Ironically, he became teammates with Minnesota QB Daunte Culpepper, whom he had intercepted more times (five) in his career than any other pivot.

Sharper made a stunning debut with the Vikes, returning a pick for an 88-yard TD. That came in the opening quarter and put Minnesota ahead 7–0 in what eventually became a Week 1 loss to Tampa Bay (24–13).

He showed that afternoon—and throughout the season—that his penchant for stealing passes is still very much part of his arsenal.

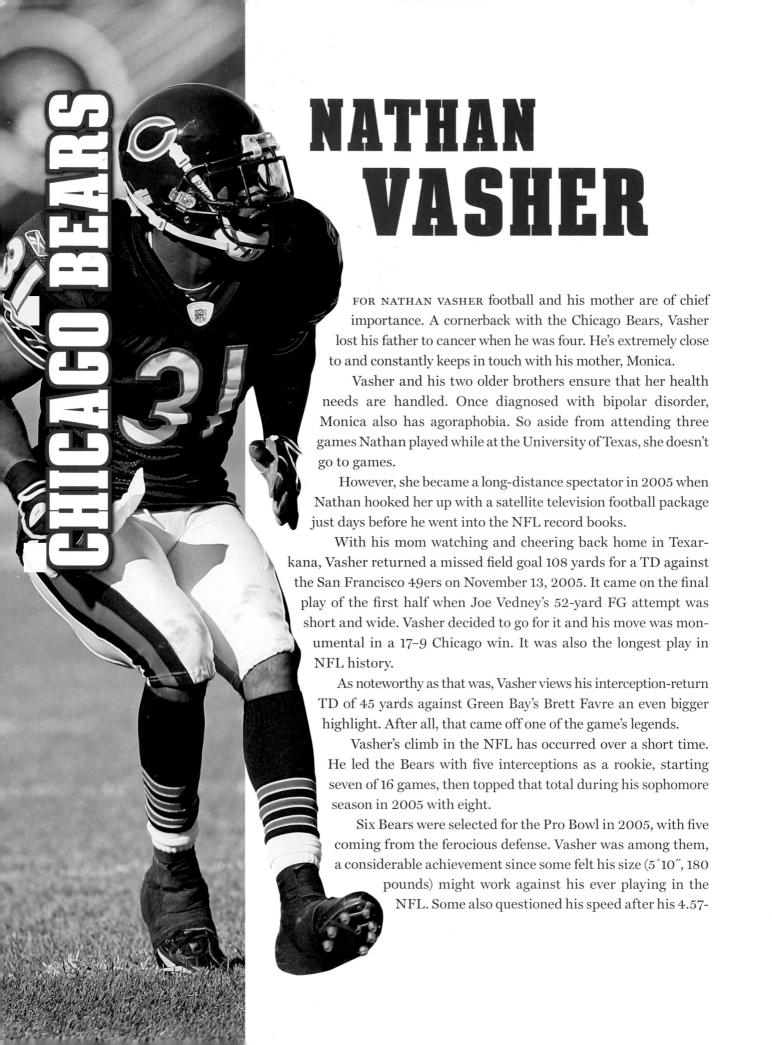

NATHAN VASHER

FOR NATHAN VASHER football and his mother are of chief importance. A cornerback with the Chicago Bears, Vasher lost his father to cancer when he was four. He's extremely close to and constantly keeps in touch with his mother, Monica.

Vasher and his two older brothers ensure that her health needs are handled. Once diagnosed with bipolar disorder, Monica also has agoraphobia. So aside from attending three games Nathan played while at the University of Texas, she doesn't go to games.

However, she became a long-distance spectator in 2005 when Nathan hooked her up with a satellite television football package just days before he went into the NFL record books.

With his mom watching and cheering back home in Texarkana, Vasher returned a missed field goal 108 yards for a TD against the San Francisco 49ers on November 13, 2005. It came on the final play of the first half when Joe Vedney's 52-yard FG attempt was short and wide. Vasher decided to go for it and his move was monumental in a 17–9 Chicago win. It was also the longest play in NFL history.

As noteworthy as that was, Vasher views his interception-return TD of 45 yards against Green Bay's Brett Favre an even bigger highlight. After all, that came off one of the game's legends.

Vasher's climb in the NFL has occurred over a short time. He led the Bears with five interceptions as a rookie, starting seven of 16 games, then topped that total during his sophomore season in 2005 with eight.

Six Bears were selected for the Pro Bowl in 2005, with five coming from the ferocious defense. Vasher was among them, a considerable achievement since some felt his size (5´10˝, 180 pounds) might work against his ever playing in the NFL. Some also questioned his speed after his 4.57-

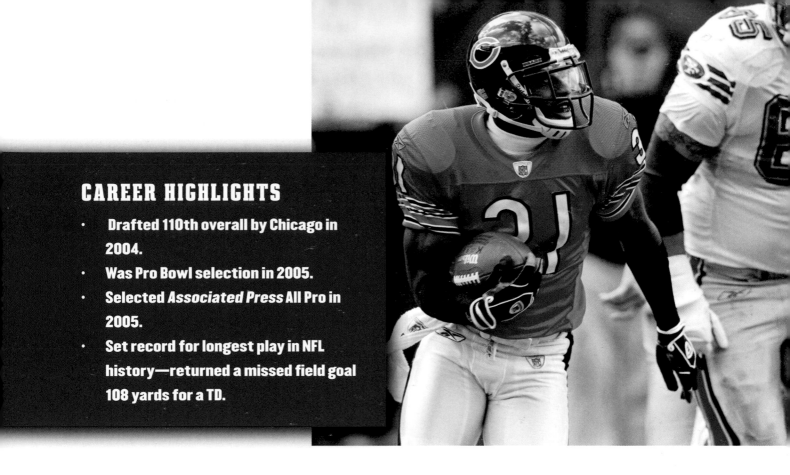

second time in the 40-yard dash in pre-NFL-draft drills.

But Vasher knows how to survive. His eight interceptions combined with Charles Tillman's five resulted in a total of 13 interceptions by the Chicago cornerbacks in 2005—the best in the NFC (along with the Carolina tandem of Chris Gamble, with seven, and Ken Lucas, with six). The NFL best in 2005 was 15 and came from the AFC—a tie between Cincinnati's corners Deltha O'Neal (10) and Tory James (five) and New York Jets corners Ty Law (10) and David Barrett (five).

Vasher's interception total in 2005 was two shy of the Bears' record (10) set by Mark Carrier in 1990, the last time the Bears had six Pro Bowlers in one season. Carrier and Vasher had the most interceptions in one season by a Bears player since 1963, when Roosevelt Taylor topped the NFL with nine.

It's no surprise then that Bears head coach Lovie Smith has taken to calling Vasher "The Interceptor," a moniker that certainly fits his leading ball hawk.

What's more, after a record of 5–11 in 2004, the Bears used their defensive strengths to the max and finished 11–5 in 2005. After smothering the Carolina Panthers in the regular season, however, the Bears couldn't contain Steve Smith and company in their Divisional Playoff rematch, and Chicago's season ended with a 29–21 loss.

IN THE HUDDLE

Nathan Vasher dreamed of playing in the NFL as a child, telling his mother that one day he'd play for the Cowboys. He's fulfilled his aspirations, albeit with the Bears instead of the Cowboys.

Yet the Bears advanced noticeably in 2005 and Vasher did as well. After tying the Longhorns' record with 17 career interceptions, Vasher became a fourth-round selection of the Bears in the 2004 NFL draft. He started seven of 16 games as an NFL freshman and became a full-time starter in 2005.

DEFENSIVE

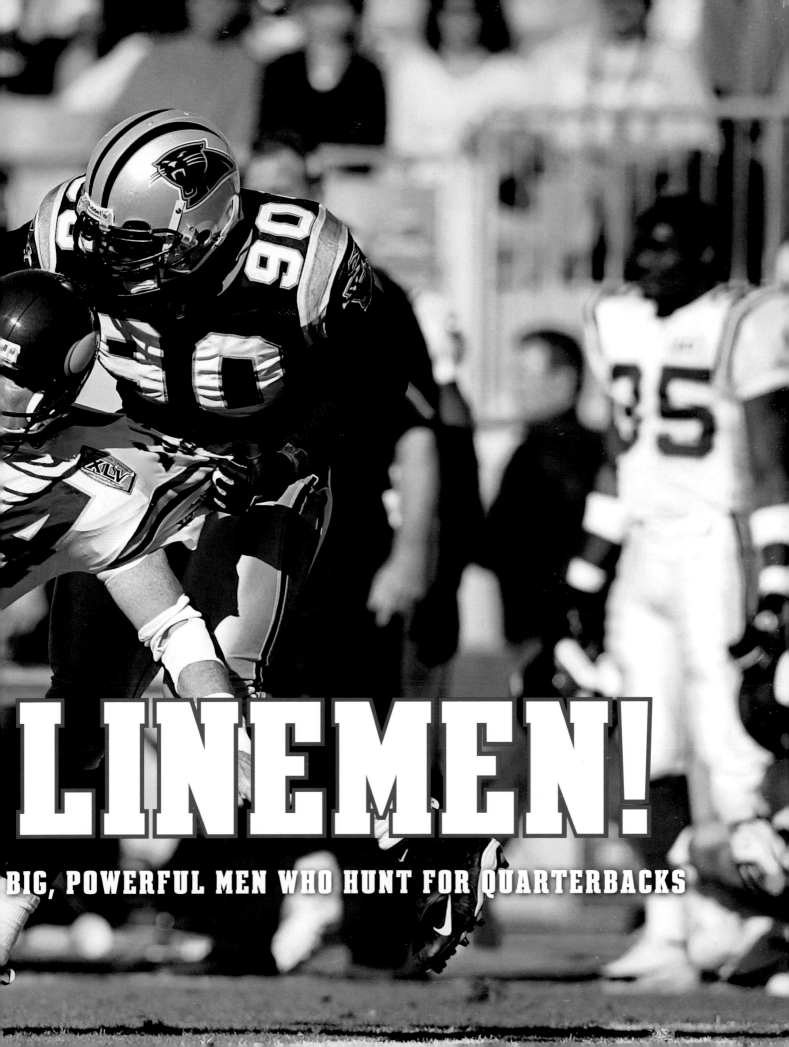

LINEMEN!

BIG, POWERFUL MEN WHO HUNT FOR QUARTERBACKS

INDIANAPOLIS COLTS

DWIGHT FREENEY

DESPITE HIS PASS-RUSHING magic with the Syracuse Orangemen, some doubted that defensive end Dwight Freeney could perform that way in the NFL.

The Indianapolis Colts thought otherwise. They ignored the knock on Freeney's size (6'1", 268 pounds) and went on the theory that speed kills. Freeney possessed an enormous amount of that along with an incredible spin move, overall skill and the will to silence his detractors.

Freeney has been a cornerstone of the ever-improving defense for the Colts. At 15.4 points per game allowed in 2005, the Colts ranked second in the NFL to the Chicago Bears (12.6). Freeney, who became the first Colt to lead the NFL in sacks, with 16 in 2004, finished ninth in 2005 (11). The fact that he was double-teamed and drew extra blocking attention allowed teammate Robert Mathis to pick up a team-high 11.5 sacks.

The Mathis-Freeney total of 22.5 sacks in 2005 was second in the NFL by a tandem, surpassed by the 26 sacks of the New York Giants duo Osi Umenyiora (14.5) and Michael Strahan (11.5).

Through 2005, Freeney had 51 sacks in 63 NFL games for an average of .81 sacks per game. That

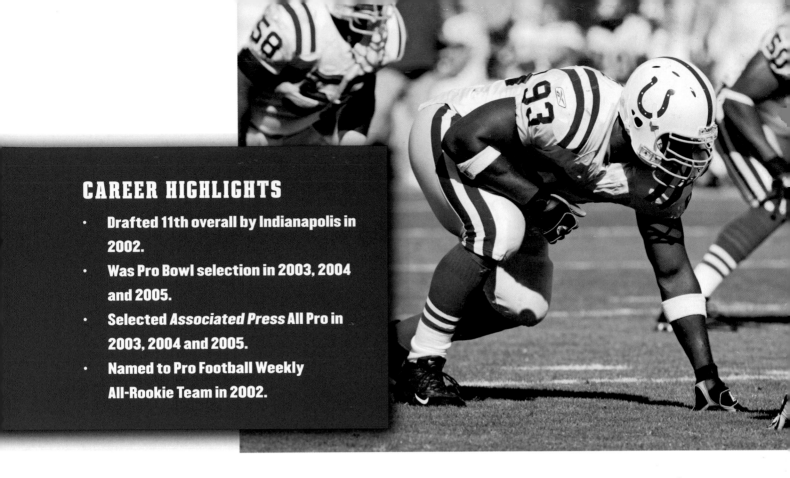

CAREER HIGHLIGHTS

- Drafted 11th overall by Indianapolis in 2002.
- Was Pro Bowl selection in 2003, 2004 and 2005.
- Selected *Associated Press* All Pro in 2003, 2004 and 2005.
- Named to Pro Football Weekly All-Rookie Team in 2002.

places him second all time to the .87 sacks per game accumulated by Reggie White of the Green Bay Packers.

Freeney has reached double-digit totals in sacks in each of his first four NFL seasons—the only member of the Colts to achieve that since sacks became an official NFL statistic in 1982.

He arrived with an attitude to succeed. Although he started only the final eight games of the 2002 season, Freeney set the Colts' record (he's since broken it) with 13 sacks—the second most ever earned by an NFL rookie; in 1999 Jevon Kearse of the Tennessee Titans had a record 14.5 sacks.

Freeney was twice named AFC Defensive Rookie of the Month in 2002. That title helped to establish him as one of the NFL's most feared pass rushers.

Injuries that he sustained in 2003 affected his sacks total, but he still put up 11 and became the first Colts defensive player to make the Pro Bowl since 1987. Playing his first NFL season with starts in every game in 2004, Freeney averaged a sack per game, although he picked up three sacks in back-to-back games against Tennessee and Houston during December. His dominance earned him the AFC's Defensive Player of the Month selection for December/January.

Freeney set the defensive tone for the Colts from the get-go in 2005, when he was selected as the AFC's Defensive Player for September. He averaged a sack a game through the first five games in which Indianapolis allowed only 29 points and no more than 10 in any of those games. At season's end, Freeney received four votes and was runner-up to Brian Urlacher for the *Associated Press* NFL Defensive Player of the Year award.

A quiet leader who studies game film intensely, Freeney takes the same approach in virtually anything he does. For instance, he's a multi-champion in the John Madden NFL video games—and he works as hard at preparing for that as he does for the real game action.

JULIUS PEPPERS

THE NATIONAL FOOTBALL LEAGUE is filled with very many great players and athletes, and few would argue that Carolina Panthers defensive end Julius Peppers does not fit perfectly into both categories. Peppers is a player who can do virtually everything from his position after only four years in the league. Panthers head coach John Fox thinks there is no limit to what Peppers can accomplish, and he likes the approach his defensive star takes to the game of football. The coach knows how to handle his defensive stalwart and gives Peppers enough challenges (including some work on offense) to keep him focused. Fox thinks that Peppers lacks only experience, but that he is mentally strong enough to remain a star player and perhaps become the best defensive end in the NFL.

One reason why Fox is so impressed with Peppers is that he can line up in so many different spots along the line of scrimmage, and that always keeps the opposition guessing. He has outstanding quickness and can get into the other team's backfield to disrupt a play before it even gets going. Peppers can roam all over the field to make a tackle, since his speed keeps him in every play (many offensive tackles have nightmares trying to keep up with him). He knows how to use his hands effectively to shed blockers and has more than one technique to get to a quarterback. In two of his first three years as an NFL starter, Peppers recorded

IN THE HUDDLE

Julius Peppers is one of only two defensive linemen in the Carolina Panthers' history to record two interceptions in one season (in the 2004 season).

double-digit sack totals (recording 11 sacks in 2004, a year that also saw him get credited with 31 quarterback hurries), setting a standard by which the rest of his career will be measured by. Peppers believes that he must carry out all his assignments effectively rather than focus just on getting sacks.

Peppers was selected second overall by the Panthers in the 2002 draft after the 6′6″, 283-pound end had finished his junior year at the University of North Carolina. He won or was nominated for just about every defensive award available to college players, including the Lombardi Award, given to the top lineman. He started 12 games for the Panthers as a rookie in the '02 season and promptly recorded 12 sacks and was named the Defensive Rookie of the Year by many publications. His second season saw him record seven sacks, and he was in on 65 tackles (second-best total of Panther linemen) and helped his team to a Super Bowl appearance, where they lost to the New England Patriots. The '04 regular season saw Peppers make all the end-of-year All Pro teams as he bettered his tackle mark with a total of 85, and he even recorded two interceptions (one was returned for a touchdown).

The 2005 season started out rough for Peppers, who was not producing to his usual standards on account of nagging injuries. Teammate and fellow defensive lineman Kris Jenkins was lost for the season because of an injury, and that hurt Peppers, since the offense had one less player to worry about. As the year wore on, Peppers got better and finished with 12 sacks; the Panthers made the playoffs (as many expected). Peppers and fellow defensive end Mike Rucker wreaked havoc on many Panthers opponents and helped the team to an 11–5 record, earning a Wild Card spot in the playoffs. A couple of wins followed in the postseason, but the Panthers were humbled by the Seattle Seahawks in the NFC Championship Game. If the Panthers make it back to the Super Bowl, it is a certainty that Peppers will help lead the way.

DETROIT LIONS

SHAUN ROGERS

DETROIT IS KNOWN as the Motor City and, with that in mind, rivals must think they're staring down a truck or an SUV when lining up against Lions defensive tackle Shaun Rogers.

He's huge (6′4″, 345 pounds), re- markably quick for his size, capable of charging swiftly on the snap of the ball, then employing his exceptional strength to overpower opponents.

Rogers broke into the NFL in 2001. He was teamed on the interior of the Lions' defensive line for three seasons with Dan (Big Daddy) Wilkinson, a 12-year NFLer who was released in 2006. The duo held up extremely well doing lots of grunt work for a franchise short on bite.

The Lions were 21-59 from 2001 through 2005. In 2004 (6-10) and 2005 (5-11), Rogers distinguished himself as a bright light in the midst of all the losing by earning trips to the Pro Bowl.

IN THE HUDDLE
Shaun Rogers collects throwback jerseys and is a fan of *The Lord of the Rings* trilogy.

He was in Hawaii in 2003 as well, as a Pro Bowl alternate. He used the time to observe the goings-on with the best in the game, and he also got to spend time with defensive tackle Corey Simon, then with the Philadelphia Eagles (now with the Indianapolis Colts). Rogers and Simon were once collegiate teammates with the Texas Longhorns.

Seeing Simon participate in the Pro Bowl and soaking up the atmosphere inspired Rogers to do all he could to earn his way there as well. In 2004, he fulfilled that objective by playing with such intensity and inspiration that his teammates voted him Defensive MVP. He had 68 tackles (his highest number since notching 81 as a rookie), added four sacks to equal a career high, and blocked three kicks.

One of his two blocked field goals that season resulted in an NFL record 92-yard TD return by Bracy Walker in the season opener at Chicago. A season later, Rogers was off to the Pro Bowl once again after registering a career-high 5.5 sacks and blocking another field-goal attempt, raising his career total for blocked kicks to eight—seven field-goal tries and one point-after attempt.

He also scored the first touchdown of his pro career, a 21-yard fumble return against New Orleans at San Antonio, Texas, on December 24, 2005. Rogers had several Saints draped over him as he rambled into the end zone to score the only TD of the game in a 13–12 win.

Signed to a six-year contract extension on January 1, 2005, Rogers also carries a fair bit of the franchise's weight on his shoulders as it delves for better motoring ahead. The Lions still feel fortunate to have landed the Longhorns star in the second round of the 2001 NFL draft.

Reaching the pro level has allowed Rogers to complement and enhance the football legacy his father, Ernie, set years ago. Drafted by the Dallas Cowboys in 1979, Ernie Rogers played in the Canadian Football League and the United States Football League.

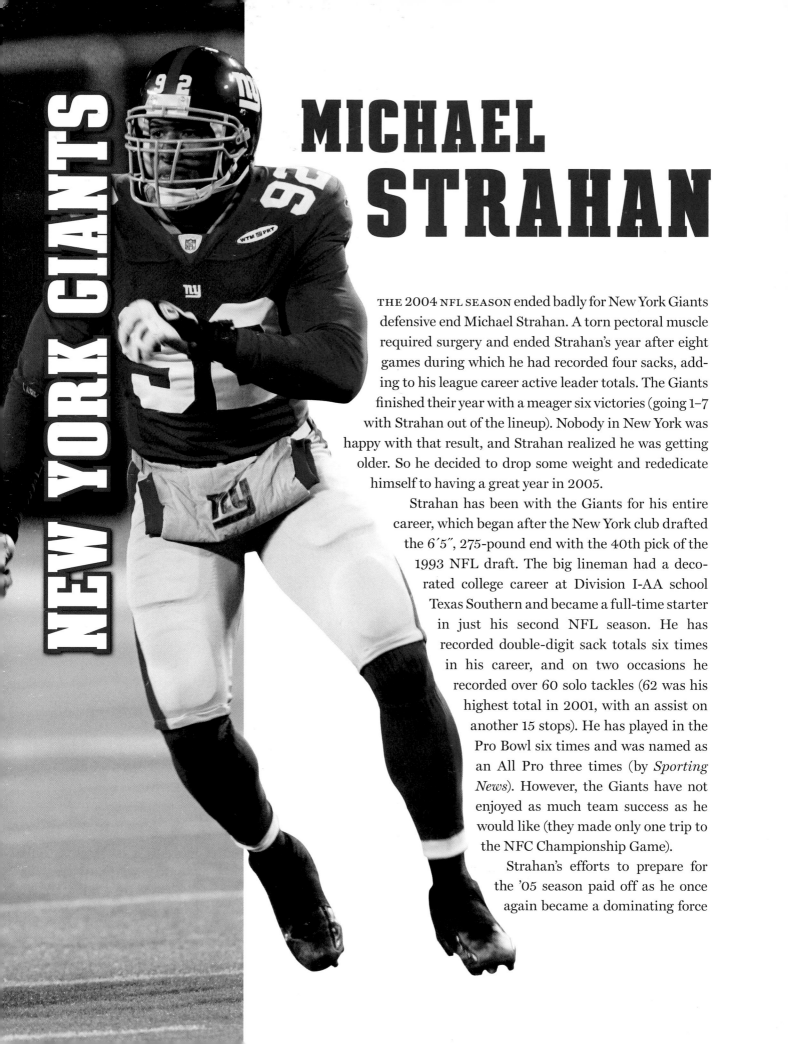

NEW YORK GIANTS

MICHAEL STRAHAN

THE 2004 NFL SEASON ended badly for New York Giants defensive end Michael Strahan. A torn pectoral muscle required surgery and ended Strahan's year after eight games during which he had recorded four sacks, adding to his league career active leader totals. The Giants finished their year with a meager six victories (going 1–7 with Strahan out of the lineup). Nobody in New York was happy with that result, and Strahan realized he was getting older. So he decided to drop some weight and rededicate himself to having a great year in 2005.

Strahan has been with the Giants for his entire career, which began after the New York club drafted the 6´5˝, 275-pound end with the 40th pick of the 1993 NFL draft. The big lineman had a decorated college career at Division I-AA school Texas Southern and became a full-time starter in just his second NFL season. He has recorded double-digit sack totals six times in his career, and on two occasions he recorded over 60 solo tackles (62 was his highest total in 2001, with an assist on another 15 stops). He has played in the Pro Bowl six times and was named as an All Pro three times (by *Sporting News*). However, the Giants have not enjoyed as much team success as he would like (they made only one trip to the NFC Championship Game).

Strahan's efforts to prepare for the '05 season paid off as he once again became a dominating force

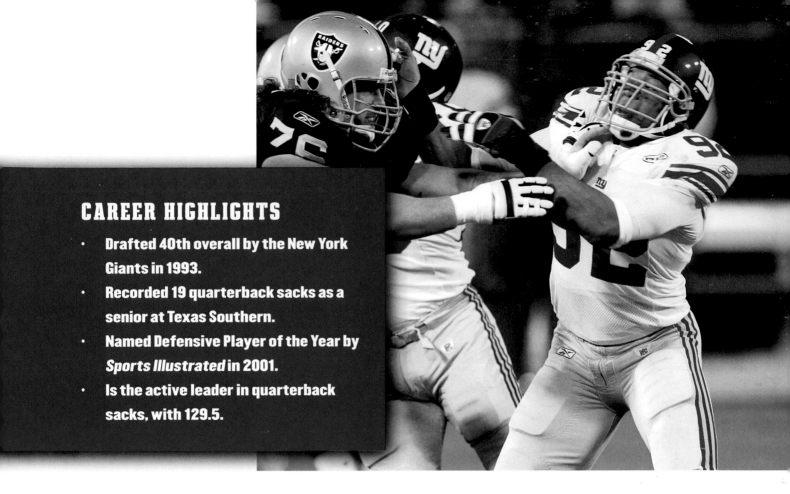

CAREER HIGHLIGHTS

- Drafted 40th overall by the New York Giants in 1993.
- Recorded 19 quarterback sacks as a senior at Texas Southern.
- Named Defensive Player of the Year by *Sports Illustrated* in 2001.
- Is the active leader in quarterback sacks, with 129.5.

along the line of scrimmage. His well-known quickness and explosiveness returned, and his creativity was still a strong factor. Strahan uses his long arms and hands to great effectiveness, and his determination has never wavered. He also knows that it's the quarterback sacks that get him all the attention. But Strahan has come to realize that a good defensive end does his best to contain the other team's running game. His own teammates have come to see that Strahan is not out just for the statistics but for the victories. Strahan does not have many years left in the game and wants to get a Super Bowl ring on his finger before he leaves (it still irks him that the Giants were beaten badly by Baltimore in the one Super Bowl he played in). He is glad to help out the younger players as long as they listen.

One of the youngsters heeding Strahan's advice is fellow defensive end Osi Umenyiora. The opposition now has to worry about two quality defensive ends, and Strahan might not always be the one getting the double-team attention. The emergence of Umenyiora was the perfect tonic to get the best out of Strahan, and he enjoyed a great year in '05, with 11.5 sacks during the season. The rejuvenation of the Giants seemed to go right up and down the team, and they finished with an 11–5 season to make the playoffs (although they were wiped out 23–0 by the Carolina Panthers right in Giants Stadium in one of the Wild Card games).

The team was more ready to respond to the demands of coach Tom Coughlin in his second season in New York, and defensive coordinator Tim Lewis seems to have designed a system that allows players like Strahan (who was named to the Pro Bowl for his '05 season) to excel. A potential future Hall of Fame player, Strahan must hope that the Giants can take another step up during the playoffs if he wants to get back to the Super Bowl.

MIAMI DOLPHINS

JASON TAYLOR

THE MIAMI DOLPHINS were not expected to beat the Denver Broncos on the opening day of the 2005 season even though they were at home. New Miami coach Nick Saban wanted to get off to a good start with his first NFL game, but not many were thinking he could outdo the Broncos' veteran head coach, Mike Shanahan. However, Dolphins defensive end Jason Taylor had other ideas when he was able to strip Denver quarterback Jake Plummer of the football. Taylor then picked up the loose ball and scampered 85 yards for a touchdown. It was a big play in the Dolphins' surprisingly easy 34–10 win, and Saban's career got off to a good start.

What is not surprising to anybody who watches Taylor consistently is his great effort to make an important play. The 6´6˝, 255-pound defensive end has been making such plays since he came into the NFL after the Dolphins drafted him 73rd overall in 1997. New England quarterback Tom Brady thinks Taylor is the toughest player he faces year after year (Taylor has now completed nine NFL seasons) because he plays hard on every play, setting the tone and style of the Dolphins' defense. It's easy to see why Brady is very concerned about Taylor: he's always on the field and is just as tough against the run as he is against the pass. Taylor exhibits good anticipation and can accelerate very quickly, especially when he has his sights on the quarterback. He has 92.5 career sacks as of the end of the '05 season and he is a perennial Pro Bowl player. When Saban first arrived, he decided to change Taylor's role somewhat. In addition to instilling more team discipline, Saban also

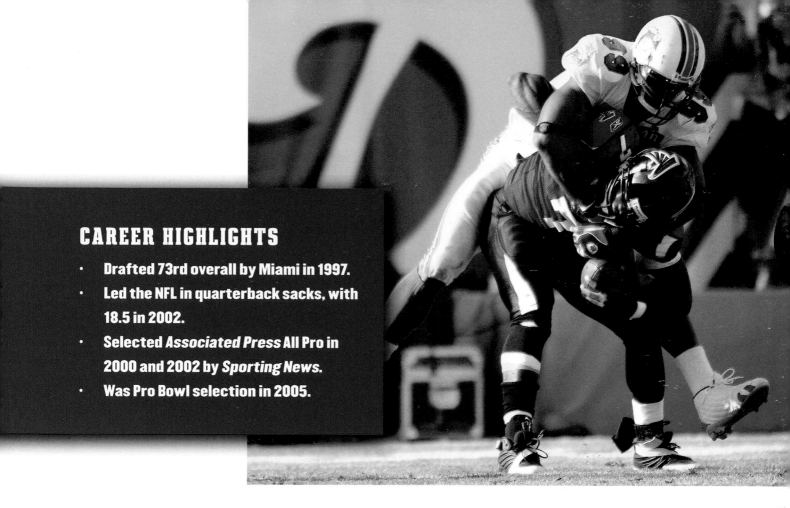

created more defensive schemes that could be switched in and out of very easily. Since Taylor does not carry a lot of bulk, as many of the other defensive ends in the league do, Saban tried Taylor in more of a rush-end position (sometimes acting as a coverage linebacker) to take advantage of his great athleticism. Saban's idea is to free Taylor up and give him more leeway to roam all over the field. On occasion Taylor might overrun a play, but he has the speed to make up ground and displays good hands that can corral a ball if he has to. Some might think a star player like Taylor should never be tampered with. However, Saban sees more possibilities for someone he believes to be one of the best in the NFL. Early in the year Taylor embraced the new role and loved to jam receivers, whom he does not consider the toughest guys in football!

A native of Pittsburgh, Pennsylvania, Taylor attended Akron University between 1993 and 1996 and received many accolades. He started 11 games for the Dolphins as a rookie (in '97), getting in on 42 tackles while recording five sacks. At one point in his career, Taylor was designated the Dolphins' franchise player (in 2001); it was a designation that was well deserved. The Dolphins look to more success under Saban (the

IN THE HUDDLE

In February of 2005, the University of Miami's Jackson Memorial Medical Center renamed its learning center the Jason Taylor Children's Learning Center in recognition of Jason Taylor's contributions and support.

first year ended with a 9–7 record), and that will give Taylor a chance to see more postseason action (they have not made the playoffs in five years).

NEW YORK GIANTS

OSI UMENYIORA

HIS LAST NAME ISN'T an easy one for rival NFL coaches and players to pronounce. They tend to refer to Osi Umenyiora as "number 72." Whatever you call him, the right defensive end for the New York Giants fast-forwarded himself to Pro Bowl and All Pro status in three short seasons.

His parents envisioned him becoming a doctor. However, Umenyiora majored in business administration while he set his sights on pro football at small Troy State in Troy, Alabama.

Credit the Giants for doing their homework. They realized he was raw, but, believing pass rushers can't be manufactured, they jumped at the chance to draft Umenyiora in 2003 (during the second round).

Giants GM Ernie Accorsi has said that the trade with San Diego for quarterback Eli Manning in 2004 would not have occurred if the Chargers hadn't dropped their request for Umenyiora. Since then, the Giants have reportedly turned down calls from other clubs attempting to acquire Umenyiora.

Although he started only once in the 13 games during his rookie season, his performance in the season finale against Carolina was an indicator of his potential. He

IN THE HUDDLE

Born in London, England, to parents of Nigerian descent, Osi Umenyiora spent seven years in London and seven in Nigeria before joining his sister in Auburn, Alabama. A high-school classmate named Marcus Washington, now a linebacker with the Washington Redskins, encouraged Umenyiora to try football in his junior year.

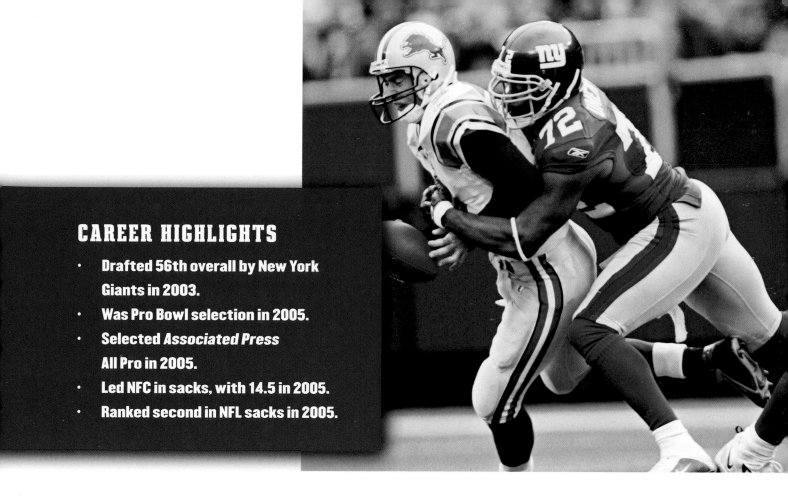

blocked two punts (the first time in 60 years that the Giants had two blocked punts in one game) while adding one sack and one forced fumble. His excellence factored into all three TDs for the Giants that day.

Umenyiora's development has been largely influenced by his mentor, Giants left defensive end Michael Strahan. Heeding Strahan's advice, Umenyiora has learned to commit himself to being the best he can be—on and off the field.

Umenyiora made seven starts in 16 games played in 2004, becoming a regular when Keith Washington was sidelined. After he led the Giants with seven sacks as a sophomore, he blasted his way into prominence with 14.5 sacks in 2005, second in the NFL to Derrick Burgess of the Oakland Raiders, who had 16.

Add the 11.5 that Strahan accumulated to tie for seventh in the NFL and the Giants' bookend defensive ends tallied the best combined total of any duo in the league. At 26, the Umenyiora–Strahan duo outdistanced the 22.5 total of Indianapolis tandem Robert Mathis (11.5) and Dwight Freeney (11).

Umenyiora's sacks parade was made all the more impressive by the caliber of the opponents attempting to block him. He netted two against Seattle by going head-to-head with perennial Pro Bowler Walter Jones; it was the first time Jones had been victimized in a season and a half. Umenyiora notched sacks in nine of his 16 starts in 2005, landing two sacks per game five times. Just before Christmas 2005, news broke that the Giants had locked Umenyiora up with a six-year contract extension.

Usually soft-spoken, Umenyiora caused a stir in the week leading up to the Wild Card game against the Carolina Panthers. He called the Panthers' duo of Julius Peppers and Mike Rucker the second-best defensive-end tandem in the NFL, clearly implying he and Strahan ranked number one.

PLAYERS WHO ROAM FROM SIDELINE TO SIDEL

LINE

, LOOKING TO CRUSH OPPONENTS IN THEIR TRACKS

BACKERS!

PITTSBURGH STEELERS

JAMES FARRIOR

OPPONENTS CAN ATTEMPT to run against the Pittsburgh Steelers, but with left inside linebacker James Farrior a force among the fierce defense, there's not much to be gained.

The Steelers ranked third in the NFL in 2005, yielding a meager 86.0 yards rushing per game. Overall, the Steelers' defense, with an average of 284.0 yards surrendered per game, was fourth in the NFL and first in the AFC.

Farrior's performance in 2004 led to a Pro Bowl selection and a runner-up finish for the NFL Defensive Player of the Year Award. He followed that by once again leading the Steelers in tackles, with 119 in 2005. Farrior also had two sacks, and he combined with right inside linebacker Larry Foote (102 tackles, three sacks) in support of an imposing defensive line,

IN THE HUDDLE

Born in 1975—a year after the arrival of the hit sitcom *Happy Days*—James Farrior picked up the nickname Potsie after the Anson Williams character on the show. Why? Well, his parents, James and Rebecca, liked the show and their son had a pot belly at the time.

which consisted of nose tackle Casey Hampton and ends Kimo von Oelhoffen and Aaron Smith.

The defense had a great deal to do with the Steelers, becoming conquering road warriors. Their success led them to the AFC Championship and a 21–10 victory over Seattle in Super Bowl XL.

A two-way football star during his high-school days in Ettrick, Virginia, Farrior went on to a stellar defensive career with the University of Virginia Cavaliers. A first-round NFL draft selection of the New York Jets, Farrior supplied 75 tackles in his 1997 NFL rookie season.

Although Farrior racked up 142 tackles and started all 16 games for the first time in his career in 2001, the Jets cut him loose following the season—a move for which they have since been criticized. He became a strategic free-agent acquisition for the Steelers, providing nine tackles in his Pittsburgh debut at New England.

Farrior has evolved into an important part of head coach Bill Cowher's defense and is one of the Steelers' leaders. The Steelers won their final four games of the 2005 season to finish 11–5, second to the Cincinnati Bengals in the AFC North.

That set up a Wild Card showdown against the Bengals and a confrontation pitting two NFL stars from Ettrick, Virginia—Farrior of the Steelers and running back Rudi Johnson of the Bengals—against each other.

Farrior and Johnson chatted the day after the playoff matches were set up. There's a mutual respect between the two players. Johnson even said he would make sure Farrior's family was well taken care of, since the game was in Cincinnati.

But both emphasized they'd do everything in their power to lead their teams to victory. After a strong beginning by Johnson and the Bengals, the Steelers' defense bent but never broke in the 31–17 win. Farrior's fourth-quarter interception set up a field goal that helped seal the deal. The defense held the Bengals to 84 yards rushing and repeatedly blitzed Jon Kitna, who had replaced the injured Carson Palmer, with relentless pressure.

And the momentum just built from there.

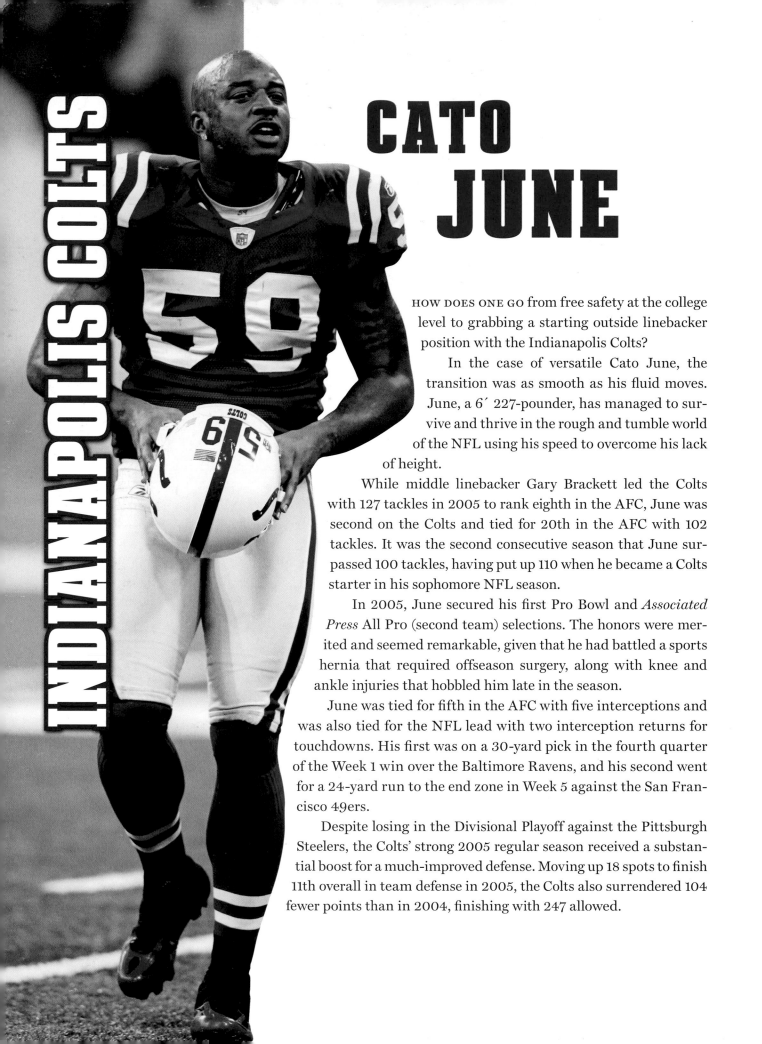

INDIANAPOLIS COLTS

CATO JUNE

HOW DOES ONE GO from free safety at the college level to grabbing a starting outside linebacker position with the Indianapolis Colts?

In the case of versatile Cato June, the transition was as smooth as his fluid moves. June, a 6´ 227-pounder, has managed to survive and thrive in the rough and tumble world of the NFL using his speed to overcome his lack of height.

While middle linebacker Gary Brackett led the Colts with 127 tackles in 2005 to rank eighth in the AFC, June was second on the Colts and tied for 20th in the AFC with 102 tackles. It was the second consecutive season that June surpassed 100 tackles, having put up 110 when he became a Colts starter in his sophomore NFL season.

In 2005, June secured his first Pro Bowl and *Associated Press* All Pro (second team) selections. The honors were merited and seemed remarkable, given that he had battled a sports hernia that required offseason surgery, along with knee and ankle injuries that hobbled him late in the season.

June was tied for fifth in the AFC with five interceptions and was also tied for the NFL lead with two interception returns for touchdowns. His first was on a 30-yard pick in the fourth quarter of the Week 1 win over the Baltimore Ravens, and his second went for a 24-yard run to the end zone in Week 5 against the San Francisco 49ers.

Despite losing in the Divisional Playoff against the Pittsburgh Steelers, the Colts' strong 2005 regular season received a substantial boost for a much-improved defense. Moving up 18 spots to finish 11th overall in team defense in 2005, the Colts also surrendered 104 fewer points than in 2004, finishing with 247 allowed.

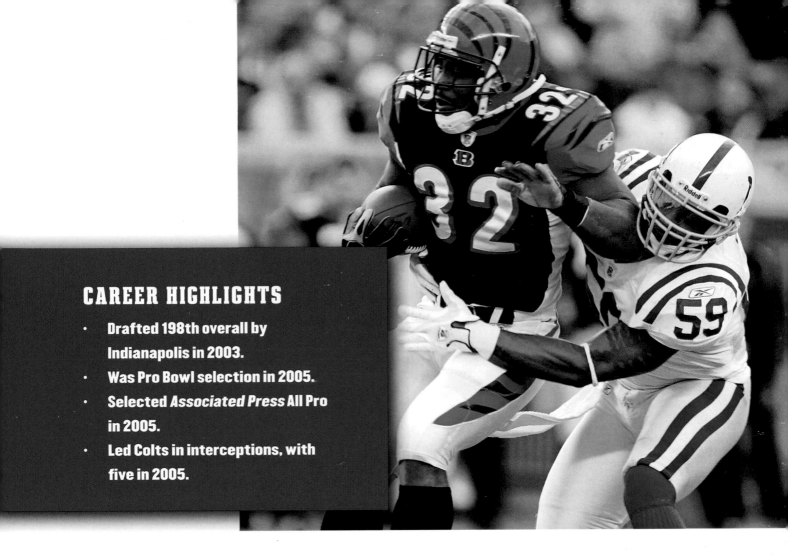

Those following the Colts detected substantial advances by the linebackers and defensive backs in support of the hard-charging line. Anyone believing their lack of overall size would hinder the Colts forgot to take the team's fleet-footedness into account.

Head coach Tony Dungy was known for his defense, but until 2005 the Colts won mostly because of their offense. The maturation of youngsters such as June factors into the evolution of things on the Colts' defensive scene.

Given that Brackett was undrafted and that June was selected in the sixth round of the 2003 NFL draft by the Colts, the franchise has been fortunate to see them both blossom as big-play performers.

As a rookie, June didn't even dress for five games the Colts played; he was primarily used on special teams for the 11 games he did play. But he had achieved his goal of playing in the NFL, and next he went about trying to establish himself.

IN THE HUDDLE

Talk about two-way impact! Cato June played defensive back (with 22 interceptions and 354 tackles) and running back (with 26 touchdowns and 2,033 yards on 234 carries) at Anacostia High School in Washington, D.C.

That came in 2004, when he proved he could handle the position switch and make up for his lack of size with speed and intelligence. His growth continued in 2005, and he reinforced the trust the Colts showed in him.

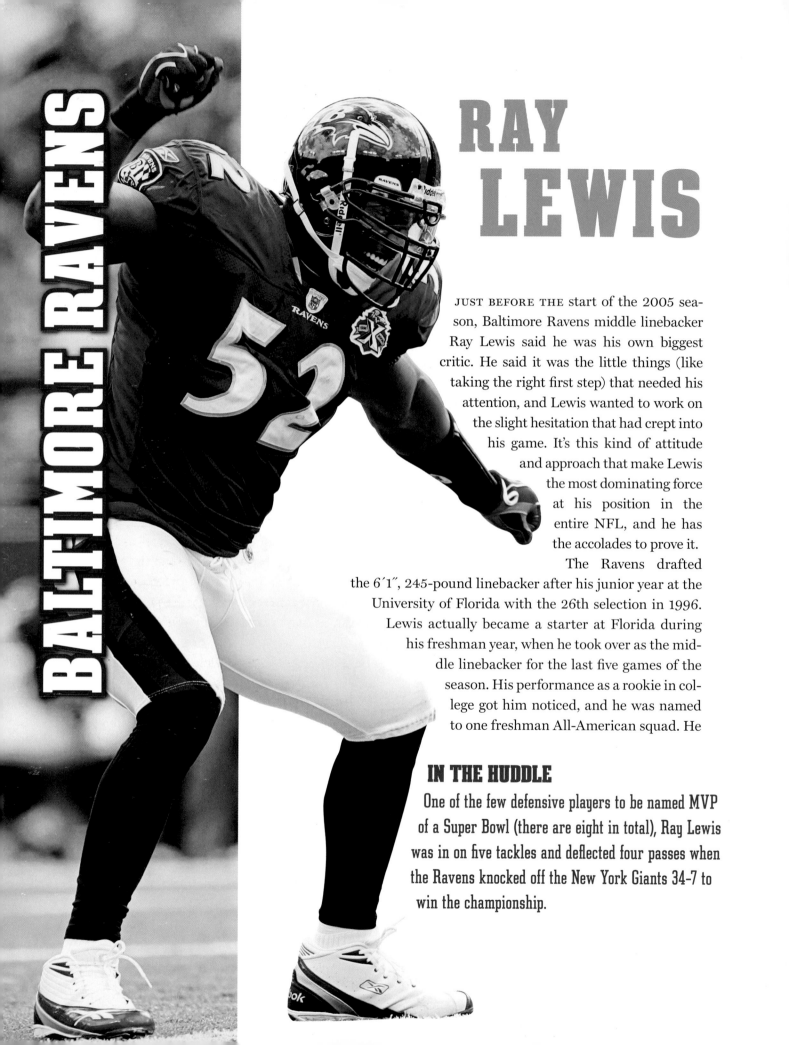

BALTIMORE RAVENS

RAY LEWIS

JUST BEFORE THE start of the 2005 season, Baltimore Ravens middle linebacker Ray Lewis said he was his own biggest critic. He said it was the little things (like taking the right first step) that needed his attention, and Lewis wanted to work on the slight hesitation that had crept into his game. It's this kind of attitude and approach that make Lewis the most dominating force at his position in the entire NFL, and he has the accolades to prove it.

The Ravens drafted the 6´1˝, 245-pound linebacker after his junior year at the University of Florida with the 26th selection in 1996. Lewis actually became a starter at Florida during his freshman year, when he took over as the middle linebacker for the last five games of the season. His performance as a rookie in college got him noticed, and he was named to one freshman All-American squad. He

IN THE HUDDLE

One of the few defensive players to be named MVP of a Super Bowl (there are eight in total), Ray Lewis was in on five tackles and deflected four passes when the Ravens knocked off the New York Giants 34-7 to win the championship.

was a consensus All-American in his final year as a Hurricane and led his team in tackles in 22 consecutive games. He had 160 total tackles in his last year at college, and only one other Hurricane ever recorded more stops in one year (back in 1965). Lewis stepped right into the Ravens' lineup and led or was tied for most tackles in 10 of Baltimore's games in the '96 season. His performance got him named to one all-rookie team, and a legend was born. By 1997 he was the Ravens' best player, and he began to dominate every game.

Lewis can impose himself on a game like few other players. He is high on intensity and roams from sideline to sideline hunting down the opposition. Lewis is a hard tackler who lets any runner know he has been rocked. His mean streak helps him to deliver hits with a great pop, and he does not mind playing to the crowd. Lewis is the type of player who makes others around him better, and his teammates tend to respond to his leadership (or else!). He is quite capable of taking a team on his back and is considered an all-round force, since he can play the run or pass equally well. His aggressive nature can sometimes lead him to overrun a play, but that's really a minor problem compared with the havoc Lewis can impose on any team he lines up against.

By the 2000 season the Ravens were ready to contend, and it was the defense led by Lewis that took the team all the way to the Super Bowl. Balti-more finished the season with a 12–4 record and then demolished Denver, Tennessee and Oakland to advance to the big game for the first time in team history. During those three games, the Ravens gave up a grand total of 16 points and allowed the New York Giants seven points (on a kickoff return) in a 34–7 romp over their NFC opponents in the Super Bowl. In fact, the Giants gained a mere 152 yards of offense and turned the ball over five times as the Baltimore defense completely suffocated the New York attack. It was as dominating a performance in a championship game as anyone has seen, and the most valuable player of the contest was none other than Ray Lewis.

Since the Super Bowl victory, the Ravens have still played well on defense, with Lewis as imposing as ever. However, it's a different story on offense, where the lack of a quality quarterback has hurt the club badly. Two playoff appearances since the 2000 season have not led the team back to former glory, and the 2005 campaign was a nightmare for both Lewis (who played in only seven games because of injury) and the Ravens (a terrible 6–10 record). If the Ravens rebound in the near future, one can be certain that Lewis will be leading the charge back to respectability.

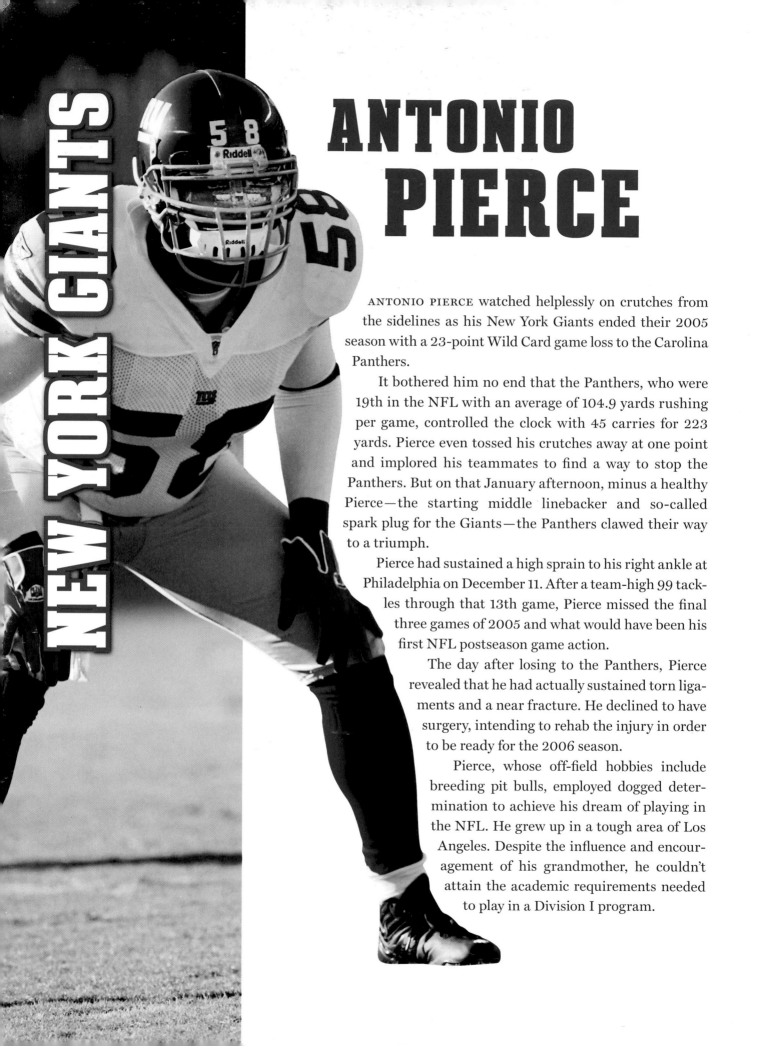

ANTONIO PIERCE

NEW YORK GIANTS

ANTONIO PIERCE watched helplessly on crutches from the sidelines as his New York Giants ended their 2005 season with a 23-point Wild Card game loss to the Carolina Panthers.

It bothered him no end that the Panthers, who were 19th in the NFL with an average of 104.9 yards rushing per game, controlled the clock with 45 carries for 223 yards. Pierce even tossed his crutches away at one point and implored his teammates to find a way to stop the Panthers. But on that January afternoon, minus a healthy Pierce—the starting middle linebacker and so-called spark plug for the Giants—the Panthers clawed their way to a triumph.

Pierce had sustained a high sprain to his right ankle at Philadelphia on December 11. After a team-high 99 tackles through that 13th game, Pierce missed the final three games of 2005 and what would have been his first NFL postseason game action.

The day after losing to the Panthers, Pierce revealed that he had actually sustained torn ligaments and a near fracture. He declined to have surgery, intending to rehab the injury in order to be ready for the 2006 season.

Pierce, whose off-field hobbies include breeding pit bulls, employed dogged determination to achieve his dream of playing in the NFL. He grew up in a tough area of Los Angeles. Despite the influence and encouragement of his grandmother, he couldn't attain the academic requirements needed to play in a Division I program.

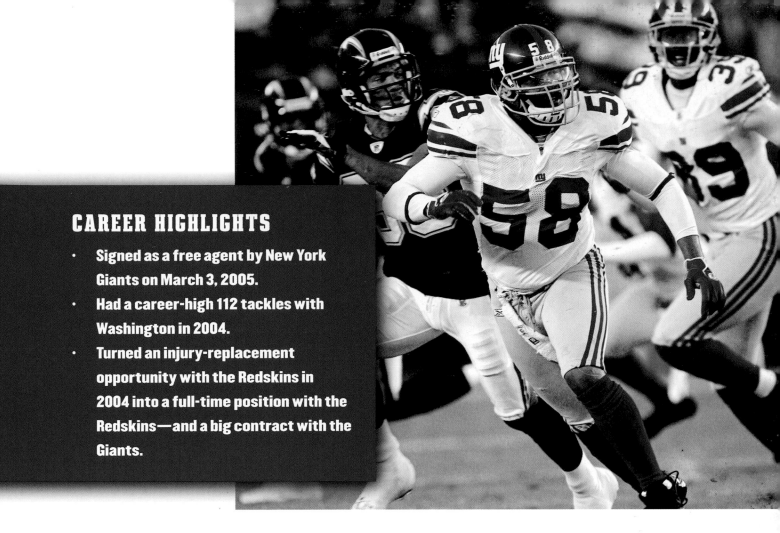

He instead spent two years at Mount San Antonio College in Walnut, California, before transferring and playing two seasons at Arizona. When the NFL draft came in 2001, he watched 30 linebackers have their names called while he was not asked to come forward.

Overcoming that frustration, he caught on with the Washington Redskins, winning over his coaches with enthusiasm and a willingness to do whatever was necessary. For three seasons, he filled in as a linebacker and played on special teams. Then, in 2004, when Mike Barrow was sidelined, Pierce became the starting middle linebacker for the Redskins, playing all 16 games. Pierce finished with 112 tackles and had two interceptions for 94 yards, returning one 78 yards for the first TD of his NFL career.

His leadership and performance as a starter paved the way to a lucrative six-year deal with the Giants. In 2005, the Giants surrendered 33 fewer points than the season before, and the defense showed a new-found nasty edge.

Once overlooked in the NFL, Pierce had reached new heights. He's kept tabs on the list of 30 linebackers drafted in 2001 and notes that

IN THE HUDDLE

Antonio Pierce is an old-car buff. Some of his most-prized possessions are a 1964 Chevy Impala and a 1968 Volkswagen Bug. Pierce told *Sports Illustrated* he gets a kick out of driving the Impala on game days. It has a red body and a white top.

only about half remain in the NFL. Then there's that "undrafted" one named Antonio Pierce, who has become a central figure for the Giants.

SHELTON QUARLES

DEFENSE HAS BEEN the trademark of the Tampa Bay Buccaneers, who have ranked in the top 10 in that department for nine consecutive seasons (from 1997 through 2005), an NFL best.

Whether it's a coincidence or not, that's exactly the length of Shelton Quarles' tenure with the Buccaneers. Now the middle linebacker and defensive quarterback, Quarles is a perennial standout, a fact known best by his teammates and by Buccaneers fans.

While other middle linebackers and defenses won accolades in 2005, Quarles and his unit led the NFL with only 277.8 yards allowed per game. The Chicago Bears were next at 282 yards allowed per game.

Quarles finished eighth with a personal-best 129 tackles; he then added a team-high 11 in Tampa Bay's disappointing 17–10 loss to the Washington Redskins in a Wild Card showdown. The Redskins won,

IN THE HUDDLE

While middle linebackers are known as stoppers rather than throwers, Shelton Quarles did toss the first pitch for the Tampa Bay Devil Rays baseball club on Opening Day in 2003.

despite a meager 120 yards on offense. That represented the lowest yardage total for a winning team in the NFL postseason.

Washington running back Clinton Portis, who entered that game with five consecutive 100-yard rushing games, was held to 53 yards on 16 carries. Wide receiver Santana Moss, who like Portis had set a Redskins' yardage record in 2005, led his team with 18 yards receiving against Tampa Bay!

The Redskins were opportunists, however, converting two first-quarter turnovers into touchdowns. Still, the defense kept the Buccaneers alive right until the bitter end.

The fact that Quarles is now firmly established as a leader of the Buccaneers and is one of the most active and recognizable figures in the Tampa community seems surprising.

The four-year starter at Vanderbilt wasn't drafted. The Miami Dolphins signed him in on April 29, 1994, and then cut him during training camp that August. Not about to pack in his pro career, Quarles headed to Vancouver and the Canadian Football League, where he spent two seasons with the B.C. Lions.

In 1997, he signed with the Buccaneers, making the roster as a backup to Derrick Brooks and proving himself a valuable contributor to the special teams. His contagious determination and progress resulted in more time as linebacker in 1998. He also continued to play on the special teams and had a team-leading 20 tackles to lead that unit for a second year in a row.

He finally won a consistent job as a strongside linebacker in 1999 and started all 14 games he played, including both in the postseason. He remained a strong-side linebacker until 2002, when he was moved to the middle. He finished with a then career-high that season, capping his season with the individual honor of Pro Bowl selection and the ultimate team prize—the Super Bowl title.

The 6'1" 225-pounder from Whites Creek, Tennessee, is an inspirational force and serves to ensure that the Buccaneers' defense remains near the head of the NFL class.

SEATTLE SEAHAWKS

LOFA TATUPU

THE SEATTLE SEAHAWKS finished the 2005 regular season with the best record in the National Football Conference with a 13–3 mark. Few experts thought they would have such a good year, considering the team was only 9–7 in 2004 and bounced from the playoffs for the second straight year in the Wild Card weekend. In fact, the Seahawks had not won a postseason game in 21 years (the longest any NFL team has gone between playoff victories). But head coach and vice-president of football operations Mike Holmgren believed he could get more out his key veterans, while new president of football operations Tim Ruskell made the right changes to the roster, elevating the Seahawks to the status of true contenders.

One newcomer to the Seahawks was rookie middle linebacker Lofa Tatupu. Ruskell was criticized for taking the undersized Tatupu (6´, 240 pounds) with a second-round pick choice (trading two fourth round picks and a second-round selection to get the linebacker) in the 2005 draft.

However, he was soon earning accolades for his in-spired choice. Tatupu has good football bloodlines: his father, Mosi, was a former NFL player (running back and special teams) with the Patriots and the Rams. Lofa attended the University of Maine for one year (in 2001) before switching to the University of Southern California, and he led the Trojans in tackles (in 2003) when he returned to football after sitting out one year. After his junior year at USC, Tatupu declared himself eligible for the NFL draft, and the Seahawks pounced on him while he was still available when they secured the 45th pick overall.

When Tatupu arrived at the Seattle training camp for the '05 season, he promptly beat out Niko Koutouvides for the starting job at middle linebacker and never looked back. Although Tatupu is not big or especially fast, he makes up for it with great instincts and a drive to succeed. He is very aggressive and energetic in carrying out his duties but not to the point where it becomes a problem. Tatupu reads the play well and can make a tackle with good authority once he sheds his blocker. He also shows good hands and can handle the ball if it's in his reach. In addition to his natural physical skills, Tatupu is a very intelligent player who has shown he can handle all the defensive calls for his team. Considering the Seahawks have added many younger players to their team, Tatupu's leadership is even more valuable to the team.

Linebacker Leroy Hill, defensive tackle Rocky Bernard and cornerback Jordan Babineaux were

CAREER HIGHLIGHTS

- Drafted 45th overall by Seattle in 2005.
- Recorded 12.5 quarterback sacks and 10 interceptions in a three-year college career.
- Led the Seahawks in tackles in 2005, with 104 (85 solo).
- Recorded four quarterback sacks in 2005.

also young players who made significant contributions to the Seahawks' defense in 2005. There may have been some doubt about whether the youngsters could handle a long NFL season. But players like Tatupu proved they could go the distance by making a strong contribution to a franchise-best 13-win season.

IN THE HUDDLE

During his two years at USC, Lofa Tatupu played on two national championship teams (in 2003 and 2004). He finished his career as a Trojan with nine sacks, seven interceptions, three fumble recoveries and one touchdown.

Tatupu did more than his share of the work by leading his team in tackles and also recording four quarterback sacks. His play drew comparisons with Tedy Bruschi of the New England Patriots—high praise indeed.

Although a strong candidate for Defensive Rookie of the Year honors, Tatupu was beaten out for the award by Shawne Merriman of the San Diego Chargers. The Seahawks, however, made it all the way to the Super Bowl.

MIAMI DOLPHINS

ZACH THOMAS

THE ONLY WAY to meet a problem is head-on and that's what Zach Thomas did from the moment he assumed his starting position at middle linebacker for the Miami Dolphins in 1996.

He had a team-high 13 tackles and one sack against New England in his first game as a pro. The following week at Arizona, he had a team-high 15 tackles and a forced fumble that he recovered to set up a Dolphins TD.

By season's end, the Dolphins had him listed for 180 tackles, 131 solo. Seemingly undersized at 5'11" and 228 pounds, nothing has stopped him from fulfilling his desire to provide the Dolphins with a steady performer.

Out of Texas Tech, he has operated with a telling motto, which he shared with nflplayers.com: it's not the size of the dog in the fight, it's the size of the fight in the dog.

Although banged up from a series of injuries in recent years, Thomas has managed to rebound and continues to pile up Pro Bowl appearances. When he was selected for his play in 2005, it was the sixth time he had received this honor. In Dolphins history, only two other players have surpassed this number. However, Thomas holds the record among the club's defensive players and has now moved ahead of Jake Scott, Bob Baumhower and John Offerdahl.

Fittingly, Thomas was a finalist for the Dick Butkus Award as the nation's top collegiate linebacker. When NFL historians think of linebackers, of course, Butkus is among the first names to come to mind. The long-time middle linebacker for the Chicago Bears epitomized the position, and Thomas is a throwback to that type of passion and consistency.

Thomas recorded double figures in tackles 12 times in the 14 games he played in 2005 and 28 times in a 31-game stretch. In Week 14 at San Diego,

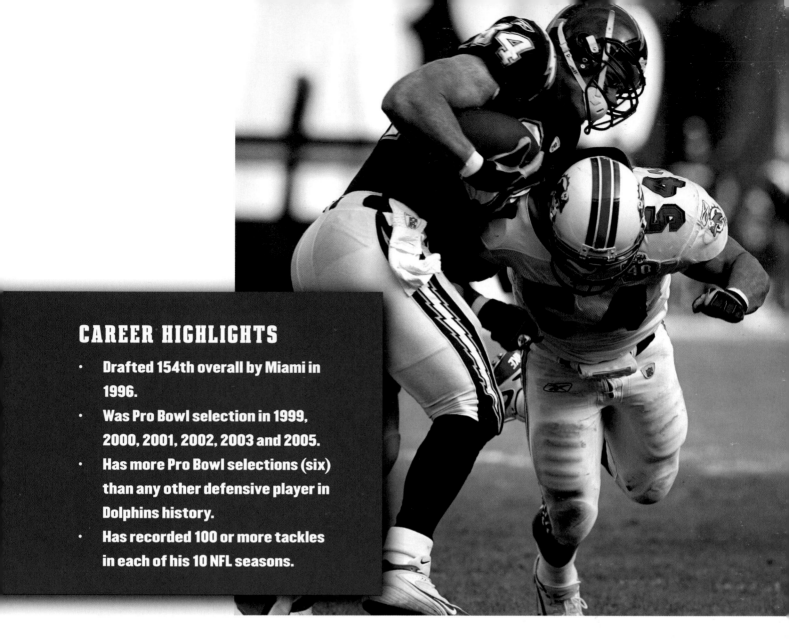

CAREER HIGHLIGHTS

- Drafted 154th overall by Miami in 1996.
- Was Pro Bowl selection in 1999, 2000, 2001, 2002, 2003 and 2005.
- Has more Pro Bowl selections (six) than any other defensive player in Dolphins history.
- Has recorded 100 or more tackles in each of his 10 NFL seasons.

Miami's defense—with Thomas in the middle and his brother-in-law, Jason Taylor, at defensive end—held the Chargers to under 100 yards rushing during a 23–21 win. Thomas was selected AFC Defensive Player of the Week after providing 11 tackles and an interception, the 16th of his career.

That was a stunning way for Thomas to return to the lineup after missing the previous two games because of shoulder and ankle injuries. After a poor start to the 2005 season, the Dolphins finished strongly with six consecutive wins and an overall record of 9–7.

Thomas, who ranked fourth with 145 tackles in 2004, climbed to second in 2005, with 158 tackles, 11 fewer than league leader Jonathan Vilma of the Jets. However, both those seasons saw Thomas sidelined for a combined five games.

IN THE HUDDLE

The passion Zach Thomas brings to his game is reflected in his favorite movies (*Braveheart* and *Scarface*) and in one of his favorite TV shows, *The Sopranos*.

Playing middle linebacker takes its toll, but Zachary Michael Thomas attacks it with all he's got. That's why number 54 has entrenched himself as one of the Dolphins' all-time standouts.

BRIAN URLACHER

CHICAGO BEARS middle linebacker Brian Urlacher had a lot to prove as the 2005 NFL season began. He had missed the final seven games of the 2004 season with a hamstring injury that had been bothering him all year long, and some critics were suggesting Urlacher was a little overrated (it is interesting to note that the Bears lost six of the seven contests Urlacher missed). Expectations for Urlacher have been high since he burst onto the scene as a rookie in 2000, earning a starting position just three games into his first year. In 2001, he became one of the top five players in the entire NFL by finishing fifth in MVP voting. It's easy to see why so much was placed on his shoulders after such a notable performance early in his career. In addition, Urlacher played one of the most glamorous positions in Bears history, that of middle linebacker, which was previously manned by legends like Dick Butkus and Mike Singletary.

There is no doubt Urlacher is the leader of the Bears' defense and has been so since he arrived in Chicago after he was selected ninth overall in the '00 NFL draft.

The native of Lovington, New Mexico, had a great college career. He attended school in his home state and was a second-team All-American in his final year. The 6´4˝, 258-pound Urlacher also played the strong safety position at New Mexico, in addition to his linebacker duties, and he saw some action on offense as well. The Bears liked him for the middle of their defense, and he showed he was up to the task. Urlacher is

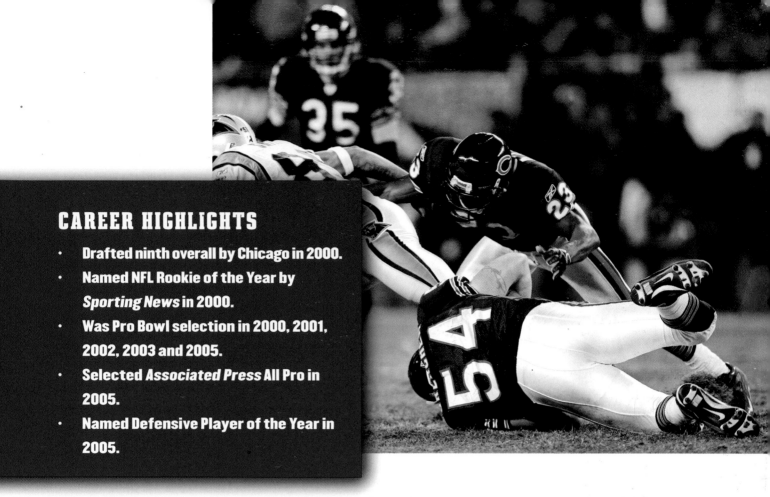

CAREER HIGHLIGHTS

- Drafted ninth overall by Chicago in 2000.
- Named NFL Rookie of the Year by *Sporting News* in 2000.
- Was Pro Bowl selection in 2000, 2001, 2002, 2003 and 2005.
- Selected *Associated Press* All Pro in 2005.
- Named Defensive Player of the Year in 2005.

very quick and moves well laterally. He is explosive going to the ball and likes to be very aggressive. The rough linebacker can read a play well and can keep up with most backs coming out of the backfield. He finishes his tackles effectively, but sometimes the very motivated Urlacher tries to do too much. He works better when the defensive line is doing its job (giving the line plenty of credit for his success). In the '05 season, the Bears' defense seemed to jell just right.

Under the tutelage of defensive coordinator Ron Rivera (a former Pro Bowl player for the Bears), Chicago's defense was so dominating in the '05 season that comparisons were being made to the Bears' vaunted 1985 Super Bowl defense, which lost only one game.

Such discussions might be great for the legions of Bears fans who long for the days of their only Super Bowl win, but the defense goes out in blue-collar fashion and does its best to keep the team in the game. There was little to the Bears' offense led by rookie quarterback Kyle Orton (the expected starter, Rex Grossman, was injured for most of the year). So Urlacher and his defensive cohorts knew any success the team would enjoy in '05 rested on their shoulders. In eight of the Bears' games, the defense gave up 10 or fewer points (seven of those games were wins), and in three others, the opposition was held to 20 or fewer points (two of those games were victories). Maybe the Bears of '85 are indeed back!

Urlacher's performance helped lead the Bears back to the playoffs (with an 11–5 record), and he loved the role of underdog the Bears embraced for the entire '05 season. Urlacher was so dominating from his linebacker position that he was named Defensive Player of the Year. Ironically, the Bears' defense had a let-down during their 29–21 playoff loss to the Carolina Panthers. However, with greater offensive output in the future, the Chicago club might get back to the Super Bowl quicker than expected.

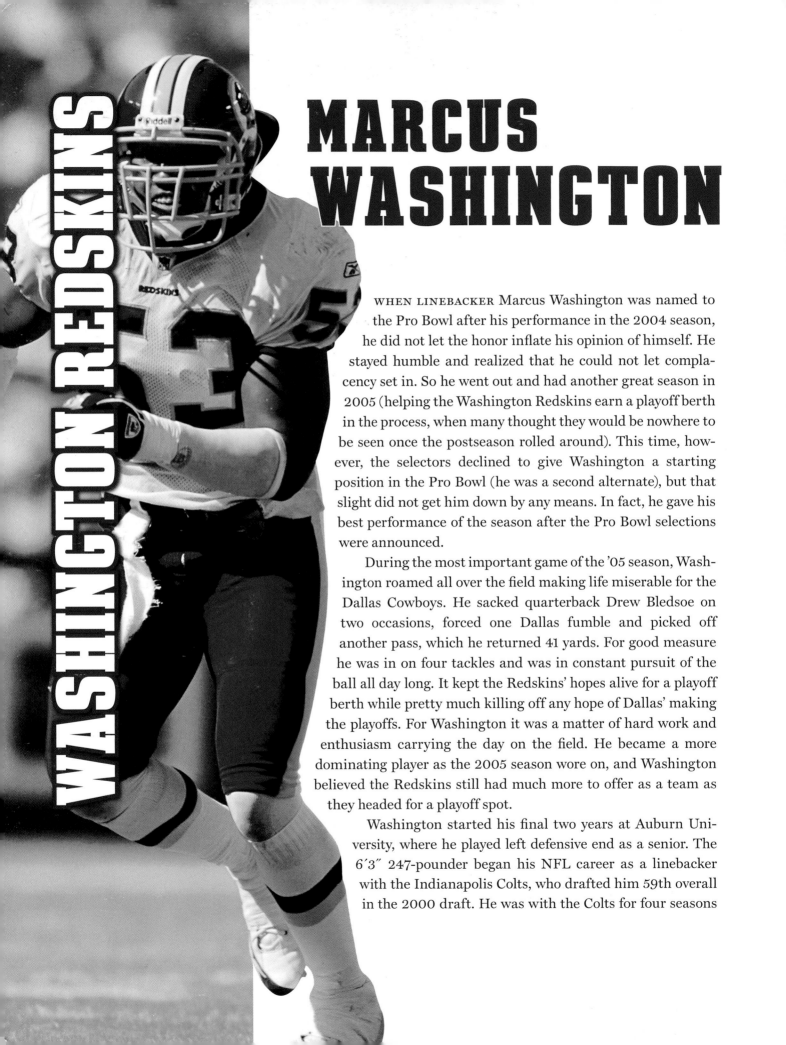

MARCUS WASHINGTON

WASHINGTON REDSKINS

WHEN LINEBACKER Marcus Washington was named to the Pro Bowl after his performance in the 2004 season, he did not let the honor inflate his opinion of himself. He stayed humble and realized that he could not let complacency set in. So he went out and had another great season in 2005 (helping the Washington Redskins earn a playoff berth in the process, when many thought they would be nowhere to be seen once the postseason rolled around). This time, however, the selectors declined to give Washington a starting position in the Pro Bowl (he was a second alternate), but that slight did not get him down by any means. In fact, he gave his best performance of the season after the Pro Bowl selections were announced.

During the most important game of the '05 season, Washington roamed all over the field making life miserable for the Dallas Cowboys. He sacked quarterback Drew Bledsoe on two occasions, forced one Dallas fumble and picked off another pass, which he returned 41 yards. For good measure he was in on four tackles and was in constant pursuit of the ball all day long. It kept the Redskins' hopes alive for a playoff berth while pretty much killing off any hope of Dallas' making the playoffs. For Washington it was a matter of hard work and enthusiasm carrying the day on the field. He became a more dominating player as the 2005 season wore on, and Washington believed the Redskins still had much more to offer as a team as they headed for a playoff spot.

Washington started his final two years at Auburn University, where he played left defensive end as a senior. The 6′3″ 247-pounder began his NFL career as a linebacker with the Indianapolis Colts, who drafted him 59th overall in the 2000 draft. He was with the Colts for four seasons

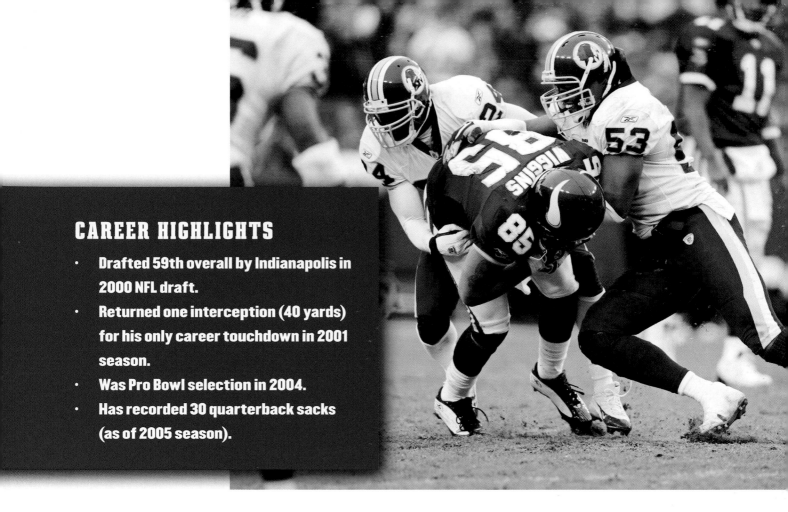

(the last three as a very productive starter) before he was declared an unrestricted free agent and signed with the Redskins in March of 2004. The Redskins liked the superior athletic skills of the outside linebacker and were very impressed with his ability to go from sideline to sideline. Washington has the speed to run a play down and has the size to shed blockers straight up. He is also considered a top pass rusher because of his speed. When head coach Joe Gibbs returned to coach the Redskins, he added Gregg Williams (former head coach of the Buffalo Bills) to coach the defense, and Washington likes the fact that his defensive coach has a warrior's mentality. Williams likes to turn the defense loose, and Washington appreciates the opportunity to just go out and play the game. Signing with the Redskins has been a good move for all concerned.

In the '05 season, Washington was second (to middle linebacker Lemar Marshall) on the Redskins in total tackles, with 93. He also had 7.5 quarterback sacks and forced three fumbles during the regular season. The Redskins made the playoffs with a 10–6 record and won their first postseason game (against Tampa Bay) for the first time since 1999. A loss to Seattle ended the season for the Redskins, but Washington and

IN THE HUDDLE

Marcus Washington was named the Player of the Year by the Washington Redskins Quarterback Club for the 2005 regular season.

his defensive teammates were vital in the win over the Buccaneers. The Redskins appear to have drawn out the potential that so many see in Washington, and that will likely mean more Pro Bowl appearances in the future for the outstanding linebacker.

ON THE

AN EXCITING TALENT POOL — ON THE VERGE

RISE!

OF BECOMING TOMORROW'S STARS AND SUPERSTARS

OFFENSE

RONNIE BROWN
RUNNING BACK, MIAMI DOLPHINS

- Drafted second overall by Miami in 2005.
- Attended Auburn University, rushing for 2,697 career yards.
- Rushed for 907 yards on 207 carries for Miami in 2005.
- Recorded 32 catches for 232 yards and scored a total of five touchdowns.

LARRY FITZGERALD
WIDE RECEIVER, ARIZONA CARDINALS

- Drafted third overall by Arizona in 2004.
- Named All-American while attending University of Pittsburgh.
- Caught 58 passes as a rookie in '04 for 780 yards and eight TDs.
- Caught 103 passes in 2005 for 1,049 yards and 10 TDs.

SAMKON GADO
RUNNING BACK, GREEN BAY PACKERS

- Signed as a free agent by Green Bay in 2005.
- Rushed for 901 yards on 138 carries as a senior in college (Liberty).
- Rushed for 582 yards with a 4.1-yard average per carry in 2005.
- Scored a total of seven touchdowns as a rookie in '05.

JULIUS JONES
RUNNING BACK, DALLAS COWBOYS

- Drafted 43rd overall by Dallas in 2004.
- Rushed for 819 yards as a rookie in '04 with seven TDs.
- Rushed for 993 yards on 257 carries in 13 games during 2005.
- Caught 35 passes in '05 for 218 yards.

LAMONT JORDAN
RUNNING BACK, OAKLAND RAIDERS

- Drafted 49th overall by New York Jets in 2001.
- Signed as a free agent by Oakland in 2005.
- Started 14 games in '05, rushing for 1,025 yards and nine TDs.
- Caught 70 passes for 563 yards in '05.

HEATH MILLER
TIGHT END, PITTSBURGH STEELERS

- Drafted 30th overall by Pittsburgh in 2005.
- Caught 149 passes and 20 touchdowns during career at University of Virginia.
- Started 15 games in '05, catching 39 passes for 459 yards.
- Scored six touchdowns in '05 and was a member of Super Bowl winning team.

SHANE OLIVEA
TACKLE, SAN DIEGO CHARGERS

- Drafted 209th overall by San Diego in 2004.
- Attended Ohio State University.
- Started 16 games as a rookie in 2004.
- Started 15 games in 2005.

ROB PETITTI
TACKLE, DALLAS COWBOYS

- Drafted 209th overall by Dallas in 2005.
- Attended University of Pittsburgh from 2001 to 2004.
- Earned second-team All-American honors in 2004.
- Started 16 games in '05 for the Cowboys.

CHRIS SIMMS
QUARTERBACK, TAMPA BAY BUCCANEERS

- Drafted 97th overall by Tampa Bay in 2003.
- Attended the University of Texas.
- Started two games in 2004 for Tampa Bay.
- Started 10 games in 2005, completing 191 of 313 passes for 10 TDs.

CARNELL "CADILLAC" WILLIAMS
RUNNING BACK, TAMPA BAY BUCCANEERS

- Drafted fifth overall by Tampa Bay in 2005.
- Earned All-American honors at Auburn University in 2004.
- Rushed for 3,831 career yards at Auburn.
- Rushed for 1,178 yards in '05 and named NFL Offensive Rookie of the Year.

MIKE WILLIAMS
WIDE RECEIVER, DETROIT LIONS

- Drafted 10th overall by Detroit in 2005.
- Made 176 career receptions and recorded 30 TDs at Southern California.
- Gained 2,579 yards in receptions in two years at USC.
- Started four games in '05, making 29 catches for 350 yards and one TD.

DEFENSE

JARED ALLEN
DEFENSIVE END, KANSAS CITY CHIEFS

- Drafted 126th overall by Kansas City in 2004.
- Started 10 games as a rookie in '04, recording nine QB sacks.
- Recorded 11 QB sacks in 2005.
- Has recorded 77 career solo tackles as of 2005 season.

LOUIS CASTILLO
DEFENSIVE END, SAN DIEGO CHARGERS

- Drafted 28th overall by San Diego in 2005.
- Attended Northeastern University between 2001 and 2004.
- Recorded 49 total tackles in '05.
- Recorded 3.5 QB sacks in '05.

DOMONIQUE FOXWORTH
CORNERBACK, DENVER BRONCOS

- Drafted 97th overall by Denver in 2005.
- Attended University of Maryland between 2001 and 2004.
- Recorded 70 total tackles in '05.
- Recorded two interceptions in '05.

MARLIN JACKSON
DEFENSIVE BACK, INDIANAPOLIS COLTS

- Drafted 29th overall by Indianapolis in 2005.
- Earned All-American honors at University of Michigan in 2004.
- Recorded 58 total tackles in '05.
- Recorded one interception in '05.

SHAWNE MERRIMAN
OUTSIDE LINEBACKER, SAN DIEGO CHARGERS

- Drafted 12th overall by San Diego in 2005.
- Recorded 22 career QB sacks at University of Maryland.
- Recorded 10 QB sacks in '05.
- Named NFL Defensive Rookie of the Year in '05.

MARCUS SPEARS
DEFENSIVE END, DALLAS COWBOYS

- Drafted 20th overall by Dallas in 2005.
- Attended Louisiana State between 2001 and 2004.
- Recorded 19 career QB sacks in college.
- Recorded 31 total tackles and 1.5 QB sacks in '05.

ODELL THURMAN
MIDDLE LINEBACKER, CINCINNATI BENGALS

- Drafted 48th overall by Cincinnati in 2005.
- Attended University of Georgia in 2003 and 2004.
- Recorded 64 solo tackles in '05.
- Recorded five interceptions with one TD in '05.

CHARLES TILLMAN
CORNERBACK, CHICAGO BEARS

- Drafted 35th overall by Chicago in 2003.
- Started 13 games as a rookie, recording four interceptions in '03.
- Played in 15 games in 2005, making 82 solo tackles.
- Recorded five interceptions with one TD in '05.

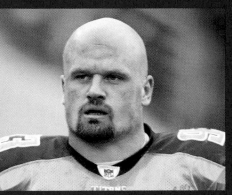

KYLE VANDEN BOSCH
DEFENSIVE END, TENNESSEE TITANS

- Drafted 34th overall by Arizona in 2001.
- Started 16 games for Arizona in 2002, recording 3.5 QB sacks.
- Signed as a free agent by Tennessee in 2005.
- Recorded 12.5 QB sacks in '05.

JONATHAN VILMA
MIDDLE LINEBACKER, NEW YORK JETS

- Drafted 12th overall by New York Jets in 2004.
- Started 14 games as a rookie, recording two QB sacks and 77 solo tackles.
- Recorded three interceptions and returned one for a TD in '04.
- Recorded 124 solo tackles in '05.

DeMARCUS WARE
DEFENSIVE END, DALLAS COWBOYS

- Drafted 11th overall by Dallas in 2005.
- Recorded 27.5 career QB sacks at Troy College.
- Started all 16 games as a rookie for the Cowboys in '05.
- Recorded eight QB sacks and 47 solo tackles in '05.

ACKNOWLEDGMENTS

The authors would like to acknowledge (and thank the contributors to) the following sources, which we consulted while writing this book.

NEWSPAPERS

Boston Globe, Chicago Sun-Times, Chicago Tribune, Cincinnati Enquirer, Cincinnati Post, Dayton Daily News, Denver Post, Fort Wayne Journal Gazette, Fort Worth Star-Telegram, Globe and Mail, Houston Chronicle, Indianapolis Star, Los Angeles Times, Milwaukee Journal Sentinel, Newark Star-Ledger, New York Daily News, New York Post, New York Times, Pittsburgh Tribune-Review, Rocky Mountain News, San Jose Mercury News, Seattle Post-Intelligencer, Seattle Times, Texarkana Gazette, Toronto Star, Toronto Sun, USA Today, Washington Post. In addition, many stories from the *Associated Press* appeared in these newspapers and on a variety of websites.

WEBSITES

http://www.cbs.sportsline.com
http://www.coltpower.com
http://www.edgerrinjames.com
http://www.ESPN.com
http://www.FOXsports.com
http://www.indybluecrew.com
http://www.jacksonsun.com
http://www.nfl.com
http://www.nflplayers.com
http://www.packersnews.com
http://www.redskins.com
http://www.saukvalley.com
http://www.Seahawks.net
http://www.scout.com

http://www.si.com
http://www.Tennessean.com
http://www.WKRN.com
http://www.wikipedia.org.
In addition, many NFL team websites were consulted beyond those listed here.

RECORD BOOKS

2005 NFL Record & Fact Book, Sporting News 2005 Pro Football Register. In addition, many NFL team media guides were consulted.

MAGAZINES

Andy Benoit's Touchdown 2005, Anthlon Sports Pro Football 2005 NFL Preview, Fantasy Football Weekly, New York Magazine, Pro Football Digest, Pro Football Weekly, Sports Illustrated, Sporting News, Sporting News Scouting Guide 2005, Street and Smith's Pro Football 2005 Yearbook.

TELEVISION

ABC's *Monday Night Football*, ESPN's *GameDay*, ESPN's *Sunday Night Football*, FOX Sports, *The NFL Today* (on CBS), *The NFL on Fox.*

PLAYER LIST

Alexander, Shaun, 34
Allen, Jared, 169

Bailey, Champ, 114
Barber, Ronde, 116
Barber, Tiki, 36
Bledsoe, Drew, 8
Brady, Tom, 10
Branch, Deion, 60
Brees, Drew, 12
Brown, Ronnie, 166
Burress, Plaxico, 62

Castillo, Louis, 169

Dawkins, Brian, 118
Delhomme, Jake, 14
Dunn, Warrick, 38

Faneca, Alan, 86
Farrior, James, 146
Fitzgerald, Larry, 166
Foxworth, Domonique, 169
Freeney, Dwight, 132

Gado, Samkon, 166
Galloway, Joey, 64
Gates, Antonio, 66
Glenn, Terry, 68
Gonzalez, Tony, 70
Green, Trent, 16

Hall, Dante, 100
Harrison, Marvin, 72
Hasselbeck, Matt, 18
Hutchinson, Steve, 88

Jackson, Marlin, 170
James, Edgerrin, 40
Johnson, Chad, 74
Johnson, Larry, 42
Johnson, Rudi, 44
Jones, Adam "Pacman," 102
Jones, Julius, 167
Jones, Thomas, 46
Jones, Walter, 90
Jordan, Lamont, 167
June, Cato, 148

Kreutz, Olin, 92

Lewis, Ray, 150

Manning, Eli, 20
Manning, Peyton, 22
Mathis, Jerome, 104
McGahee, Willis, 48
McNabb, Donovan, 24
Merriman, Shawne, 170
Miller, Heath, 167
Moss, Santana, 76

Nalen, Tom, 94

Olivea, Shane, 167
O'Neal, Deltha, 120

Palmer, Carson, 26
Parker, Willie, 50
Peppers, Julius, 134
Petitti, Rob, 168
Pierce, Antonio, 152
Plummer, Jake, 28